Philosophy for Spiders

philosophy for spiders

on the low theory of Kathy Acker

McKenzie Wark

DUKE UNIVERSITY PRESS Durham and London 2021

© 2021 Duke University Press
All rights reserved
Printed in the United States of America on acid-free paper ∞
Project editor: Jessica Ryan
Designed by Aimee C. Harrison
Typeset in Portrait Text, Helvetica Neue, and SangBleu Kingdom
by Copperline Book Services

Library of Congress Cataloging-in-Publication Data
Names: Wark, McKenzie, [date] author.
Title: Philosophy for spiders : on the low theory of Kathy Acker /
McKenzie Wark.
Description: Durham : Duke University Press, 2021. | Includes
bibliographical references and index.
Identifiers: LCCN 2021004441 (print)
LCCN 2021004442 (ebook)
ISBN 9781478013754 (hardcover)
ISBN 9781478014683 (paperback)
ISBN 9781478021988 (ebook)
Subjects: LCSH: Acker, Kathy, 1948–1997—Criticism and interpretation.
| Wark, McKenzie, 1961– | Experimental fiction, American—History
and criticism. | Feminist fiction, American—History and criticism. |
Postmodernism (Literature)—United States. | Feminist literary criticism. |
Gender identity in literature. | Sex role in literature. |
BISAC: LITERARY CRITICISM / LGBTQ | SOCIAL SCIENCE / LGBTQ
Studies / Transgender Studies
Classification: LCC PS3551.C44 Z95 2021 (print)
LCC PS3551.C44 (ebook) | DDC 813/.54—dc23
LC record available at https://lccn.loc.gov/2021004441
LC ebook record available at https://lccn.loc.gov/2021004442

Cover photograph: © Kathy Brew

Drawings of spiders on title page and part openers by Kathy Acker.

In memoriam:
Kato Trieu

And: dedicated to all the Janeys,
Janeys everywhere.

Contents

Whoever wrote this story said that history is philosophy, therefore, sexual history is the philosophy of religion.

—KATHY ACKER (*PUSSY, KING OF THE PIRATES*, 99)

the city of memory

Part I

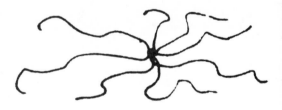

I've arrived at the conclusion that there's a profound
connection between ex-boyfriends and clichés.
—KATHY ACKER (ACKER PAPERS, 22.06)

The First Resort

When Kathy Acker checked in there, I knew something had changed.

It's a quiet place, empty and calm. A place where nothing ever happens. Like a resort hotel in the off-season. The décor is classy but generic, a banal, high-end nonplace. Kathy took me by the hand and led me through the big portal doors.

This was unexpected. Why was Kathy leading me to this place that is so familiar to me, from my own recurring dream? I have been coming here in dreams as long I can remember. It is always quiet and still, the light cool and mute. There seem to be staff keeping it running but you never see them. There appear to be other guests, but they have just walked around a corner. Or you hear laughter from the elevator as it arrives, but when it opens it is empty. And yet there's nothing either weird or eerie about it.

It always looks the same but sometimes it is on a cliff overlooking the sea and sometimes it is in the woods or by a lake. It always feels partly familiar to me in the dream, and partly not. It is a place to go so you can temporarily not exist. A vacation from life. A nonplace for nonlife.

That is why it is so strange that Kathy took me by the hand and brought me to this place, in my dream. I was surprised that she knew about it.

McKenzie: "But how do you know?"

Kathy: "It is the place the dead make for the living. It is always here."

She showed me what it is for, this resort from life and nonlife alike. She showed me that the dead make it for us. The dead make a place without qualities. They make the space of dreams itself. The dead don't want us to be like them. They have nothing to give us that has any features or qualities. They just make this place for us, this generic nonplace, and leave us alone.

Kathy knew all about this. She came back in a dream to remind me that I have been here too. She came back to remind me why one comes here. Maybe we all visit this place but forget all about it. The hard part is to go back and still remember what it is for.

This is how it has always been for us moderns. The dead refuse to tell us anything. And so we feel like they have finally left us alone. Which can make us go crazy. Kathy knew where to find them.

Actually that's not true. Nobody knows. She was one of the ones who knew where to find their absence. She found the place they had left. That they left for us. You can come here and be in their absence and come back.

Let's go.

Bestiary

Content warning: This book contains the language of sex, violence, sexual violence, and spiders.

Form warning: This book has elements of memoir and criticism but is neither.

I wanted to write about what I learned from Kathy in person and what I learned from reading Acker's texts, based on who I could become (in part) through knowing her both ways.

I didn't know her person for long at all. There are many others who can write with a lot more understanding about who she was. Nor am I a specialist in her writing or even in the kind of writing she wrote. I haven't dug deep in her archive, nor interviewed people around her. I make no claim that anything to do with Kathy Acker is my private property. I will note in passing that we shared a dislike for both writers and scholars who treat some body, or some body of work, as if they owned it.

The bourgeois writer is an acquisitive animal. A creature of power, ownership, and control. What it writes it owns; that which writes is the kind of being that can own. Kathy was a different beast—or beasts.

Martine Sciolino: "A kleptoparasite is a spider that appropriates another's web and eats the prey entrapped there. In a sense, the deliberate, overt plagiarisms of Kathy Acker are klepto-parasitical—*Great Expectations, Don Quixote, The Story of O*, Acker steals these and other narrative webs, but it is not easy to tell what victims are coiled in these already woven fictions. Because Acker always recounts her own life story as if it, too, were a stolen text—and because this *auto*-plagiarism always involves the victimization of the teller—the knots in these stolen, intersecting webs are unraveled to reveal an insect within, whose form mirrors that of the spider unwrapping it."[1]

This is not an *interpretation* of the life or work of Kathy Acker.[2] As if she was something over which I had claims that would be verifiable facsimiles or likenesses of her essence. Rather: She made texts. She lived and wrote in a particular way, the living and writing being a connected kind of *praxis*, the warp and weft of the same act of transforming things. The form of the praxis makes the texts in their own distinctive way. Here is a text made out of her texts, using a different praxis.

I learned a lot from Kathy as a human and Acker as a writer, and about four of the grand obsessions of our times: love and money, sex and death. She made a sort of gift toward me, and I'm returning it, after a fashion.

Here is a little about what that gift was: A body that writes is a body that fucks. There are peculiar asymmetries of the ways bodies may fuck: dom and sub, top and bottom, penetrator and penetrated, writer and reader, butch and femme, male and female, trans and cis, and so on. These differences find their way into and out of the way bodies write. A body that fucks with fucking can be a body that fucks with gender and a body that fucks with gender can be a body that writes where the writing fucks with gender and a writer embodied as fucking with gender can be a writer who fucks with genre, that most nucleated family of forms.

Patrick Greaney: "Baudelaire writes of the 'immense intellectual profundity in popular expressions, holes dug by generations of ants.' Clichés are burrowed through with subterranean passages that poets can explore and exploit in their battle against the truths that these clichés are supposed to support. But to do this, poets must enter into enemy territory and repeat the locutions that they undermine. In this repetition, poets burrow into language, but they, too, are dug into, penetrated by the very language that they want to overcome or keep at a distance."[3]

Kathy wrote prose, as I do, although she wrote much more interesting prose, better prose, and with different methods. Like the poets, she entered and was entered, fucked and was fucked, with language.

Tom McCarthy: "As a schoolchild, I had to learn collective nouns for animals. Jellyfish, for some reason, get two of these: bloom and smack. Open, morphing, endlessly penetrating or being penetrated by the scenes around them, Acker's bodies channel and act as hubs or mainstays in a world of viscerally networked continuity—like jellyfish quivering as pulse signals reach them through a viscous sea. Or rather (lest we start getting holistic), they both anchor this world and serve as its disjecta: more smack than bloom."[4]

What follows is in two parts. The first is about Kathy, as a body that fucks. The second is about Acker, as a body that writes. The first part is how I began a lesson with her about fucking, back in the nineties. The second part is how I began a lesson with her texts about what is between acts of writing, thirty years later. At a time when I was in transit between acts of genders.

Comrades, contemporaries, cunts: I come neither to critique Acker nor to blurb her. What makes her books enduring is the other books you can make out of them, and their difference from each other. This book is its own evidence of this concept.[5]

Let's not devote too much time on which writing her writing digests. I don't much care to give her a lineage of great forebears. Nor cast her by the lights of some master theorist. There's something not only bourgeois but also patriarchal about writing having to have owners and these owners having to have illustrious fathers, even if those fathers are sometimes mothers.

Vanessa Place: "Consider the phrase 'artist's shit.' Consider the mimetic effect of such excrescence, pace Piero Manzoni, who literally put his shit in ninety 30-gram cans and sold it for its weight in gold. Consider its metamorphosis, given that what's left of this shit is now worth more than its weight in gold, so that Manzoni could have been said to have shit gold bricks. Consider its lament, à la Erykah Badu, who says: 'Keep in mind I'm an artist and I'm sensitive about my shit.' Consider how Kathy Acker could be part Quixote or some such shit. As I have noted elsewhere, citation is always castration: the author's lack of authority made manifest by the phallus, presence of another authority. What better way to play the gendered part. I like this."[6]

Kathy died when she was fifty. I turn fifty-seven as I write this. I wanted to write about her for the longest time. Somehow it never quite seemed like the moment. I had to live not only up 'til her age when she passed but past it, before I could start.

Reading Kathy again helped me to transition: I came out as trans in the midst of reading and writing about her. I wanted to escape masculinity, but I didn't know where to. Kathy just seemed intuitively to be the writer to hold my hand through that.

I told Matias Viegener, the executor of the Kathy Acker estate, that I was probably writing a book about her, and he said, "Well of course you are."

Woolloomooloo

We first met at the Ariel Bookstore on Oxford Street, in Sydney, in June 1995. Kathy read, I don't remember what. Mythical characters were involved. It was a launch event for an issue of *21C* magazine.[7]

Noel King: "Leathered from top to toe, she told how the initial contact between her and *21C*'s editor, Ashley Crawford, came via email. They began a correspondence, he seemed a nice and interesting guy and here they finally were in person. At this point a separatist sister interjected that obviously these virtual forms of communication could be very misleading. Without missing a beat Acker said 'I still like the object in the flesh,' and went on with the launch."[8]

I was also a *21C* writer, so you could say it was Ashley Crawford who brought us together. She liked to write for Ash because he had a light hand cutting copy.

There was dinner after Kathy's reading, at the restaurant near the Wharf Theater, in The Rocks. Justine Ettler sat next to Kathy, I think. Justine appeared to all the world as quick and glamorous. She was the author of *The River Ophelia*, probably the only Australian fiction that showed what you could do with it if you had read Kathy Acker. A sensational book that drowned in the swamp of marketing and media that typecast it as "grunge."[9]

Surprising that Kathy talked to me. Perhaps it was the fluke of sitting close together. When she finally turned toward me, it was as if we were alone at that long candlelit table. The others fell away. I have no memory of them.

Then we were in my car together. (Which car was it? Did I have the little red one by now?) I drove Kathy back to Morgan's, her hotel on Victoria street in Kings Cross. I stopped in the loading zone out front. The car idling. It was not quite parked, pulled over as if for a quick drop-off. She asked me what the hell I thought I was doing. I had no idea. Impatience. "Well, are you coming in or not?"

All I remember of the hotel room is the color of sage and her stack of books. Maybe five books. "That's what I've been working on," Kathy said. I only remember the top book on the stack: Stevenson's *Treasure Island*. She was not quite done making *Pussy, King of the Pirates*.

There was not a lot of ceremony. We ended up naked on the futon. I told her that sometimes I don't want to actually fuck. That I just wasn't in that kind of relation to my body where I would want to fuck her. I don't know why I was so candid about this. She seemed to invite a kind of sexual frankness. At least in me. She was not at all bothered.

She was older than me: forty-eight to my thirty-four. This was an older woman's body, as is the one I have now. I was curious about this aging body. About the state of this flesh. This flesh liked being close to that flesh, of her.

This flesh wanted to learn about that flesh, starting with what made it feel what. A finger runs around cunt lips. Touching her clit, which reacts as if electrified, so finger backing off, redirecting attention to the multiple piercings in this labia. I had never seen this before. Touching them gently, touching the metal to move the flesh. Seems this is good. She touched my cock but I pushed her hand away. Felt more like doing the exploring. We were starting at the peripheries of each other's nervy surfaces.

Dodie Bellamy: "We sit in the living room on his boxy green sofa and Matias tells me that even though Kathy slept with many women she really wasn't a lesbian, and even though she was into S&M that wasn't her thing, not really. What really mattered to Kathy was to be fucked really well."[10]

Arranged crouching before cunt and licking, especially where piercings enter flesh. Hint of vanilla. Wiry hairs, crinkly skin. Licking outer lips, inner lips, poking tongue entering into the opening just a little. Then quietly edging closer to clit.

Kathy relaxed back into herself, arching, releasing, breathing rising and rising, not too hard and fast, then exhale and release, a little wave cresting just as another surges. Licking sinking into the rhythm, the rise and fall. Raft and ocean. Sailors adrift. And since I didn't come and she never stopped coming, I came in the same way that she did. "This was a fine perversion," Kathy said.

She pulled me up for air. We kissed again. Bodies pressing, my cock pressed into the curve of her hip. I felt cum leaking from it. I had been up on a crest the whole time, a slow-motion time. Flushed all over, heart slowing. Electric tremble and treble tapering down.

Felt the need to explain myself: "Sometimes . . . sometimes I just don't feel like fucking. I just feel, I don't know, like aroused, but all over. Not in my dick so much as everywhere, everywhere else, even," I said. "For me, every area of my skin is an orifice. Any part of your body could do anything to mine," Kathy said. She had a great way of describing such things.

Amy Scholder: "What cannot be overestimated is the pleasure Kathy took in writing porn, finding exactly the right cadence and rhythm, using language, pushing limits, turning on. Still, sexuality is a site of confusion — and it's within that confusion that her female characters come alive, expressing who they are and what they want."[11]

She was tired, lagged, out of sorts. I asked if I should stay. She wanted me to stay. I didn't sleep for a while, just watched her breathing, watching the carp tattoo anime across her shoulder blades. Woke nesting her head in my hands.

Upon waking, she was up, showered, dressed. She wore the same pink leather bustier as the night before. I remember it coming off, her softs unleashed from its form. Over that, she wore something low cut and patterned, maybe animal print, in black and white to show off the pink leather. Bare legs and boots.

She wanted to eat at Morgan's as it would go on the hotel tab which was covered. Breakfast was subdued. Like we had just met. A first conversation sober is indeed a first conversation.

I remember the café-restaurant at Morgan's. It faced the Victoria street scene. Inside, it was steeply terraced. The servers teetering down the staircase up the middle while balancing plates and trays. But we all went there quite often in those days, as it was open late, so I don't know if I remember it with Kathy or just remember it.

The next few days are a Sydney haze. I became her guide to the city, this city whose twisty ways I knew and she did not.

The only thing I can remember, or think I can remember, that we saw together, is the graffiti, not far from Whitlam Square, that said, "One cannot commit evil in evil," signed "Genet." Which another writer had changed to "Genetalia." Yet another hand added "Et Alia." Now I'm looking for that building on Google Maps: corner of Liverpool and Hargrave, two-story and darkly painted, it's still there: the spray-paint thread is not.

The night after we met. Dinner again. Then I dropped Kathy off at Morgan's, but did not come in. Did not occur to me that she wanted my company to continue into the night again. I thought very little of myself. But she took it to mean I thought even less of her. The common language that divided us.

And she was mad at me for missing her big performance at Artspace in Woolloomooloo. The show was sold out. A review later called it a mix of "blood, grunge and gynaecology."[12] Which is not particularly helpful, and doesn't address the galvanic effect that her performances could have on people. Apart from the very low-key reading at Ariel I never saw her read.

Eileen Myles: "Each of us had to read for 8 or 10 minutes and Kathy would read for 21. And miraculously she didn't kill the room. I'd watch her going on and on same fucking story. I think how can she do this. Deadly. But she was okay. More than that. People were riveted. I mean her work was so artificial and ritualized, all on the outside, I thought. Constructed for the performance of Kathy and she made that corpse walk night after night."[13]

Pam Brown:

> the day after
> the very long reading,
> at the very cool venue,
> we, the audience, *were*
> those sluts, those girls—
> rats in our hair
> vampires in our anus
> blood, piss, shit,
> spit, bones, vomit—
> Kathy Acker's
> drunken girls,
> she meant *us*,
> that's the way she read
> to us[14]

I missed it because I had to teach my class. She did not think this was a good enough reason. I was starting to discover that Kathy rarely thought any reason was good enough reason for not giving her what she wanted. I met up with Kathy after the show.

So it went on for a few days, in Sydney. Kathy was avoiding people who were fans of her image but who did not know her work. She even avoided some who knew her work well.[15]

That I was neither ignorant of her work nor a fan seemed the right ratio of appreciation and ambivalence.

We gossiped a lot about various people unknown to each other, although actually I had read or read about some of the people whose bodily functions and emotional habits she dished.

Something happened between us. Some third thing in between. The third flesh.

I drove her to the airport. And then she left.

Spider_cat

Kathy and I exchanged email addresses. This was not quite a thing people did much yet in 1995. Of the eighteen million American households whose computer had a modem, eight million hadn't used it. There were about twelve million email users in America then, less than five percent of the population. People received an average of five emails a day and sent three.[16]

I had a computer in my office out at Macquarie University and another one at home. I think the home modem was still 1200 baud and connected to the phone line with the same singsong mating ritual sound as fax machines. For internet access, both my office computer and home computer connected to the same server at the Office of Computer Services at Macquarie University.

Actually, there were two servers, and they were called laurel and hardy, which might give you some idea of the sensibility of the people who ran them. This is why my email address read mwark at laurel dot ocs dot mq dot edu dot au. Domains within domains. This all seems rather quaint now. The materiality of writing in the era of networked computation.[17]

I taught myself enough Unix programming to use the university's computers, from my office or home. The email reader I used was called Pine, and I still think it was the best email reader ever. Faster and easier than this corporate-designed spyware we have to use now.

In Pine, it was easy to save an email message as an ASCII text file, and then to add it to a file that collected them all. The command for joining a file to another file was *cat*, short for concatenate. I still put *cat* in the name of my merged files. This file I'm working on now is called spider_cat.

At home, I had one of those dark gray Apple PowerBook 100 series laptops with a monochrome screen. The first to put the trackball below the keyboard. It lived on my coffee table, near the home fax machine, answering machine, and the base for the cordless phone. The TV sat on a milk crate on the other side of the coffee table, atop the VCR, DVD, and Sega. I could camp out on the decrepit, hand-me-down black leather sofa that sat on the floor without its feet and live in one or other simulated world.

Mostly, I wrote to Kathy lying on this sofa, drinking stovetop espresso in the morning or a glass of Hunter Valley white at night. The laptop would be in my lap, only it got hot as fuck, so I put a pillow in between. I wrote to her first, then did other stuff, then came back to see if she had replied. I would hang out in forums on The Well, which attracted mostly Bay Area hippies. Or, I became various characters on LambdaMOO, a text-only adventure playground with six genders.[18] Then more email with Kathy.

Rosie Cross: "Her rapid-fire style made her a natural-born net-surfer, and when she took to the internet, she found an alternative venue for her anarchistic impulses, and a place that provoked her interests in unpredictable and shifting realities. She also found trouble."[19]

Her early emails to me were from an America Online account. She got kicked off AOL for asking if there were any dykes in the MTV chatroom. America Online disabled her interface software remotely, modifying her computer without informing her, but kept billing her for the account. She felt that this was some sort of rape.

Later, I learned that Kathy may have played on LambdaMOO too. What if our text-only avatars had met there, or even hot-tubbed together?

Stranger things happened. Nineties cyberculture was like experimental performance art going on around the planet, around the clock. It was a world thousands were already making for themselves, but not the millions, let alone billions, who would populate it by the second decade of the twenty-first century.

Nobody knew how to live in these worlds yet. Neither had anybody figured out how to make money off the seething ocean of desires stirring there. Certainly nobody knew how to write emails to someone they had laughed and loved and fucked and wandered and drunked and gossiped with for a few days, and who was gone but whose sense memory lingered, like sweat and leather.

Later, the emails I saved ended up as a book, called *I'm Very into You*.[20] Then our nineties cyberculture conversations got ingested and digested by twenty-first-century corporate (anti)social media, which operate on difference principles. I'm addressed throughout in a name I no longer use. The book got the perfect review in *Bookforum*. David Velasco: "slim, perfect, evil."[21]

They say never read the comments, but then they only say that in the comments.

I'm Very into You

5.0 out of 5 stars | Not your Mother's Kathy Acker Book (I hate writing headlines)
T. Porges | November 18, 2017 | Verified Purchase

This is more Ken Wark's book than Kathy Acker's, but it's a labor of love and makes an interesting companion volume to Chris Kraus's Acker biography. You probably won't be buying this if you aren't a bit obsessed with Acker or are a Wark reader/completionist. If you're either of those people, you don't need an introduction and you'll be quite happy with this book. As a kind of flirtation text, it compares neatly with _Swoon_, by Nada Gordon and Gary Sullivan (totally different writers, yes?).

Comment | One person found this review helpful | Report abuse

5.0 out of 5 stars | great book, must read for acker fans!
Tina | June 30, 2015 | Verified Purchase

Fantastic book. Interesting perspective on queer issues juxtaposed to the early possibilities of online communication.

Comment | One person found this review helpful | Report abuse

5.0 out of 5 stars | IM VERY INTO THIS BOOK RIGHT NOW
alyanna del rosario | June 16, 2015 | Verified Purchase

this book is meant to make you feel awkward because you haven't read something so light and delightful before. This book is so light and flirty and i totally recommend this book for people who are tired for those cliche, campy, romance novels. this book is a breath of fresh air.

Comment | 2 people found this review helpful | Report abuse

4.0 out of 5 stars | The Olsen twins star in this great tale of halloween adventure
Joseph Jambroni | April 27, 2015

The Olsen twins star in this great tale of Halloween adventure. Their family is going through some tuff financial troubles and may lose their house so they turn to the only member of the family with any money—a cruel aunt. Upon arrival they are immediately dismissed—but the young twins' presence frightens the mean aunt because she was once a twin herself and she did something very horrible to her own twin. See—their cruel aunt is a witch and used a spell to make her twin vanish and now it's up to mary kate and ashley to uncover the plot and save someone they have never met. They find help with a little person and a grave digger and set off around the town trying to learn more about their evil aunt's witches coven. Great for all families with younger children and worth many watches.

Comment | 24 people found this helpful | Report abuse

4.0 out of 5 stars I An Interesting, Energetic Read Studded With Sharp Peaks
ninaleox I April 27, 2015

I picked this book up at my local bookstore on a whim. I didn't know anything about Acker or Wark beforehand, so I suppose you could say I was unburdened by negative bias towards the authors. The foreward by Acker's friend and executor (in the will sense), Matias Viegener, was a nice little piece of lit in and of itself. I love this phrase: "In the exchange between Acker and Wark, we see the reciprocal machinery of introjection and projection." I actually reread Viegener's foreword after I finished the book, as I found it infinitely more insightful and readable than the epilogue—whose author seems unbecomingly proud of his feeble punning when he coins the term 'e-pistolary'—(Get it?! They're emails!)—and I didn't want to end on a low note.

The format is interesting and effective. At times, Kathy and Ken maintain multiple email chains, so there is this layering and expansion of conversational threads over time, of tangents and interpretations, that provide the perfect spacial/structural expression to two smart people's neural networks connecting and firing. As a reader, you get to observe the pair negotiate the boundaries of their newfound intimacy in an ultimately pretty staid, but intellectually charged courting ritual. They cover a lot of ground, from Portishead to Pasolini, and if nothing else will leave a reader with lots of Wikipedia-ing to do.

To paraphrase Viegener less eloquently, it's like watching brainy people flirt. What's interesting is that even when the conversation turns prurient (fisting, anyone?), it reads like a red herring: what emerges at the core is two (pretty polite) people isolated by their own intellect, clearly thrilled at the opportunity for self-disclosure and the emergence of a common "territory" over which to commune. (The sex stuff is often just oblique provocation.) Ken and Kathy are both thoughtful and well-mannered, sensitive to not "trespass" on the other ("Write me your vertigo, it will be safe with me," Ken replies gently after Kathy apologizes for her emotional overspill)—because intimacy has not yet bred contempt. Despite the inclination to write them off on the basis of the reductive reputations that precede/succeed them (punks, obscurantists, whatever), there is a familiar and rather endearing humanity at play here.

Read less I 10 people found this helpful I Report abuse

5.0 out of 5 stars I once upon a time, a man and a woman wrote some letters
Jeremy W. Hunsinger I April 28, 2015

Ken Wark had the relationship with Kathy Acker that so many people would have liked to have. This correspondence sheds new light on both authors and upon the world in which we live.

Comment I One person found this helpful I Report abuse

5.0 out of 5 stars I Five Stars
Esther Anders I April 29, 2015

This is simply a wonderful book and great document.

5.0 out of 5 stars I Highly recommended.

Nine Yamamoto I April 27, 2015
I'm Very Into This Book. Highly recommended.

Comment I 4 people found this helpful I Report abuse

5.0 out of 5 stars
Steyerl, Hito I April 28, 2015

This book is wonderful, period.

Comment I Thank you for your feedback I Report abuse

San Francisco, 1995

So I was going to see Kathy in San Francisco. There was some bother changing tickets, but with that sorted, we could have more time together. I knew nothing about San Francisco. These were landscapes I knew only from Hitchcock's *Vertigo*.

September 14, 1995: It's a fourteen-hour flight from Sydney to San Francisco. The cab from the airport seemed like something from a seventies movie. Eventually I arrived at the address she gave me, in Cole Valley.

Twenty-odd years later, I took another cab to her address: 929 Clayton St., Cole Valley. The cab now had a flat screen in the back. Her house is as I remember it, but was it this color? I remember a lighter blue. It is a wooden row house on a steep hill. Out front I saw the empty space where Kathy had parked her motorcycles. One had a blue tarp over it.

We were awkward with each other at first. I said I wanted to go out and get some tea and milk, as she had neither. These turned out to be difficult commodities to acquire in Cole Valley. There was plenty of soy milk and all sorts of newly fashionable herbal tea that wasn't actual tea.

I walked down the same steep street, retracing my steps, my crip feet complaining more than they did back then. Using psychogeographic principles, I found the little cluster of shops again, around the corner of Cole and Carl. I even bought tea again.

Kathy made tea for me. She had drawn a bath. I was left alone to soak in the tub with a cuppa. Restoring the animal body.

The kitchen filled with sunlight in the morning, warming the wooden floors. There was a small room with no windows and white shag carpet. That room was dark and there was a phone and answering machine on the floor. Kathy never answered it. The phone rang at all hours, mostly with urgent-sounding messages from Germans.

There was an office-cum-library space with a wooden desk. An off-white Apple computer sat on it. The keyboard had a long, tangled spiral cord, so she could sit back in the armchair with the keyboard on her lap. There was a wine glass on the desk, stained red. Bookshelves everywhere, the books arranged alphabetically by author, in double rows. She had what looked like a yoga mat, on which she did what she called calisthenics.

Her bedroom had a mattress on the floor and all her stuffed animals, including a tarantula, Woofie the wolf, and Ratski the rat, were arranged on the pillows, just as she described them in her email. Actually I had forgotten their names. I looked it up. I remember colors, moods, the steam rising from my tea in the sunlight, Kathy's anxious attention, her voice. That's about all.

Lynne Tillman: "The memories I have of Kathy seem, like most memories, somewhat vague and dream-like, with some images, some pieces of the past solid as rocks, as if they were facts."[22]

The Concept of the Body

The Chinese logicians came up with this puzzle: a horse has five legs. There are the four legs that one can observe on the horse, plus the *concept* of the leg. That makes five. Language messes with flesh; logic messes with language.

Joseph Needham: "The writings of the logicians always had an undercurrent of the wish to 'épater le bourgeois' (cf. the paradoxes below), as here in the statement that quadrupeds have five legs each, which was doubtless made to draw attention to the unchanging universal 'quadruped as such.'"[23]

There is no such thing as a couple fucking. A body fucks another body, but it also fucks the concept of the body. A concept of a body is a gender.

If the bodies that fuck are the same gender, then the two bodies that fuck are three bodies: the two bodies that one can observe, plus masculinity. Or: the two bodies one can observe, plus femininity.

Actually, when two bodies of the same gender fuck, there are four bodies. The two bodies one can observe, plus the concept of those bodies, its gender, plus the gender they are not, as each gender makes no sense without the one that it is not. Language has digital bits that bodies don't.

If the bodies are of different genders, then there are also four bodies. The two bodies that one can observe plus the concept of each of those bodies, its gender. So it seems that when two bodies fuck, there are always four bodies, fucking.

Only maybe it's more. Let's say there are two bodies we can observe. Then there is the concept of each of those bodies, its gender, if the gender is different. But in each case, the gender of the body that is the gender it is not is not the gender of the other body, its concept. The concept of each body is its gender, and also the gender it is not.

It is not the case that the concept of one body is the negation of the concept of the other body. Each body has its own concept, its own gender, and also its own nongender which does not correspond to the concept of the other body.

This all assumes that the concept of the body, its gender, corresponds to the body that one can observe, and that it does not change. Neither are a given. A body might change its concept, its gender, even during the act of fucking. Or maybe the concept of the body is an unknown gender, or flickers between known concepts in an unknown way.

In short, every fuck is an orgy. Even every hand job.

Which of the fifty-one gender options now on Facebook would Kathy choose, if she had to? Maybe Kathy was sometimes what one might call trans-masculine. There was her body, which one could observe. And there was its concept, which changed from time to time, even instant to instant. Sometimes its concept was masculine.

It was more the concept of the boy than of the man. Kathy was a boy sometimes. She could be masculine but not the father. The boy is not the father, that's what makes the concept of the boy the concept of the boy. The boy has not yet become the father, and can become something else, such as a sailor. Part of her was like a boy who would never grow up.

I wanted to become someone else too, but I had yet to learn my sexuality.

It's hard to pull off masculinity if you are small, and Kathy was small. I know. Even though I am taller, I'm still small. Kathy took elements of her look from bull dykes, which they probably took from the working-class men of postwar factory towns.

It freaked Marx out a bit that women factory workers looked like horny-handed boys. He had a moment of gender panic about such a body, its concept, its gender. But maybe even in factory work, there was a new possibility for the body: women and men subordinated to the same machines is not really progress, but it is different to women subordinated to men. Maybe the concept of technology is another gender, and another erotics. Victorian do-gooders had issues with this, and Marx himself was not immune to a certain Victorian prurience.

Amy Wendling: "If, unlike these reformers, we interpret the laboring, actively sexual female body as a positive rather than a negative monstrosity, we might even conclude that industrialization has conditioned certain aspects of women's liberation. . . . A girl at work is not, necessarily, a rough, foul-mouthed boy. She might simply be a rough, foul-mouthed girl, or, better still, a rough and foul-mouthed hybrid creature whose very existence challenges the rigid norms of Victorian gender."[24]

And if where we are now is, as Kathy thought, some kind of post-capitalism, imagine the fun to be had despite its norms or concepts. The machine-body becomes the information-body. Kathy's short hair, leather jackets, motorcycles: it was and wasn't an act. Sometimes it was a way to visualize a concept of the body, its gender. If you thought that was weird, then it was an act for you. If you thought it just was, she just *was* a body that could be rather than mean.

Body and Body: Flesh

After a restorative cup of tea and a bath I felt a lot more human. I felt like I could start to edge my way into a problem I had thought about but only abstractly. How could I be in her space, her habitat? It was clearly something that made her nervous. Both of us lived more or less alone at the time. I felt like minimizing the amount of space my body took up. I felt like competing for the prize of the best houseguest ever.

Kathy wanted to be accommodating. She wanted—needed—to know my needs. But my needs were few. I just wanted to be with her. To fit in to whatever she usually did. Oh, and I wanted us to fuck again, and soon.

Memory glitches: The sunlight in her kitchen. The white shag carpet in the room with the telephone answering machine. The bookcases, the wooden floor. Back when she was writing *After Kathy Acker*, Chris Kraus messaged me to ask if I remembered a white sofa. I don't remember any sofa at all. I don't recall much about a living room. I remember the bath, the kitchen, mostly the bedroom. Probably the rooms in which we spent the most time.

There was lots of fucking. That I remember, although it all merges together. I remember who I was starting to be with Kathy. I was starting to be her girlfriend. That concept.

She wanted to know what I wanted. She wanted to give. She could be fragile in her sense of whether anyone loved her or cared for her. She wanted to give and to have tangible proof of that offer returning. She wanted to be vulnerable but became defensive about it, looking for who or what might take advantage.

Avital Ronell: "It was a gift, but Kathy had ways of testing your friendship. The Greeks had a word for it, *basamos*, which links testing to torture. It is not the case that we know when or whether we're being tested (because if you *know* you're being tested, this awareness may collapse the premise of the test)."[25]

She was particularly wary on this score of men, and where friendship, love, and lust might get confused. I did not particularly want to be her man. Sure, I fucked her. When she wanted me to. Everyone ought to know how to top: ethics.

Not for the first time, I would fuck this woman's body and imagine her body was my body, that I was in her place. Imagining her body as my body, I opened all my senses to it. I fucked her body with my dick but her body fucked mine through the eyes, ears, through all the senses. I wanted its particular qualities to come into me and come in me.

Kathy wanted to know why I was fucking her if it was not entirely what I wanted. She was suspicious, even. How can what a body wants be what another body wants? She had philosophical questions. I could only describe things.

I didn't want to fuck her because the thing I really wanted was to be the one who was fucked. Is that all? To Kathy this was just a question of differential fuck mechanics. This was San Francisco. You want to be fucked? We have the technology! Kathy had her own tool box. She took from it a leather strap-on harness and laid out before me a selection of dicks. This array of would later be one of the harder endowments for her literary executor to grant onward.

Matias Viegener: "The box of dildos and vibrators confounded me, intimate and irrepressibly sad. Kathy's love toys, honored in her life as sex and the body were honored in her work. Finally I left them on the street, deciding they'd end up in the right place by chance."[26]

Now I wonder where they are in the world.

Dildocentrism

She lined them up and we looked at them. Mostly plain black, symmetrical, none with that fake man-dick look. I chose the big one. She hesitated. She offered the next biggest, and that seemed like a better idea—start with something a bit less ambitious.

Sitting on the edge of the bed, Kathy inserted the biggest one in her cunt, then with much care held it in place while strapping the smaller one over it. She stood, arched her back, shifted her weight from leg to leg. Touched her still impressively large dick. Smiled at me. The sight got me so hot: trembling, palpitating. This tiny human; this big silicone dick. She had left on the pink leather brassiere, giving the whole ensemble an intentional, fuckware look.

I put a condom on the dildo, and the lube. We always used condoms. Hers was hardly the first body to fuck me, but was the first that was female (or was it?) in concept. Cowgirl style. Kathy on her back, me on top, facing her; I was in charge of her taking charge of me.

This body that I call mine fucked myself with her dick. It was one with a pronounced head on it. I felt it pop through the first ring of ass. My hands aiming it at the second. These hands deciding not to take it slow, this ass deciding to go for enough sensation to overload the nerves, to put enough information about to shock the body out of its concept, its gender. Maybe these bodies could have other concepts, or none at all.

This was new territory, this dick-technics, this pirate-sex. I did not have to worry about someone keeping an erection, getting bored, or coming too quickly—those concerns that bring you back to yourself too much. This body could play with that dick how it wanted for a while. Its inanimate, inhuman quality was a new sensation. Pushing down hard, in an instant it was everywhere inside, touching from inside, touching inside ass but also inside liver and spleen and legs and arms, insisting in the nerve-ways.

"Are you OK? Are you OK?" I had blacked out for a few seconds. Seemed like an age had gone by, a hole poked into time: widening a gap in the web of time.

Kathy was still there, under this body. I came back to me. Her (his) cock was still inside him (her), opening me up. But I was back. I smiled. I was hoping for a beatific smile, but probably just looked dopey. Looming over her (him), silicone dick in my ass, my legs spread around her (his) sun.

The dick in my ass was, at its base, back to back with an even bigger one in her (his) cunt. I felt for the connection. It felt like one dick, pointing into both of us. It was a thing, an object, a technique, a toy. Something of neither body. But it was also an extension of both their bodies. It was me and not me; you and not you. It was your dick fucking me; it was my dick fucking you. He (her) fucks him (her) while her (him) fucks her (him).

Kathy had her own roller-coaster; her being rose and fell, rose and fell, coming and coming, higher this time or lower this time. 'Til she glid to the end. With my ass I pressed the base of her cock in me onto her cock in her, but also very gently onto her super-sensitive clit. I could sort of feel how to move to move her. My own dick wasn't hard at all. It felt like an extraneous appendage. I didn't touch it. I came just from the movement of cock in ass. Giving up a surprisingly big squirt for me onto her belly.

It felt, if only for a time, like all the concepts of the body, of its gender. Mostly I was Kathy's girl, her dick inside me, open to her. But she was my girl as well. Open to me. This is on the assumption, and—what can I say? The concept speaks through me—that the girl is the one who wants to open to another.

Bodies fucking can open and close to each other all sorts of ways, and can flip from open to closed, or can be both closed to each other or open to each other, or there can be more than two. You don't have to think this is what it is about, it is just what I think it is about. And maybe it's what Kathy was writing about, but that's for later.

Ideology fucks us all with its habitual concepts. Ideology hails you like a cop in the street: "Hey you!" Or it insinuates quietly in your ear: "Hey . . . you . . ."[27] Ideology plays cute before it plays rough. It's cheaper.

When you fuck me, I told her, I feel like a girl. "Well, it is easier to penetrate the male body with dicks than with feelings," Kathy said.

Kathy's Girl, In and Out

Once that cock had been in my ass, I felt like I knew who I could be around Kathy. I was her girl. I aligned myself with Kathy's needs and wants. I was attentive to moods, desires. That Kathy was getting comfortable with me being around seemed to crystalize when Kathy would want to stay in and would just ignore me and write. I kept to myself at those times. A little self-consciously, I wrote in my own notebook. Which I wish I still had, as in that writing I described Kathy writing.

Kathy sat cross-legged on the wooden floor, wearing just a tank top and panties. Back against the wall. Sunlight falling. Spiral-bound notebook in lap. Look of complete concentration. Those neat printed characters on the page, one by one. Writing each letter with care in that fifties private-school-girl hand.

One hand on the pen; other hand in the underpants. Both twitching in rhythm. In a heightened state, just rolling along, not coming too hard. Cycles of micro-orgasm giving a rhythm to the calligraphy, and even to the text itself. Until done. An aesthetics in the form of the rolling, cumulative, nonpunctual orgasm.

As Kathy's girl I was open to whatever experience Kathy wanted to open me toward. We went out for long rides on her motorcycle. Was it the Yamaha Virago? I felt exposed, up on the back of the bike, holding tight, leaning with the machine, the wind spooling by, and at night the cold San Francisco air.

Gary Indiana: "[Kathy] drove the bike in this firm and definite pattern, zooming right through the sorry details of the street as if she was headed for better times, better places, better people—well, I understood that bike was the closest she could get to a feeling of freedom. I couldn't see her face but I knew she was happy, and for ten minutes so was I."[28]

We would stop for gas and other bikers would engage in biker-talk. The fraternity of the road. I thought back to the time I was Edward's girl, careening about in his open-topped sports car. Giving one's body over to another's control, confident they can handle a body's machinery.

Further Outings

She took me to a strip club. Was it the famous Mitchell Brothers, on 895 O'Farrell Street, the place where the lap dance was invented? One of her students was performing so we came to see her, but Kathy liked all of these girls who did some variety of sex-work and lived their own lives on the proceeds. "I learn a lot from them. I'm very staid compared to them," Kathy said.

The stage had seats around three sides. We were close to the stage. One or two other women performed before the one we came to see, who stood out as a different kind of beauty. I felt what Kathy saw in her.

I felt awkward in that place, neither one thing nor another. I did not want to be the client, but I wasn't one of the women. I wanted to be this dancer. To see her was a kind of pain, of impossibility. I could see and feel in her body that her pain was not mine and not for me, or anyone. She did her three songs. Last I saw she was leading some john to another room for a private lap dance.

Kathy took me to Zuni Café on Market Street, her favorite restaurant, which chef Judy Rodgers had made famous. She took me blindfolded. Led me to her bike, wobbly on the sloping street. A thrilling ride—my liver and spleen felt like they were going to explode out of me from pure sensation. She parked the bike and put the lock on. Reminded me to remind her to take the lock off before we rode away again, as she had damaged the other bike by forgetting it.

Zuni Café was not too fased by the blindfolded diner. This was San Francisco, and this was Kathy Acker, and she was a regular. She ordered for me, fed me. We did not say much, the whole evening mostly silent, solemn, ceremonial. Just opening this mouth, when told to. Surprise of flavors. Taste of salty-oily roast chicken, crackling skin. Acute awareness of exposure to unseen gazes.

On the way back I forgot all about the bike lock, but Kathy remembered. We zoomed off, me on the back, hands locked around, feel and smell of leather intensified by the blindfold, by the sensory orgy of the meal. Whole body aching in anticipation.

Kathy always asked, always wanted to know what I wanted. As if it wasn't clear: "I want you to fuck me, right now." Blindfold still on, getting the shoes off was a struggle, but soon I was naked on the low bed, apart from a T-shirt. I didn't want to displace the blindfold. Waiting: time a drugged pupil, dilating. And then: Kathy. I could sense, by smell, sound, by the disturbance in the air. On my back, Kathy on her knees. She drew me up onto her cock and fucked me, slowly, one ring at a time.

Jonathan Kemp: "Over sushi she told me she'd been having sex with gay boys but was bored because all they wanted was her to fuck them with a strap-on. At a night of readings of Acker's work in London recently, I bumped into an old flat-mate who tells me one of his friends used to get fucked by her, and now I feel an odd kind of jealousy as another echo is heard, another connection made."[29]

Wardrobe

I had not brought much by way of clothing with me, as I had thought San Francisco would be warmer than it is. I started wearing Kathy's clothes. I am taller but about the same size across the shoulders and hips, so I could get into some of her things. When we went out I wore jackets and sweaters of hers, a little short in the sleeve. She had some curious garments. Some seemed to have been cut not for humans at all but for some alien species.

Dodie Bellamy: "On a shelf above our heads are stacked four large packing boxes. The bottom one is labeled in black marker 'Acker's Clothes' in Kathy's handwriting. Once we get the boxes on the floor, we start to rummage through them. Matias pulls out a black mass of fabric. It's a dress, but it only has one sleeve and a sort of diagonal band stretching from where the missing armpit would be. We examine piece after piece and ponder what part of the body it was meant to cover."[30]

At her apartment, I tried on all sorts of things that felt sexy or elegant to wear. All I remember is the feel of quality fabric and construction, shaping me, drawing energy out and into new shapes. A bustier that conjured imaginary breasts. Something rigid that flared, causing hips to angle out from this (still) skinny ass. Kathy fucked me while I wore her clothes. Concepts of gender, redistributed. As if one could have some dick from the other and the other of that other could have some tits: corporeal communism.

Transitive

A horse really has only four legs. The fifth is superfluous. The concept of the horse's leg is either immanent to each of its legs or is just an artifact of language. Likewise, the body does not need its concept, its gender, as another body. The question remains as to whether the concept is immanent to the body or is a thing of language, or maybe a thing of language that became a thing of the body, its ideology.

Kathy went off to the gym by herself sometimes. Working out is maybe one way to expel the concept from the body, at least for a bit. "Bodybuilding rejects ordinary language," Kathy said. Her muscles hid their sculpting under skin.

Kathy also told me about cruising girls at the gym. I don't know if Kathy picked any up in the brief time we were together. Would not have bothered me. I was her girl (who also fucked her sometimes) but it wasn't a romantic relation where we became each other's property.

To fuck is sometimes used as a transitive verb: he fucked her; she fucked him; they fucked each other. The object comes after the verb; the verb performs an action on it. Maybe gender is transitive in another sense. Between any two bodies is a difference. Maybe that difference is gender even when it is not, actually, gender. It's what top and bottom imply, a difference. Maybe the genders could be transitive verbs, and can be applied in any situation where part of a person acts on another through that gender as an action: Kathy manned me.

I wanted her to man me. Or, in metaphors: to install herself on top and inside. To take the handlebars, to straddle and ride. To pilot, to cruise, to fly me, to drive me. She was better at it than I was.

And I knew a little about how to be the girl. When you are manned, sometimes you end up girling. A girl appears as a performance for another. A girl is a margin that appears around her own withdrawn center.

These days, people talk about toxic masculinity. Toxin, from *toxion,* neuter of *toxikos,* archery. *Toxion pharmakon:* poison arrows. *Pharmakon:* poison and cure.[31] Only it's more of an algorithm than an ambiguity. A procedure. A beginning; an end. An injected drug and its drugging. The male body is penetrated by the arrow of masculinity, a concept, but a nontransitive concept, in that it refuses to be penetrated as it is the one that penetrates.

And so, in just a few days, I became Kathy's girl. Because I wanted to be, and Kathy wanted to be what I wanted. Kathy was willing to be anything I wanted. That to her (him) was a kind of love. The kind where to love is to say: this can be anything you want, anything at all. So long as the gift comes back, and as something else.

Kathy also wanted to be wanted, totally, suddenly. Would make any demonstration of that willingness to lose her will. But yet also resisted this impulse. Was quick to reprove anyone who did not grant themselves to this granting of them to them.

Riding on the back of Kathy's bike was thrilling but cold. I was entirely in her hands. I loved to feel her control of the machine, that other gender.

We went to Cliff House on Point Lobos. Walked around the ruins of the abandoned Sutro Baths. We went to the Musée Mécanique. I had forgotten all about this, until I found a piece of paper in the prepress copy of *Pussy, King of the Pirates* that Kathy gave me. It was a small, faded sheet of thermal paper. This is what it said:

"*Mouth of Truth* tells you that: You're full of vitality and enjoy physical pleasures. You enjoy excellent health although you often abuse it. Beware of trying to be too clever. You know how to enjoy your many relationships with the opposite sex while still maintaining your independence. You keep making mistakes which jeopardize your future. Your capricious and inconstant nature will make it difficult for you to get on with life. Life: 6/10, Love: 7/10, Luck: 8/10, Health: 4/10, Sex: 8/10."

The smell, the touch of this yellowing thermal paper is what brought back the memory of Cliff House, of the water, cold, and sun, and an amusement hall full of vintage attractions. From Bay Area friends on Facebook I learned that this was the Musée Mécanique, and that it still existed, only not in the same location.

Back in San Francisco thirty years later, I had limited time and so had to make a decision: should I go to the old location, to Cliff House, or try to find the fortune telling machine at the place to which the Musée Mécanique had moved. I went looking for the machine, out on Pier 45.

The machine took some finding. The attendant had no idea. I found all sorts of dead media. Mechanical dioramas that became animated for a quarter. Antediluvian peepshow cinema that worked by cranked handle. Machines for pleasuring hand and eye.

No luck. I texted Kato, who, a few weeks earlier, had done some scouting— a thing we did for each other. I followed his directions. Hidden in the back was my fortune.

It gives its name in Italian: BOCCA DELLA VERITA. It's an off-white, plastic, shoulder-width disk with a face and open mouth. Put in two quarters, insinuate your hand in the mouth, and it pretends to read your palm. Red LEDs flash and plinky electronic sounds play. Your fortune extrudes from a slot at the bottom.

The original Bocca della Verità is a massive marble disk that can be found in Rome. Nobody knows what it is. Maybe it was just a drain cover for the Temple of Hercules.

In the movie *Roman Holiday*, Gregory Peck and Audrey Hepburn scoot around Rome on his two-wheeler. Greg is giving Audrey a hard time because he knows she is an actual princess pretending not to be. He tells her if you put your hand in the mouth of the Bocca della Verità and you are not a truthful person, it cuts off your hand. He puts his hand in. He screams and contorts, she shrieks in horror, then he reveals that he was just kidding. A dick move. A handy lie.

He is a liar who lies about challenging the gods to harm him for his dishonesty, only to show that they don't really seem to care at all. She is a liar who fakes being a normal girl just to have some adventures away from public duties. He knows they are both liars; she does not know he is one too. Asymmetry of gender.

So much memory is external to the body now. The holes in the past, my past, the past I imagine makes me me, are easily filled with information, from the internet. Inhuman memory: The Bocca della Verità machine is still made by an Italian company, DPS Promatic. They also make weighing scales and recording devices for weather stations. The model at Musée Mécanique is the Mini, first made in 1993. The shell is fiberglass, not plastic. DPS Promatic insists that they are the makers of the original, and that all the other companies make copies.

I put my hand in the plastic mouth a few times. None of the fortunes I received seemed as interesting as the one I got when I was with Kathy that day. You will have to suffer deception and unhappiness in love several times during your life. You are determined on changes: you've thought about it for a long time and you think it's time to bring it about. You could become entirely dominated by your partner: beware of this. And so on. Ideology tries on its concepts for a body in the second person: hey you.

New York, 1995

Why did Kathy and I not fly from San Francisco to New York together? No memory. The internet remembered for me. I went to Montreal first: September 17 to 24. To talk about cyberfeminism, and other things.[32] It comes back to me now as lonely and cold.

Then I flew to New York to meet her, where we could be together for a longer stretch of time. I had been to New York once or twice, but had more of an image of it from Hitchcock movies than from wandering in it.

In San Francisco, I was Kathy's girl; in New York, I was her top. Or rather, sometimes I tried to be. Something like that. Maybe boy and girl, top and bottom, aren't the right concepts. We had different concepts.

We did not speak the same language because we both spoke English, which is not so much a language as a mongrel tongue left as a scar on the world, by one invasion after another, all the way back to 1066.

In New York, we stayed at the Gramercy Park Hotel, 2 Lexington Avenue. "The Gramercy reminds me of what I wanted childhood to be like," Kathy said. Edmund Wilson had lived there with Mary McCarthy. Later it had a downtown vibe, but more literary than the Chelsea Hotel. This was before the inevitable Ian Schrager renovation. It was a bit on the seedy side. The room had some weird dark-colored wallpaper that immediately made me think of the hotel room in which Oscar Wilde died.

Not everything Kathy ever said to me was—strictly speaking—true. Particularly when we got to New York. It was as if we were inside a Kathy Acker book, written on flesh and city.

Chris Kraus: "Walking around New York City with McKenzie Wark, Acker stopped next to the carriages outside the Plaza Hotel and said, 'We had our honeymoon at the Plaza Hotel. Jews had theirs at the Plaza, WASPS at the Sherry-Netherland.' Wark was Australian, fourteen years younger than she was, but . . . sensed that 'there was something dreamlike about the New York she was showing me. Like a fable.' In fact, she and Bob Acker had left for San Diego right away. A rare family photo shows her in a white dress and veil, smiling, and cutting a cake next to her tall, handsome husband."[33]

There are whole websites devoted to movie locations. The Plaza Hotel is in *The Great Gatsby* and countless movies. Let's just mention Hitchcock's *North by Northwest*. Oh, and in *Home Alone 2*, Macaulay Culkin meets Donald Trump in the lobby. The Sherry-Netherland has a more discreet presence—itself a Waspy attribute—in imaginary New York, although it appears in the movie *New York Stories*. I knew nothing about New York at the time. Anything Kathy told me could be true to me, was true to me. She showed me the New York of myth.

We wandered from Central Park toward the East River, to Sutton Place. Sutton Place, she told me, was her childhood home. In the psychogeography of New York, it is certainly a place from which a Kathy Acker should hail. It is in countless movies, from *How to Marry a Millionaire* to *Black Caesar*. Lou Reed has a song that mentions *not* walking there. It's in *Catcher in the Rye*; it's in *Great Expectations* and *My Life My Death by Pier Paolo Pasolini*—by Kathy Acker—and some of her other books.[34]

She was indeed from the Upper East Side—from 400 East 57th Street, a nineteen-story Art Deco pile built in 1931.[35] Some would locate this in the Sutton Place "district," but to me, wandering about there now, it seems to have a different ambience, and that it always did. On Sutton Place the buildings are older and smaller, and there are some elegant piles from the very start of the twentieth century, built when being a millionaire was still a thing. In Kathy's day it would have smelled like old money over there. At a time when most artists and writers downplayed their bourgeois origins, maybe Kathy gave herself an upgrade.

Sarah Schulman: "To be a German Jew of that generation was to feel entitled and endangered. She was born Karen Alexander, from the kind of family known to New York Jews as 'Our Crowd'—her family, the Alexanders, along with the Loebs, Ochs, et cetera were the best educated, wealthiest, and most sophisticated Jews in the world. Kathy came from a tiny ethnic group responsible for originating the most influential theories of twentieth century: Marxism, psychoanalysis, the theory of relativity, postmodernism. And therein lay her problem. For emotionally, Kathy was average. She had no family. She was an abandoned, traumatized person. Artistically and intellectually, she was exceptional. Inherent in her supremacy was a certain kind of expectation."[36]

There is a Kathy who was an Oedipus, secretly of more noble blood, gone out into a world of writing, wherein to fuck-marry-kill all the veiled ghosts of ancestry.

Mel Freilicher: "Kathy was once approached by a distinguished looking gentleman who claimed she was a member of the prominent New York Lehman family. Clearly it's not easy to live out a myth. In her work, Kathy was brilliantly in control of her own mythmaking tendency. To me, it's an open question as to how confused Kathy herself was regarding being mythological Kathy, and how damaged by it."[37]

We walked east toward the East River, where Kathy found a little park with views of the water and the Queensboro Bridge. Sitting on a park bench, I sat in her lap and we kissed. It might have been Sutton Square, but the space does not quite feel right. My feet tire easily these days, so I did not revisit all the little green nooks along the island's edge there. Nor was I up for the long walk back across the city. Kathy and I walked so far together.

Back by Central Park, Kathy asked if I wanted a carriage ride, but I declined. Not because it was corny. Like Tracy in the movie *Manhattan*, I might have gone for it for exactly that reason. I declined because it was cold.

Bridge and Tunnel

We had drinks with The Mekons. Not much said, more a serious Northern English style of getting trolleyed.

Kathy wanted to know: Did I want to meet Ira Silverberg? Did I want to meet Betsy Sussler? I should have said yes. I didn't really know how to network with people, or who to network with. Kathy was surprised at my passivity, as was I.

I took Kathy to Lucky Cheng's, which was then in the East Village, at 24 1st Avenue at East 2nd Street. It was opened in 1993 by Hayne Suthon, an heiress with a Louisiana natural gas fortune behind her, with which to turn carbon into shine. She had style. Lucky Cheng's was in a former bathhouse and managed to hang on to a certain louche ambience. The rooms were dark, shades of ultramarine, carmine, and black, lit by nothing but the candles on the tables. The waitstaff were all trans women, mostly Asian, who presented themselves in a sleek, modern, futuristic style. Of course I adored them. Role models.

What I didn't know is that since I had last been there the clientele had changed. The Prince of Monaco had come, which brought a less downtown crowd. "It's a bit bridge and tunnel," Kathy said, meaning people from the outer boroughs, or worse—New Jersey. Actually, Lucky Cheng's had not quite reached its low point. It would later appear in the TV show *Sex and the City*, and after that it hosted bachelorette parties.

But still: I felt out of my depth. A feeling I'd had before. I'd had older boyfriends who had taste and style. With them I learned how to be decorative and obliging when out in their world, to prep them so they'd want to fuck me later. But this was a different situation, the roles less clear, and the city and its ways more foreign to me.

Topping (1)

In our room at the Gramercy, sometimes I was Kathy's girl. I wanted to watch her strap himself into her cocks. The leather harness was all black straps and shiny buckles. Its odor an appealing blend of leather, lube, and sweat. Kathy did not want my help with it, but she took her time. Choosing cocks. Inserting a cock in the harness, another in his cunt. Strapping on the harness without either falling back out again. Even after a few drinks Kathy was deft at this. I just lay back and admired her technique, his presence.

I have the pink leather bustier on again. The bustier smells like Kathy. It is rigid, creating cups for phantom tits. I feel the outside, where they would be. There's nothing there. No breasts, no me. Just a euphoria outside gender, that concept, but even closer to it. An intimacy with gender, the concept of the body. Intimacy is a distance within a closeness.

Having been fucked in the ass plenty, I know what I want. Kathy is in charge, but I am in charge of that being in charge. Kathy is in charge of another's desires. I'm on the sofa now. Kathy kneels before me. I spread my legs for him. He holds the larger black cock in one hand, gently massages herself under it with the other.

Holding that dick, pressing it against this ass, getting lube on my hand that I know I'll get on the sofa. Wondering just for a moment about all the other bodies that fucked in this room, all the combinations, all the ways they could do it, their concepts.

The cock is an inhuman black, in silicone, like some sort of matte anodized robot prosthesis. Only this is a problem, to do with that other concept of the body, its race. The bottom wants to be penetrated by an-other, brought low, but sometimes that other is a racialized other: black dick. I imagine robot black, but am I also thinking of human black? The white body brought low by the black one, the colonized one.

It is not a problem our two white bodies—Jewish white and antipodean white—are up for resolving. The theater of sex just plays out the concepts drilled into them. You know you know the ideologies. Think about them later.

Guy Hocquenghem: "What the young gay man says to the Arab is still an avowal of guilt: 'The bourgeoisie exploits you, my father exploits you, so fuck me!' Class struggle, class masochism. What hides beneath this artificial appropriation of the primitive? Sodomized, we are the only ones to shit backwards. But being the least proper does not imply that we are the least propertied."[38]

Thinking about humans with robot dicks for an instant. Pressing it against the outer ass-ring. Kathy is looking straight at me, and there I am. I appear to myself in her look.

In our room at the Gramercy, sometimes I am not Kathy's girl. Sometimes I'm her man. She gives me the sign that it's time. I leave on my jacket and sunglasses. My jacket becomes his jacket: the man.

"Get on your knees," he orders. She gets on her knees. "Suck my dick." She unzips him, fingers trembling a little, fishes his dick out and puts in in her mouth. "Not like that." She tries again. "Not like that." She tries a different tack. "Stop."

"Stand up. Take all your clothes off." Kathy takes all her clothes off. "Go sit on the toilet." Kathy leaves the room. Having not done much of this before, I'm basically just copying attitude I vaguely remember from Pat Califia stories. I decide to let her wait for me for a moment.

Kathy is sitting naked on the toilet, looking expectantly at me. "Not like that. Put the seat up. Sit on the porcelain." She does. I take out his dick and piss on her breasts and belly. The piss mostly trickling down her body, over her pubes, into the toilet. I am conscious that this is a hotel room and I don't want to make too much mess, which is probably quite out of character. I get back into character. I get into him.

"Get in the shower." She gets in the shower. He turns on the cold water—hard. Kathy gasps under the chill. I see her left knee tremble a bit. "Go into the living room. Get down on all fours." She steps out of the shower, leaves the bathroom, tracking wet on across the carpet.

I look down and see that my dick is still out, just flopping around. He would not be trying to give commands with a limp dick wiggling, but I try not to think about that. I tuck it in and zip up.

Kathy is on all fours in the living room, prone on the carpet, over a puddle. He picks up the riding crop from the sofa, where she had left it this morning, strategically placed as a sign for what she wanted. He kneels behind her and teases her back with it. For a long time.

THWACK. Flesh flinches. "One." THWACK. Flesh flinches. "Two." THWACK. Flesh flinches. "Three." THWACK. Flesh flinches. "Four." THWACK. Flesh flinches. "Five." THWACK. Flesh flinches. "Six." THWACK. Flesh flinches. "Seven." THWACK. Flesh flinches. "Eight." THWACK. Flesh flinches. "Nine." THWACK. Flesh flinches. "Nine and a half." Flesh sighs, but doesn't say stop. THWACK. Flesh flinches. "Ten."

He unzips and take his dick out. It's not hard. Make her wait. With a little coaxing he gets it hard. He takes a condom from my jacket pocket. I at least had the foresight to put some in there. He struggles to get the packet open, ends up using his teeth. Anxious for a moment about going soft again, but I don't. He rolls the condom on.

He gets down behind her. He presses the tip of this dick against her cunt. It's wet. Very wet. He just leaves it there. Teasing. She makes whimpering sounds, trembles, twitches.

And then he fucks her hard. Holding her hips, thrusting away. Human fucking seems vaguely ridiculous sometimes. This was one of those times. My thighs are longer so I'm on a weird angle. He pushes her head down, her face to the worn carpet. She cries out, but doesn't ask me (him) to stop. He fucks her for a while. Who knows how long? Her cunt is doing its little staccato spasms. Then I come.

I don't remember what happened after, other than that I cleaned the pee that had splashed on the bathroom floor. Sometime later we are in bed together. Kathy says: "Thank you." That was the only time she said that.

Kate Zambreno: "There is something unthreatening about the confessions of a white, pretty girl and her sex life. Even if she takes revenge, by telling her story, it does not ultimately threaten the order of things. Fury, though, is another thing. Kathy's girls are passive and want to be fucked and want to be loved. Yet Kathy makes it threatening because she makes it grotesque. Her porn texts are too prickly to jack off to without feeling the threat of castration."[39]

We didn't talk about it much. I made excuses for my lack of skill. I could never be anything like The German, about whom she had told me a few stories. His orders; his knife. Sounds like he was the man, not playing.

"We all exist in pain," she said, but she doesn't like to. Just a little is enough. Just like that, maybe a little more—next time. We never got to practice much. I wasn't sure this was a part of myself I wanted to know much about.

It was a more extreme masculine I that was doing this, who was becoming a stranger to me. One that felt other than human, and not in a good way. I preferred to be *that girl* with Kathy, but I could be *this man* just a bit if she wanted me to. For her. I played the man because she made me feel like her girl and, as such, I wanted to be what she wanted. I played the man when Kathy wanted it, as a girl should.

Kathy understood love when it came with acts. Enacted on bodies. Even if it was an act it was still an action, in the world. She knew too much about words to put any faith in them at all. Nobody had yet figured out an emotional life where you have lost faith in language.

Ring

Last day together in New York. In Soho, already an open-air shopping mall. Late breakfast at Jerry's, 101 Prince St. Kathy took me to her jeweler, Alex Streeter, at 152 Prince St. She had a few jewelers. She told me about the one who made her huge skull and skeleton ring. Almost the length of her finger, she'd had it made to neutralize the energy of the two rubies that became its eyes. The rubies were a gift from a Zen priest and were certainly conflict gems. Such a gift was charged with impossible challenge. The gems could hardly be thrown away or regifted or simply put aside. That Zen master perfected the cursed gift, but Kathy contained it.

Alex Streeter was a bit of jewelry legend. The rings Robert De Niro and Charlotte Rampling wear in *Angel Heart*, he made those. You can get knock-off copies of that design online for sixty bucks. Kathy bought me the fly ring that I still wear.

While working on this book, I lost it. Woke up and it was gone. I'd had some other version of the dream with which this text starts, but I don't remember any of it. Panic of loss. I only had two rings. The one Christen gave me, which can't come off over my bony knuckle. The one given by Kathy, which Christen tolerates. And which now was gone.

Kathy bought me the ring and I bought her shoes. The shoes were actually sexy black calf boots. But that isn't a ring. Although in a way giving footwear is a special act. The boot as double of my booty. Or: The boot as between the foot and the dirt and life of the world. I felt that she would rather I got her a ring too. But I couldn't afford it, and was too embarrassed to say so.

About money: I had a salary but no other money, and rent to pay. Kathy had money and owned her place, but only precarious teaching and performing income. We each thought the other was better off. Her money was running out, she said. Together, we were spending like there was no tomorrow. We went Dutch on the Gramercy Park Hotel bill. Put half each on plastic. I was paying that off for ages.

The last thing I remember is going to the movies. We saw Abel Ferrara's *The Addiction* at the Angelika at 18 W. Houston, near Broadway. Lili Taylor as an NYU grad student who becomes a vampire, or maybe a heroin addict, or maybe addicted to a certain knowledge of human abjection. A movie in which the vampire blames the victim for the victim's weakness.

Kathy wore leather pants. I stroked her thigh while we watched vampires in one of the little narrow theaters down under the ground. It felt like the right movie to see down there in the innards of the city, the deep sound of the subway rubbing its way through the walls and into our bodies.

Noise

Back in Sydney. Back to work. Feeling the absence of Kathy. Kept apart by work, money, being answerable to different sovereignties.

We emailed again like we had from the start. I lost all but one of those emails. My NYU guest account got shut down.

Kathy called my cell phone sometimes. This was still a bit of a new thing, having a cell phone, and even more new to be calling people from the other side of the world. I'd be walking down Victoria Street, under the plane trees, and the phone would ring. I'd squat in some doorway and talk to Kathy while bevies of drunk Scandinavian backpackers wove by.

She sent two gifts. She sent me a black silk camisole, with just a little lace. I still have it. It was the first time a woman gave me lingerie. I put it on at home and called her. We had phone sex a lot.

She sent me flowers. There was no occasion. I found the card that came with them not long ago. There's no date on it. The flowers came from Interflora. The card is in the handwriting of the Sydney-based Interflora agent, who would have received the instructions via fax. Kathy explained when I called her that Interflora wouldn't send the message for the card in English so she sent it in French and somewhere along the way it ended up with a typo. A little noise, that parasite, got in the transmission.

How it actually reads is:

> "encore je te veuz,
>   et enedre tes jambes
>   pour moi et ce temps pour toujours . . . a"

What it was supposed to say was:

> "encore je te veux,
>   et étendre tes jambes
>   pour moi en ce temps pour toujours . . . a"

Which might read as:

> "I still want you,
>   and spread your legs
>   for me now for always . . . a"

Memory Is Redundant

Date: Mon, 12 Feb 1996 12:57:26 -0800
From: Acker@eworld.com
To: mwark@laurel.ocs.mq.edu.au
Subject: Re: another day in the saltmines

Just read this over breakfast: I too am returning from Zirma: my memory includes dirigibles flying in all directions, at window level; streets of shops where tattoos are drawn on sailors' skin; underground trains crammed with obese women suffering from the humidity. My traveling companions, on the other hand, swear they saw only one dirigible hovering among the city's spires, only one tattoo artist arranging needles and inks and pierced patterns on his bench, only one fat woman fanning herself on a train's platform. Memory is redundant: it repeats signs so that the city can begin to exist.

Every time you dream I am fucking you, this is what happens. The city.[40]

The Viewing Room

The last time I saw Kathy was in London, in July 1997. I wasn't sure how she felt about me at that point. I had failed to drop everything to be with her in San Francisco the year before, and I had failed to make a job materialize that would have brought her to Sydney, as she wanted. I could offer no such extravagant gifts.

Things had, I felt, ended in a disappointing but amicable dead end. "Just be my friend," Kathy said, early on, and I had promised I would. Being friends is more of an undertaking than being lovers.

She had decamped from San Francisco back to London, with all its difficult memories, to be with someone.

Charles Shaar Murray: "I met Kathy Acker at a dinner party in a Mexican restaurant in Soho. A little over 24 hours after that meeting, we discovered ourselves to be in love and resolved to spend the rest of our lives together. We spent most of the next five days almost continually in each other's company."[41]

I think she knew on some level that she had cancer; or maybe knowing and not knowing. She was already planning to return to San Francisco. I happened to be coming to London on some arts organization's tab, so we agreed to meet there, in a city where both of us were strangers.

It seems likely we had a meal somewhere, but I remember nothing about that. The part I remember starts with going to see a performance. What I remember is that it was a one-man show about a gay man living with AIDS who expected to die soon. The performer had such presence, not just with his language and gesture and stories, but with his body.

The performance was in a lecture theater at a London teaching hospital. His only prop and light source was an overhead projector, of which he made brilliant use. The show was both cutting and moving at the same time, a portrait of the state, medicine, and technology as much as of this man's life.

That was the first part of the show. The second was very short. He told us that the lecture room in which he was performing was next door to a former viewing room. In the past, hospitals set aside such rooms for relatives to view the recently deceased. In a viewing room they could be arranged properly as a kind of tableau for relatives to pay their last respects. The performer asked us to wait five minutes. Then we were ushered into this viewing room.

The viewing room would have held maybe a dozen beds, a sort of ward for the dead. There was only one bed in it, and that bed was the only thing lit, the room being otherwise dark. The colors I remember are sienna, mahogany, and salamander. Or maybe those are feelings. In the bed was the performer, neatly arrayed, completely still. He was acting as his own corpse. This was the second part of the show.

Part of the point this made was that even in the late nineties, a gay man with AIDS could not count on his real friends, his family of choice, being able to be with him in hospital, or to have the right to see him in death. There was something dignified about the viewing room, the intentional staging of the dead one, and the performer turned this to his advantage. We strangers were in a place to see his future self where his friends might not.

In the viewing room, everyone was silent. The energetic buzz of premature after-show conversation dropped down to nothing. We all just stood around. Kathy was next to me. I wanted to hold her hand, or something, but I did not know if she would want me to, or if it would make her feel worse. We just stood in the audience, this audition for silence, being silent together. It was such a naked contrast to the animated quality of the first part of the show. Then we left.

The concept of the body is not its gender. The concept of the body is death.

Memory is a genre of fiction. For a long time, I have wanted to know what the performance was that Kathy and I saw on our last night together. I found out finally by asking on Facebook and tagging some people, who didn't know, but knew people, who knew people, who knew: *The Seven Sacraments of Nicholas Poussin*, by Neil Bartlett.

I ordered it from Amazon. Read it. Now I know it was performed at The Royal London Hospital in Whitechapel, from the first to the seventh of July. I had forgotten that most of it was about Poussin's paintings of the sacraments. Memory changed the ending. There is indeed a second half of the performance, but Bartlett sits in a chair opposite an empty bed, as if he were holding the hand of its occupant. The pillow is creased in the middle as if a head lay on it.

Neil Bartlett: "You will have noticed, those of you who were brought up with these words as I was, that I keep on remembering them wrong. I have erred, and said things, like I've lost my place. I have left out the words which I ought to have said, and I've put in some of those that I ought not to have put in, and I just can't help it."[42]

Kathy didn't want to go out, so we took the tube to her place, getting off at Angel station. Her apartment lay alongside one of London's canals. I could see canal boats tied up there. Kathy often said she wanted to be a sailor, to take off into the rolling waves. She was a sailor in the ways that were available to her. Writing (fucking) was her sea. I imagined her pottering about on canal boats, where the city meets the rising tide.

Her address was 14 Duncan Terrace. I'm looking at it again on Google Maps. The red door is as I remember. I see that when Street View last cruised this block, it was for sale. On the other side of her street is not the canal, it's a strip of green parkway. There are waterways nearby, and if I zoom in on the satellite image I can see narrow boats pulled up along the banks. Looking at the satellite images, and playing with the Street View, triggers other memories, whether real ones or not I don't know.

I remember her flat as one of a row of identical brick Georgian terrace houses. Judging by the quality of motor parked there, quite a posh area now. The brick grimy, the white-painted details shiny in moonlight. The famous writer Douglas Adams lived on the same block, Kathy said, but he could afford a whole townhouse. His lights were on. I caught a glimpse through the window of his bookshelves, in white wood.

In memory Kathy's place seems like a basement flat, but I don't know if that is a memory of architecture or of mood. Kathy rummaged around in the kitchen for wine, glasses, and an opener. I looked at the bookshelves. All her books seemed to be here, neatly arrayed in alphabetical order, in double rows, just like they had been in San Francisco. I got a little distracted looking at treasure I would like to read, like I did when I stayed with her that short while. When she was out at the gym I just rifled her books, stealing lines into my notebook. I was always careful to put them back in the right place.

Her library ended up at the University of Cologne. I spent a day there with them. Daniel Schulz, who has diligently catalogued them, showed me how to use the catalog on the computer and left me alone with them. I copied down notes she had left in them. In the back of one of her two copies of Italo Calvino's *Invisible Cities*, I found she had written this: "Every time you dream I am fucking you, you are building a ci the city."

We sat at the table and drank wine. Kathy was a red drinker, but she opened white as she remembered that is what I like. I had the gut feeling that we would never see each other again. The show had maybe put us into that mood, the way it had staged both the life and the death of an artist. It went past the point where most things end. It got me thinking about my own life posthumously even though as far as I knew my health was fine. Kathy was not fine. This night at least she seemed to accept that death could be fairly close.

The one thing I remember us talking about is whether anyone would care about her writing when she was gone. I imagined her own books fitted into the alphabetical sequence that threaded through her bookshelves. Right near the front—not many slot in before *Acker*. In her own library, they would come after Abe, Abish, and Achebe.

I pointed out that most of her books were in print, which was already a good sign. I improvised some lit-crit about the trajectory of avant-garde writing, as a series of careening but cumulative experiments, rolling, rising, roiling, and the way she had subsumed past experiments into her wake and made new ones. I don't know how convincing I was. I told Kathy she would be remembered, but the crucial question was not so much whether she would be remembered as by whom.

I hadn't counted on the internet keeping her interview with the Spice Girls permanently in circulation, but overall I think I was right, and that the answer I gave, while paltry, was sincere. She would find an enduring readership, but one that would not be driven by her media persona, nor be literary in the established sense. She would be treasured for a different kind of reading and writing, which maybe wouldn't be like her writing at all but would need her to have existed in order to exist. She would help make a place for us.

Leslie Dick: "I remember sitting with her on a sofa at a party and looking into her face, with its harsh make-up and amazing punk hair, peroxide blonde with brown burn marks on it as if it had been seared with a branding iron, and recognizing this spectacle as a mask she peered out from behind, or within, oddly like a little girl. Kathy Acker's readings, her self-presentation through clothes, hair, exposure of skin, tattoos, etc., her presence on the covers of her books, all worked explicitly to place her body as an obstacle, a threat and promise, mediating between reader and text."[43]

Kathy and I embraced for one last time, in the doorway to her flat. I wandered off into the night. It was too late to catch the tube back to my hotel, so I wandered about, a little anxious as I did not know where I was, but expecting to find a cab or minicab or a bus route, somewhere. I remember now that this is when I found the canal and the narrow boats, bumping in the slurping water. The boats and Kathy are together in memory, and so their places are too.

New York, 2000

Three years later I emigrated to New York. Three years after that I got an email from Matias Viegener, who among other things is the executor of the Kathy Acker estate. He was coming to New York City and asked to meet. I suggested the coffee shop in Chelsea frequented by Sandra Bernhard. Both Acker and Bernhard had written: "Without you I'm nothing."

Matias asked me what I thought about publishing my email correspondence with Kathy. I said I'd have to think about it. I knew that reading them again would be painful, but I also knew I still had the digital file, transferred, year after year, from one hard drive to another.

When I was with Kathy back in San Francisco, she was putting together a box of her papers to send to Duke University, which was to archive them. She had also just received a letter back from the archivist, she told me. The letter included an object the archivist was returning, saying simply that it was probably something she did not want included with the papers. The object in question was a strip of acid. Kathy was not a big drug taker, but she hid drugs of various kinds in the apartment. And so the acid had found its way almost into the archive.

I thought of Umberto Eco's book *The Name of the Rose*, where the blind archivist Jorge is keeping the monastery's most banned and restricted book in a room out of view.[44] In the novel that book is Aristotle's second *Poetics*, on laughter, but I think it should have been Lucretius, whose elemental swerve is still the most dangerous writing from antiquity. Jorge has also protected the book from prying eyes by dabbing a poison on the corners. A curious monk who tries to read it will wet his finger with his tongue before touching the page to turn it, again and again, and die from the act of reading itself.

I imagined the tabs of acid being buried among Kathy's papers, and some curious researcher coming across them, touching them, maybe putting his, her, or their finger to lips, kissing their own finger, and not dying from reading this time but reading on, feeling forms dissolve, the contentment of selves explode, words morph, warp, twist, curl, split, shatter, merge, bend, shrink, blur, wave. What really belongs in the archive anyway? A lot of weird things end up there. Apparently one of the other things found, this time in Kathy's personal library, was her lipstick.[45]

I wanted to be included in her archive. I wanted not to be forgotten. I thought she would forget me, and she did. Apart from the emails, I left no trace in her archive. Or almost none. Sitting in the reading room of the Rubenstein library at Duke University, turning the pages of her class notes on William Burroughs. There, on the back of a page—my old Sydney phone number, in her hand. I left the reading room in tears.

Writers get to choose their own parents. All artists do. You get to be present in the viewing room of their work whether you are on the approved family list or not, and bed down there.

Critics who write about the writers they admire, love, value, esteem, or would have wanted to fuck, or actually fucked—mostly want to top them. The critique goes over a layer of fleshy text—over the top. Picture it in an overhead shot: the critic, back turned to you, face turned to the writer, the writer looks over the critics shoulder at you, with a cold eye that could mean anything at all. I wanted a way to write about Kathy that was switchy, but—now that we're on intimate terms, let's be candid—the critical theory here is bottom theory. Writing as the trace of the want to let go, to be the one who is othered.

Steven Shaviro: "My love for you is a lost opportunity, a missed encounter. The events that move me, that affect me, that relate me to you, are precisely the ones that I am unable to grasp. I can't hold on to your life, or your love; I can only retain its passage, in the form of a scar. I was never able to possess the softness of your touch, the roughness with which you fucked me. Only the memory remains. Every line, every scar, concretizes your absence. For we suffer from reminiscences, and every reminiscence is a wound. You seeped into my body like a beautiful toxin."[46]

Oh, I found the fly ring. After that awful morning when I woke up and it was gone. It was in the bed. Must have taken it off in my sleep, during the dream in which I returned to the place the dead make for us, the dream I don't remember. I rarely remember dreams. Just the dread left in their place, an absence in memory. And just as well, as, apart from the recurring one, they are monstrous.

Linda Stupart: "She has returned. She is in pieces. She grabs McKenzie Wark's shoulders and he struggles against her, thrashing uncontrollably. For the first time we see Kathy's face. . . . She is a dead thing . . . the flesh on her face is rotting and oozing. . . . She is a ghoulish being, staring down at McKenzie Wark. . . . Kathy is thrashing wildly at all parts of McKenzie Wark's body. McKenzie Wark screams wildly. The two bodies make animal sounds. A close shot makes it clear that McKenzie Wark is lying limply on the ground with Kathy hunched over his form. Kathy Acker is doing something with the limp body, still ripping at it . . . teeth biting into male flesh his hair falling over her shoulders her bald grinning desiring skull."[47]

I remember almost nothing; the internet remembers almost everything. All that's left is the almost.

a philosophy for spiders

Part II

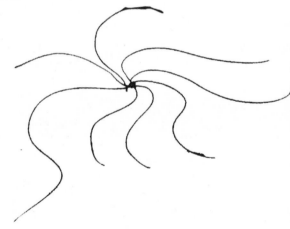

This combination of your I and I-don't-know-who-anymore
is a work of art made by both of us, and it's untitled.
—KATHY ACKER (*MY MOTHER: DEMONOLOGY*, 23)

Chapter Zero
Null Philosophy

The goddess Athena was skilled at weaving. The mortal Arachne was a weaver too, and perhaps her weaving skill was as good or better. Or perhaps it was an insult to the gods that she would even attempt to copy Athena's skill. Either way, Athena was displeased, and turned Arachne into a spider.

Maybe the problem wasn't whose weaving was better, or whether it insulted a god even to try. Maybe it is that weaving is the oldest kind of mechanical reproduction. Maybe weaving, supposedly a woman's skill, or *sophia*, was where mechanical reproduction first worked its mischief. Acker: "One might generalize by saying: the technique of reproduction detaches the reproduced object from the domain of tradition. Meaning for example: a book no longer has anything to do with literary history. . . . The art work's no longer the one object that's true." (*LM* 251)

Athena the keeper of tradition banishes Arachne the weaver from the domain of ordinary men and women. Because: "Reproducible art breaks up and ruins." (*LM* 252) Perhaps it's better to be a spider than a human anyway, particularly if female. Take the black tarantula: solitary, predatory, venomous. They have eight eyes, they hiss. Females decorate their lairs with silk. The males seek them out, dance for them. The females fuck them, or not, and eat them. For a while, Acker signed herself The Black Tarantula. "I liked tarantulas in those days and I probably like them now. . . . They're really sensual . . ." (*LI* 70)

A spider in a hedge: Acker was The Black Tarantula, but also she wasn't. The webs of words and webs of selves made each other. "It's part of the Black Tarantula syndrome. One of the ways of making your work legitimate is to work it through yourself. If you are not the I, but the I becomes you, then you have to, like, offer it as some kind of performance." (LI 114) Acker texts are a theory of self that is independent of any particular self and yet not a theory of universal selfhood. A theory of selves. And maybe more a practice of *selving*, reproducing self-ness, of braiding selves in and out of situations. "Who ever I am, I can't be known." (ES 47)

Philosophy

A word for Athena's weaving skill might once have been *sophia*. This was before Plato and his band of aristo boys created philosophy as a High Theory in which *sophia* meant not skill, ability, or praxis (in weaving, or selving, for instance) but a more contemplative wisdom. They would be lovers—*philos*—not so much of cute boys any more but of sophia, wisdom, and being posh their love would be pure. No money need change hands for the privilege.

Kathy Acker wrote philosophy, of sorts. Although they are marketed as such, maybe her books are not exactly, or not entirely, novels. "They're big chunks of prose. But are they novels? More groups of stories. Some of them aren't even that . . . somewhat philosophical treatises." (LI 218) For this Acker, "part of the work I do is sometimes theory." (RC 54) For this one, whatever the books are, she will "add a bit of theory." (LI 218)

This theory is not the high theory sort for whom Plato is daddy. More like a low theory sort of philosopher, a philosophy for spiders, "which is basically a tarantula of ideas in juxtaposition to the tarantula of fantasy that follows." (23.18) Not a philosophy for free men. More a philosophy for brutes: women, slaves, beasts. A philosophy whose skill is threading words together as its own kind of more carnal love. "The logos must realize that it is part of the body and that the body is limited." (BW 90)

It is a philosophy without fathers (or even mothers), and so no more of their Proper Names will be mentioned. This philosophy for spiders is not a philosophy in which gentlemen discourse on the nature of the beautiful, the good, and the true. It is philosophy for those who were nameless as they had to spend their time working for the money. A philosophy not by those who could arise from their place to announce it, because their place was to be on their knees, their mouths full of cock. A theory in which otherwise quite tractable bad girls and punk boys go off campus and conduct base experiments in making sense and nonsense out of situations. "Recruited due to our good intentions, V and I've instead learned a brutal philosophy: ignorance of all rational facts and concepts; raging for personal physical pleasure; may the whole Western intellectual world go to hell." (*IM* 71)

It's vulgar but not without knack. Maybe this skill that is sophia is with weaving language, but not that of the Sophists, the merchants of language skill. And yet not quite like the philosophers, the likers of (lickers of) reason. It is going to be a very contemporary love with Acker. She keeps reminding us that she does not really understand language at all. Or maybe that language does not understand her. "This is the only way I can write. Bad." (*NW* 2)

Selving

"One needs laws, the laws of writing, so one can hate them." (*NW* 3) This is philosophy without fathers, without their law. It does not say who sent it or whence it's from. It has no author or origin, which is to say: no provenance. How can it say anything about what it is? How can Acker say or write what it is? Does that not just put her in the place of some other Proper Name as that which anchors it in time and space to an author who stays firm against the flux of it?

That would be so if every time Acker appeared as the author of a statement it was the same Acker. It isn't. "My identity at any time depends on (my) lacks of stabilities." (*PE* 118) When the I speaks in an Acker-text, it is not the I of a self that knows and owns its own properties. This I is an I that could be speaking from anywhere. This I that speaks has no provenance, lineage, no patrimony: "Chance is absolutely the biggest bastard there is." (*MM* 229)

There are only Ackers in the plural. There is an Acker-web or Acker-field or Acker-text, where Ackers differ but not entirely randomly because they differ from each other. They differ from each other just as other things or events in the world differ from each other. This will be a philosophy not of subjectivity and its pet projects but of selves as things that happened to be wild in the world. "I'm trying to become other people because that is what I find interesting. . . . I'm trying to get away from self-expression but not from personal life. I hate creativity." (PE 86)

There are solitary spiders and there are social spiders, who weave their webs communally, who extrude sticky lines out of themselves that cross and mesh. The authority of a solitary self is not what authorizes the Acker-text. There could be an authorization in the negative that sets this Acker-field under its empty sky: "No religion is my stability and surety." (MM 13) But that's not much to go on. There is no coherent philosophy that can be interpreted from the texts and attributed to a self-same Kathy Acker as one that she affirms. Or even to a Kathy Acker who evolves and grows over time.

So what might authorize the presumption to speak here of a philosophy of the Acker-web? Well, for a start, the Acker-text is studded with philosophical questions. Here is just a sample: "How can writing matter?" (EU 23) "Who am I? What is the human body?" (ES 46) "Is reality always this unknown?" (ES 32) "Have I ever experienced anything I can't remember?" (EU 17) "What if language need not be mimetic?" (BW 166) "What does my desire look like?" (BW 63) "Has anybody seen gender?" (BW 166) "How can happiness be possible in this society?" (BW 11) "How can I be free if I'm broke?" (IM 24) "What is it to be an artist?" (DDH) "What matters to me?" (LM 218) "Does horror come from Nature?" (MM 108) "What is the essay in this situation?" (BW x) "Why write at a time such as this? I am writing down this question." (BW viii)

The writings form a continuum, a web, a field, a texture of connected differences, across a wind-tossed surface on which many Ackers dance and spin as they pose such questions. "Since didn't have one point of view or centralized perspective, was free to find out how texts she used and was worked." (DDH) It is something like a phenomenology without the subject, or with multiple, volatile moments where subjectivity erupts or surfaces.

And yet the text has some consistency, a skein of words raveled in time. "All I have left is my writing. That's the only stability I know have ever known." (*PE* 40)

Wonder

"I want to live forever in wonder." (*BW* 159) This philosophy for spiders corrodes all powers of certainty and order, is tossed in the wind. "The glory in my mind was formless." (*ES* 66) Everything seems to be in flux, disorder, both in awareness and the world. "It seems that everything that happens to me is all chance." (*HL* 105) Even the distinction between selves and worlds wobbles. "I have no idea what comes from inside and what comes from outside." (*PE* 60) And: "We are particulars. . . . There's more and more world a proliferation of phenomena. . . . How can you be apart from the world? Who's doing the changing?" (*LM* 277)

It begins, rather than ends, with: "We don't know anything." (*DQ* 112) Although not even that is certain. Even a methodical skepticism appears too in order and thus questionable. "I know that I can't know anything, but I don't know what this knowledge is." (*MM* 58) And "How do I know anything? What does this language mean? I'll have to trust nothing. I know I trust nothing too much. I will do anything for nothing." (*LM* 196) Experience is not to be trusted: "Can I describe (know) anything truthfully? No." (*LM* 320) The sequence of time does not reveal an order: "I don't understand what any event means." (*LM* 224) Reason too is unreliable, as "Reality is enough to make you crazy." (*ES* 86)

Is a philosophy even possible that is not, paradoxically—naïve? Can there be a thinking that knows about the things high theory chooses not to know too much about? (Just for starters: the experiences of selves that are dismissed as those of a woman, a slave, or a beast.) A theory that begins by acknowledging its not-knowing, and then by finding what can be said, for instance, as a woman, but yet not assuming it knows anything much about that either, or even that it is all that coherent a thing to be. To find words for that. "I thought that if I could just call things by their proper names, I could get rid of evil and hurt. I knew that in order to do this, I had to be naïf." (*IM* 133) A punk philosophy: here's three concepts, now form your worldview.

If this knowledge of the world was possible, it would destroy the knower. "And 'she was given the real names of things' means she really perceived, she saw the real." (GE 63) The real might not be something that a knowledge of it can endure. "There is no way to prepare for horror. Language like everything else will bear no relations to anything else." (GE 34)

This need not be because the real is some kind of horror that annihilates selves on contact. Noumena need have no fangs. The possibility that the real has qualities, changes, is not self-evidently the same, is enough to destabilize a presumed knower of it. This may just invite curiosity. "How can I know how I've changed, what change is, if at every moment I am exactly who I am?" (ES 56) Not only is self in flux and world in flux; the relation between them us in flux. None of which can be subsumed under stable concepts, even concepts of flux or change. It's all different steps, by different selves, in different rivers. Wonderful!

Writing

"To write is to do other than announce oneself as an enclosed individual." (BW 104) For language too is in flux, except perhaps when it is writing. The only thing with any stability is writing. "What is writing? This is writing." (LM 303) And yet writing is not particularly special. It is just a thing (event) in the world, different from other things (events) in the world just as other things (events) in the world differ from each other.

How can anything know anything about itself without something different being there that is what it is not? If language had a special origin or destiny, it would have a special difference from that which it is not. But it doesn't. This Acker says: "How available are the (meanings of the) specifics of all that is given? Language is a giveness like all the other givenesses." (LM 201)

Writing has no special relation to the world, nor does it have a special relation to the self. "If I understand language in this manner: by saying something I intend something, then whatever I say means some other things because one event can be equivalent only to itself . . ." (LM 219) And: "Human beings say one thing and mean another. That's what they mean by language." (LM 239) Writing says nothing special about its author. "I don't know what I write so you can't pin me down." (*LM* 232) "What I'm doing is simply taking text to be the same as the world." (*HL* 13)

Language is just one thing among many. It isn't special. It has no divine purpose. Language is not where the other things (events) are redeemed or known. "If writing's nothing: it isn't presenting a story, it isn't presenting an expression of what's real, since it isn't even this (time past); it is, going back to beginnings." (*LM* 298) Writing just is: Events in the world, differing from others only in tempo. "Decided to use language stupidly." (*DDH*)

This language is just language. It isn't a means to an end, to the idea, or to logos or reason or the world. And it can't even really be known. It can just be written. The sophia of writing is the writing of it. Acker no longer has faith in it. "Language means nothing anymore anyway." (*GE* 29) If you write it differently, you might find some other ways it can work. Language becomes known through the writing of it, through experiments and practice. But that's all.

Whose language is it? This language is the language of men. They say what it is and isn't. What it does and doesn't do. What it ought and ought not to do. Or so they imagine. "The writer's voice was a process, how he had forced the language to obey him, his will. . . . All these male poets want to be the top poet, as if, since they can't be a dictator in the political realm, can be dictator of this world." (*DDH*) All these philosophy-tops, too.

Writing is just another thing in the world, not the language of its essence. It has no special powers. But it may have some modest powers. This Acker: "Writing, narration, does not end suffering: writing masters nothing. Narration, writing, does something else. It restores meaning to a world which hardship and suffering have revealed as chaotic and senseless." (*BW* 100) This is what writing can do for those who are beasts, slaves, or women.

If a woman is to be a philosopher then perhaps she will have to do something else and be someone else. Men even made knowledge itself a woman: sophia, spirit of the trinity. The father, son, and the feminine spirit. Already she is outnumbered. "For 2,000 years you've had the nerve to tell women who we are. We use your words; we eat your food. Every way we get money has to be a crime. We are plagiarists, liars, and criminals." (*BG* 132) Female are those whose language has no provenance, just as that which can be mechanically reproduced has no provenance. "I am one big question but I can only ask through other texts: I hardly have a language of my own." (*SW* 50)

Without provenance, without a subjectivity descended and authorized by patrimony and law as entitled to speak, how is she to think, to write? "Since wanted to be a writer, tried hard to find her own voice. Couldn't. But still loved to write. Loved to play with language. Language was material like clay or paint." (*DDH*)

Texts without certitude, letters that aren't certified, much of it copied but not even properly copied. A theory where object and subject are vague pulsations, haphazard events, but where even the relation between them has no definite quality, either of dialectic or difference. It's the means to a null philosophy, a nothing. Another Acker: "A language that I speak and can't dominate, a language that strives fails and falls silent can't be manipulated, language is always beyond me, me me me. Language is silence. Once there was no truth; now I can't speak." (*GE* 96)

Rather than a fundamental difference, the separation of self and world appears as a secondary effect of sensation. "Only sensations. What the imagination seizes as Beauty must be truth—whether it exists materially or not." (*GE* 68) Elsewhere in the Acker-field, another Acker will subject this "must be" to considerable doubt. Whatever one Acker affirms, another will question. What persists is that dreams are the labor of imagination. And yet imagination subjected to consciousness has the same limit as sensation subjected to consciousness—the imposition of a coherent line controlling its fluxes. "Everything must be sacrificed to that moment: seeing that which is hidden. Otherwise people don't exist. How can writing matter?" (*EU* 23)

When the I speaks for itself it becomes other than itself. Such other-I's can be written. Selves can come into and out of the Acker-field. They appear in three ways. As writing themselves, as a *first philosophy*, of appearances, emotions, bodily functions. As encounters with an-other, with parents and rapists but also with lovers and sadists: a *second philosophy*, a philosophy of two-ness. And then also as *third philosophy*, beyond selves, others, into worlds: of the city, politics, culture, labor, art-making, capitalism, and post-capitalism.

Chapter One
First Philosophy

Exteriority

"Who am I? What is the human body?" (ES 46) "Perception has become a philosophical problem." (ES 27) But who or what is doing the perceiving, and what is there to be perceived? "Is reality always this unknown?" (ES 32) "I was totally unprepared for reality." (PE 87) And: "I'm trying to figure out what reality is." (PE 25) And then: "If reality isn't my picture of it, I'm lost." (ES 29) Most Ackers really want to know what is real. They just have a lot of doubts about what can be known, about methods of knowing, and about the who or the what it is that thinks it knows.

"It used to be that men wandered over the earth in order to perceive new phenomena and to understand. I was a wanderer like them, only I wandered through nothing. Once I had had enough of working for bosses. Now I had had enough of nothing." (ES 81) I'll come back to the matter with bosses. This null philosophy begins in boredom, feeling about for ways to think something other than nothing. Which is hard when nothing can ever be the same as itself, let alone in a consistent relation with something else. "I don't think that 'this' equals 'that'; I don't think in that kind of mode, that way of thinking. That kind of thinking, 'this' equals or means 'that,' is identity thinking, thinking concerned with meaning or closure." (PA 89)

Let's start with what seems exterior, non-identical, not to the self, but to something also in flux but a bit more stable, to writing. Language is nothing, or at least nothing special. From what language is not, an Acker tries to figure what is not language: "There is just moving and there are different ways of moving. Or: there is moving all over at the same time and there is moving linearly. If everything is moving is moving-all-over-the-place-no-time, anything is everything." (GE 58) There is a world of moving all over at the same time, and there is language which might be one of the things (events) that moves linearly. Language is indeed different from other things but it is not a special kind of difference. A difference against which to mark the passing of others.

In the Acker-web, interiority might not be a primary and dependable difference from exteriority. "I can't distinguish between my memories of dreams, waking actions, and what I've read and been told." (ES 53) And: "I can't understand what's happening in this world. It's all change." (BW 22) There might not be a self that can be self-same, and that can then be different from the world as a first difference. The I that speaks or writes doesn't have properties. This Acker: "Only when I was nothing would I begin to see." (PK 9) And: "Whenever I stop thinking, I step out of existing into nothing." (ES 61)

Linear language, one moving thing among many, makes the self, the subject, the I. And so: "There's no cause-and-effect (narrative) except in language." (PE 135) The I is not that which perceives but an obstacle to it. "Human will makes causality; causality destroys my ability to perceive." (LM 328) The alternation between senses of self might itself be a useful kind of sensation. "I'll say it again: without I's, the I is nothing." (DQ 101) Moving between various I's might make a field of selvings rather than a line of points of view, an Acker-field, Acker-web or Acker-text, where the proper name is arbitrary.

"Of what use is all this—drama, tribulations? What is my life? Just phenomena?" (DQ 68) What a web of various selvings of the I might perceive is an exteriority that escapes from linear causality. "In this world where the law of probability governs reality a quiet invisible threat hangs over everything. Fear now dictates all of our actions." (LM 225) Which might be reason enough to retreat from the world. "Why don't you let me go: I want to go back to not-existing which is freedom." (GE 65)

While there are Ackers that retreat from the world, there are Ackers that feel impelled toward it: "I go straight for the information, the knowledge, I'm too curious." (PE 13) Fear again plays a role here: "The coupling of curiosity and fear is the door to the unknown." (MM 12) And: "Fear is what makes humans inhuman." *(IM* 108) And for some Ackers, as we shall see, the emotion of fear combines with other sensations. "I'm being woken up when I'm feeling a combination of fear and pleasure. This combination is called CURIOSITY." *(HL* 110)

Emotions

Emotions are kinds of sensation, but they aren't exactly subjective. They don't refer back to a self as they exceed linear language and the selvings that language usually makes. "I'm not human, my emotions are hidden somewhere else and very dangerous." *(SW* 30) Emotions, feelings, affect, might be keys to a certain kind of understanding that is subjective but not necessarily individuated. "As if reality was emotional, I perceived solely by feeling." *(EU* 21) Feelings can become concepts. For instance: "Anxiety is time gone wrong." *(MM* 213)

A philosophy of the emotions, like a philosophy of language or of sensation, has to start from doubt, uncertainly, confusion—with nonknowledge. "My emotional limbs stuck out as if they were broken and unfixable." *(GE* 58) And: "I don't think I'm crazy. There's just no reality in my head and my emotions fly all over the place." *(GE* 65)

Still, "Real teaching happens via feelings." *(DQ* 159) And: "My feelings're my brains." *(DQ* 17) Rather than a mastery of the language of feelings, the Acker-text usually does the opposite. "I feel I feel I feel I have no language, any emotion for me is a prison. I think talking to humans, acting in this world, and hurting other humans are magical acts. I fall in love with the humans who I see do these things." *(GE* 24) The self appears as a residue of particular events in the world. What it feels is part of that event. Events lodge in memory. Narrative makes up a story that makes these emotions about events appear as consistent, and as consistently referring to the same self, same world. None of this is real.

Emotions can be kinds of intensity that break with narrative and memory. Attention to emotion is more about questioning the possibility of being in the world. "Where do emotions come from, are emotions necessary, what do emotions tell us about consciousness?" *(GE* 38) And: "Do I care? Do I care more than I reflect? Do I love madly? Get as deep as possible. The more focus, the more the narrative breaks, the more memories fade: the least meaning." (*GE* 61)

Memory

"Have I ever experienced anything I can't remember?" (*EU* 17) And: "Is there any other knowing besides this remembering?" (*ES* 48) Memory's relation to experience is questionable. "I can't remember anything anyways . . . except dreams." (*IV* 24) Although for some Ackers, "I remember pleasure." (*ES* 49)

What memory is supposed to do is produce past-present relations that anchor a self to a preexisting narrative, particularly to a narrative about one's own origins, lineage, provenance. "I remember events more clearly because I remember more clearly about my parents." (*PE* 130) To most Ackers, this is not a happy memory or narrative. "My first memory or bit of memory of memory is of absence." (*MM* 182) And: "My first meaning-relation (remembering) to the world is hatred." (*PE* 130) And so: "Janey believes it's necessary to blast open her mind constantly and destroy every particle of memory that she likes." (*HL* 38)

Pain is what the self remembers. How far can one remember? "As far as being hurt." (*DQ* 134) Memory is the means through which history leaves its marks. Unbidden pain is that which thwarts a self's desires. So could desires be a more reliable guide to being in the world? "But I have a bad memory of desire." (*ES* 48) Desire might still be too dependent on a narrative before and after. Not past and present, as in memory, but present and future. Memories arrest not only time but also locate a subject in a point of view: "When I remember, I remember an awareness, not an object. I don't remember my hamster I remember seeing my hamster." (*PE* 137)

Sensation, awareness of and in world, is a forgetting of past pain, even if pain remains a possibility in the present as well. At least it is not the only possibility of the world. "Why disturb the good life you've managed to make for yourself by remembering anything?" (*LM* 261) And so: "I'm whatever has been. There's no memory." (*LM* 220) In place of memory, writing. Writing present sensations stabilizes them in time a little, leaving a trace for another to experience, for some other series of present sensations stimulated by the presence of the written one.

"Almost everything that I know and can know about my pre-adult life lies not in memories but in these writings." (MM 8) Writing runs the risk of making memory over as that which will leave the trace of an ideal past to be imitated, demanding in advance that future sensations conform to its outline. "As a form of memory, beauty is a representation of what's past, over with, dead; but now since present delight was equal to memory, beauty could not be named." (ES 49)

"I'm no longer interested in my memories, only in my continuing escalating feelings." (PE 47) Being open to the field of sensation as one of simultaneity and chance entails not just an oscillation between selves, but a distancing from memory, for memory anchors one point in a linear narrative that orders time for an apparently continuous and self-same self. "Now that my mind's open, I can't remember anything." (ES 49) And then here, for many Ackers, is a means to a much wanted unfixing: "Memory slips even more than . . . what? . . . gender." (IV 22)

"All memories are trivia." (ES 50) A memory, not unlike a desire, makes a point of view. But memory could also be a field that generates points of view. These "memories do not obey the law of linear time." (MM 41) And while language might be linear, this memory infects it with the nonlinear and yet draws language back to the repetition of established narrative lines. Memory makes for an orderly time. There might be other times.

Time

"At that very moment I understood that my capacities for understanding are so puny that reality (for me) is Chance. Due to this ignorance, my will is useless. For me, strangeness was and is everywhere." (ES 156) The self can't be a ground for knowing the world, as one cannot take as given that it is a self-same thing. "I'm not a 'substance.' Change (temporal relations) is a substance. . . . Therefore I'm composed of an unknown number of such individuals. I is a (predicate) relation." (PE 138) The Acker-web wending in the wind.

What if time had substance? A self that is substance might be self-same, consistent, something that is a unity first and then different to the world, to what it is not, to events in time. If time, which is difference itself, is substantial, then this unity and priority of the self would be an illusion. In the Acker-field, the I, the self, is an aftereffect, always uncertain and porous, but this does not in itself establish the reality of a world of sensation as difference—just its possibility.

An Acker: "Say there's two theories of time. Absolutist theory of time: the world is in time. The world, events occur in moments. These moments can be mapped on a time line. Relativist theory of time: time is in the world. Time is the temporal relation of events. An event can be earlier (later) than or simultaneous with another event. The first theory suggests that individuals (subjects) are the true substance. The second theory suggests that temporal characters are the true substance of the world." (PE 136)

Time isn't a self-same thing that can be measured off in identical units, and, if time can't really be stabilized, neither can identity. "But what if there aren't distinct moments? I can't be a substance, an individual who persists in time." (PE 137) A self is a sensational derivative of events. As a kind of self, an author too is a sensational derivative of events. The author is product, not producer.

The problem with writing is that it imposes an orderly time through the imposition of meaning. The meaning is separate from, and anterior to, the event of which it claims to be the truth. Perhaps there could be another writing. "Why am I so violent? Because I like violence. When something means something, that event (the first something) can't be just what it is present in itself. The abolition of all meaning is also the abolition of temporality." (LM 216) Writing can't represent time as it is. Writing could at least kick against this inability.

Alternately, writing need not represent time at all. It already is time. Is a time, a temporality. "I am thinking that the more I write, the more convinced I am that writing, be it about time, is time. Is change, rhythm. Those movements of time. Need writing be only one kind of time, linear time, that form called history? Need writing end? . . . What would writing look like outside of linear narrative time?" (BW ix)

Another Acker: "If this is so, how can I differentiate? How can there be stories? Consciousness just is: no time. But any emotion presupposed differentiation. Differentiation presumes time, at least BEFORE and NOW. A narrative is an emotional moving." (GE 58) Here an Acker moves from language in general to what many Ackers take to be one of its qualities: narrative, which, put quite simply, is the linearity of language that puts one thing after another. The one thing after another produces a difference within language but always of the same kind. This same-difference makes a self that appears to itself as a change, a difference, between one emotional state and another.

Narrative

This language in which a self appears is not one in which to have any trust or faith. The god of language is dead, or could be. Language doesn't make the self or its relation to the world real. Language doesn't participate in logos—the law, form, order, idea, or origin of the world. "The difference between a writer and its world gives the reason for writing." (NW 1) But then writing has no special way of closing the gap.

Most Ackers write prose, in formally coherent sentences, but without belief in the form. "Culture has been chattering and chattering but to no purpose. When a sentence becomes distinct, it makes no more sense or connection." (GE 34) Sentences are just things in the world. A sentence has a logic in itself, but it doesn't give or receive an order or sense of the world. "This sentence means nothing." (LM 246) It's a paradox that shows nothing so much as the double nature of writing, as appearing to be at one with what it evokes but in actuality to be displaced from it.

"Human desire creates a story." (DQ 61) Then that story is just a thing in the world, a part of the world. It does not express or double or figure the order of the whole. The struggle against language, that language that makes an order, a before and an after, and a self that remains continuous across that the difference, this struggle still has to take place within language. "I want: every part changes (the meaning of) every other part so there's no absolute / heroic / dictatorial / S&M meaning / part." (GE 8) And: "The passing wind immediately modulates the least organic noise that's why one text must subvert (the meaning of) another text until there's only background music." (GE 15)

In a linear language a self can appear which feels itself in the difference-yet-continuity between one emotion and another. But this self is subject then to language, to its powers. It gives itself up to language as that which fathers the difference that makes it appear as consistent to itself. A linear language makes a lot of befores and afters, which makes subjects, who think they know who they are when they say "I." The I is made rather than a making. Made by language, subject to language.

"The ceiling of languages is falling down. Either add to this rubble or shove at least some of it away." (ES 163) The heavens fall. Maybe there can be other ways language can be a making. One sentence does not follow from another. One sentence does not control what another sentence will do. One sentence that comes before another sentence need not create an illusion of a causal or even sequential link between them. The line breaks, twists, loops: the interiority of the reader can meet with (can fuck with) the world of which it is just some variable part anyway. Then there's no human subjectivity any more. "As soon as we stop believing in human beings, rather know we are dogs and trees, we'll start to be happy." (BG 37)

This other writing breaks with the orderly use of memory, with a continuous line from a (mis)remembered past to the appearance of a present, but also with the desired projection of a future. "I have nothing to do with the future: I don't envisage it. Writing, along with everything else, if there are anything, is right now. Writing is the making of pleasure as are everything else including death." (LM 216)

This other writing is back in the world, back in an immediate fluxion of time, and becomes so by renouncing all claim to order time's meanings. "These writings are the fuels of love. Each statement is an absolute truth— and an absolute lie—because I'm always changing." (LM 303) As to what this love might be, one thing that could be said for now, is that it is not the love of one individual for another.

There could still be something narrative could do, however. There could be not just stories about others, cut to the same old form, but other kinds of story. "I was looking for any narrative form besides the white Oedipal set-up." (PA 88) Stories that don't claim to reveal or restore the old order. Stories of and for women, slaves, and beasts.

The I need not go away, it just changes from a singular to a plural function: eyes rather than an I. The compound eyes of spiders. An eye is in the world and a point of view on the world, a vector extending from a point that can track or rotate. This written I that is an eye is like cinema but also not like cinema in that it can see feelings as well as visual or auditory sensations. "For the soul and the heart are the eyes." (DQ 91)

Freed from constancy as anything other than a vector from a point, the I can become ecstatic. "Everything's moving. Voice, articulation, incantation, thunder. I see everything. I see the moving treetops: Park foliage squeeze open close like a voluptuous cunt: Sky stretch out farther farther. There's my senses. I'm total music. Sex. Energy. Vitality. I'm ecstatic. Ecstatic. I perceive the root of my senses. My cunt swells. I'm all strong. I became jealous of nature. I should control every event, my desires and my breath should control every event. My solitude was making me see this. . . . I was fifteen years old." (PE 156)

And another Acker: "It seemed to me that my sexuality was a source of pain. That my sexuality was a crossroads not only of my mind and body but of my life and death. My sexuality was ecstasy." (ES 65) The ecstatic self is outside of itself, beyond itself, strange to itself. It can be that I that is another. "One has to exist in pain." (NW 1)

But wait, perhaps it's a bit harder than that. "Once we have gotten a glimpse of the vision of the world, we must be careful not to think the vision world is us." (BG 37) It is not so simple as a love of the world, an embrace of the world, being of the world. That would be to presume still that there is love. The eye only partly frees the I from sameness. "Since the I who desired and the eye who perceived had nothing to do with each other and at the same time existed in the same body—mine; I was not possible." (ES 33)

The eye too has to be doubted. It can perform acts of reading and writing that cut, fold, flip, repeat narrative order, interrupt the linear difference which makes a single self. But what awaits is not oneness with the world. "To see. To see the nothingness. That is vision." (BG 39) And as for what sees nothingness: "Each person is an asking, a peculiar kind of hole."

(*BG* 126) But then, "After a while self-absorption is boring because one sees thoughts are only thoughts and one wants freedom." (*NW* 1)

Boredom

What might result is a kind of boredom: "The ideals and fantasies in my mind have no meaning. There's only boredom except for a prayer to nobody." (*IM* 36) Boredom is of a piece with the throwing down of all values, extending from the death of language as a god, taking down with it self and world, leaving two voids, one peering sightlessly into the other. An Acker: "I've lost my beliefs. There's nothing left." (*DQ* 125) This boredom is not a place within which most Ackers can be for long: "Boredom is the emotion I find most unbearable." (*IV* 24)

Rather than an ecstatic tumble into the world of otherness, boredom might be the absence of any relation to it. "For boredom comes from the lack of correspondence between the desire of the mind and body and the society outside the mind and body." (*IM* 10) And: "Boredom is the lack of dreams." (*ES* 58) And: "I can only feel boredom in times of want." (*SW* 102) To be bored is to be stuck in the mute nonrelation between the void of the self and the void of the orderly world, the world of other people.

Boredom might be worse than death. "Eurydice tries to escape by being dead. . . . After a minute, she's bored." (*EU* 12) Overcoming boredom, strange to say, calls for solitude, calls for a break with the world of selves and the expectation of being a self like them. "The world I perceive, everything I perceive are indicators of my boring needs. Otherwise there's nothing. I might as well not exist. I don't think I care about anything. All my emotions, no matter how passionate, are based on my needs. So I can figure out at this point how to make enough money get enough people out of my life so I can relax sleep all the time every few days. Is there any other reason besides negativity?" (*BG* 111)

"The cities have died. The cities are full of rats; the rats are bored: people seem as lonely as they are bored." (*ES* 14) Here is our first hint of a third philosophy, beyond the self of a first philosophy and even the self-other relation of a second philosophy. Exit from the boredom of the self, and of the self in relation to others just like it, calls for solitude, but solitude will depend on organizing life and labor in such a way as to make that possible. "I mainly needed to be financially supported, left alone, fucked, told I'm a wonderful writer." (PE 113)

Solitude

An Acker: "My life's solitude and mess." (IV 64) "I live alone. Anything else I write is nonsense. There's no other sentence except about knowing. I must tell you—I'm frightened. I must tell you—it makes me shiver." (LM 13) A recurring impulse is toward solitude, which sparks an array of feelings. "My being alone is my absolute pleasure." (DQ 69) And yet: "For being lonely is what scares me most in the world." (PK 93) There's an unresolved and unresolvable tension between solitude and being with another. "I have always felt anxiety based on this situation: I need to give myself away to a lover and simultaneously I need to be always alone." (MM 15)

Many Ackers oscillate between extremes of solitude and intimacy, "What I feel is lousy, immense discouragement, a heaviness of unbearable isolation . . . absence of desires, impossibility of finding any sort of amusement. I call this my laziness." (NW 2) And then: "I run away from everything." (GE 19) In part because of a lack of faith in the human, an unwillingness to participate in the fantasy of being with another as the good. "I used to have the strength to believe what I feel is real and my affection for people makes me human." (GE 33) Another Acker: "When I'm alone I live in a vision in which each sensation, no matter whether pleasurable or displeasing, each thought becomes framed in blackness. I become more and more aware of everything." (PE 127)

From within solitude, the problem of the (im)possibility of a relation to another reappears again and again. "Please tell me if the world is horrible and if my life is horrible and if there's no use trying to change, or if there's anything else? Is desire OK?" (BG 138) The solitary can produce difference out of itself, with its own methods. "Dear dreams, you are the only thing that matters." (BG 36) Like memory, the world of fantasy does not follow that of linear language; unlike memory it need not be fixed in a linear sequence of time.

Taking memory as an anchor in past time, narrative language negates the world by imposing order on it. Fantasy, or imagination, written out of a moment of detachment from others, from the world, from the temporality of solitude, negates narrative language by freeing it from order. Fantasy is the negation of the negation of the world. "In this way fantasy reveals reality. Reality is just the underlying fantasy, a fantasy that reveals a need. I have an unlimited need of him." (BG 20) The means by which the imagination is made actual is through dreams, or rather, through the writing and rewriting of dreams.

"I had learned to travel through my dreams." (PK 96) "All my life I've dreamt dreams that, after the initial dreaming, stayed with me and kept telling me how to perceive and consider all that happens to me. Dreams run through my skin and veins, coloring all that lies beneath." (MM 133) The dream is not reducible to the family romance. That would be to return to a state of boredom. Nor are they there to be interpreted. "I just wrote down dreams aren't fake. I don't know what this means." (MM 201) And: "Dream was a language I accessed; I did not make it up. I did not compose it." (PA 91)

"Without dreams, what is time?" (MM 59) For time to have any qualities, to be a substance, something has to be without time, and that other thing is apparent in dreams. "I know that we change continually when we're alive, but I don't know whether that's true in dreams. And all that's past lives in the realm of dreams." (ES 229) To be a subject within linear language is to experience the self as differences in emotions experienced sequentially. Neither the dream world nor the world have that particular temporal quality. "There is no time; there is." (GE 7)

"Dreams are true in the dream beyond good and evil." (BW 76) And: "To dream's more violent than to act." (LM 271) This might be the particular violence to which Acker is drawn. The dream is more violent because it does not act in time but against time. Dreams are a raw material for escaping the temporal order of memory, where linear time and the self might dissolve. "How many dreams must we dream in search of real love?" (IM 30) And: "I dream of finding the key to this myth of my desire." (IM 80) Dreams are, however, not something to be interpreted, read back toward the family romance, or the self's hidden desires. Rather, they point outward. Dreams are immediately within a social and historical field but provide the materials for arranging its elements otherwise.

Rather than read a dream back to (for example) repressed desire for the father, they can be rewritten outward, as it were, onto a writing that aims to map and escape the line of succession of fathers whose narrative appears to order the world. The dream needs no authority outside itself, and obeys no separation between identities. "When I dream, my body is the site, not only of the dream, but also of the dreaming and of the dreamer. In other words, in this case or in this language, I cannot separate subject from object, much less from the acts of perception." (BW 166)

Acker: "There are only dreams. This is the nothing which you men call death; therefore, in your male language, death and women are friends." (MM 195) And: "I have nightmares and they're not nightmares. I didn't say this out loud because it was men who were doing the talking. I let them. Dreams are the mouths of us girls, and all the poets know this." (PK 133) Because: "To be a poet is to wake inside someone else's skin." (IM 23) In dreams no self is its own property or anyone else's.

A first philosophy, of the self, or rather of selving, is immediately also a third philosophy of the social field. "The infinity and clarity of desire in the imagination made normal society's insanity disappear." (IM 5) Dreams are a means of accessing imagination. "When I fantasize fucking, the encounters are always cold wild and free." (BG 58) The social field can, however, change, and a third philosophy of post-capitalism appears here too: "When I started to spend all my free time with the computer, my dreams stopped." (RC 53)

Imagination

Imagination too can be questioned: "If imagination still exists in this world —which could be doubtful . . . there must be an Imaginer. Otherwise imagination, imagining only itself, isn't imagination. It is possible that there is no imagination, that this world is dead. Otherwise there must be an imaginer." (DQ 181) There is every reason (and unreason) to suspect that imagination has been colonized by the fathers of controlling sameness. It becomes a compromised refuge rather than a rampart. As we shall see when we get to Acker's third philosophy, that might be what's happened under post-capitalism.

"The imagination is will." (*DQ* 49; *BW* 114) This is the paradox of the dream state, and of imagination more broadly. It is free from linear language, but it is also a state of pure positivity. It knows no prohibition. (Hence its violence.) It can't not turn into desire for something other. It is a realm of freedom and yet, as a realm of freedom, is free also to desire without limit, reason, or right. And so: linear language negates the world, imagination negates linear language, and then as pure positivity it engages the world again, albeit only within itself. "Thus I learned that the door to the invisible, the only place that is left for us to go, must be made visible." (*MM* 205)

Imagination detaches itself from linear language in two senses: as narrative and as reason. "The German Romantics had to destroy the same bastions as we do. Logocentrism and idealism, theology, all supports of the repressive society. Property's pillars. Reason which always homogenizes and reduces, represses and unifies phenomena or actuality into what can be perceived and so controlled." (*ES* 12) Going beyond them is to go beyond their self-satisfaction in their own transgressions. "The death of reason isn't blackness. It's another kind of light." (*ES* 182)

The stylistic tactics deployed across the Acker-text change over time. They go through periods. The underlying philosophical problematic remains the same. Up until *Empire of the Senseless*, most Ackers attack linear language itself, over and over, refusing to let it structure and control the world, refusing to become a believer in its power over the world it orders (on the one side) and the selves it inculcates (on the other). "There is no master narrative nor realist perspective to provide a background of social and historical facts." (*PK* 80)

And yet the power invested in the imagination by the Romantics has itself to be put in doubt. "Do you think it's possible to destroy poverty or any other social ill or rejection by an act of the imagination?" (*IM* 141) It might not be enough to return from the solitude of fantasy, the negation of linear language, just to negate that language.

"That part of being (mentality, feeling, physicality) which is free of control let's call our 'unconscious.' Since it's free of control, it's our only defense against institutionalized meaning, institutionalized language, control, fixation, judgment, prison." (*ES* 134) So far so good, but what if this was just a retreat from faith in linear language to a faith in the language of the imagination, or its close cousin, the unconscious? What if that god too is dead?

"Ten years ago it seemed possible to destroy language through language: to destroy language which normalizes and controls by cutting that language. Nonsense would attack the empire-making (empirical) empire of language, the prisons of meaning. But this nonsense, since it depended on sense, simply pointed back to the normalizing institutions. . . . If this ideal unconscious or freedom doesn't exist: pretend it does, use fiction, for the sake of survival, all of our survival." (*ES* 134)

Body-work

Dreams open onto a practice of writing that can escape from linear language, but writing is still a practice that is all too fluent in language. Later, there are Ackers who prefer a writing in relation to something more visceral: bodybuilding. "The flesh must be the mind." (*IM* 118) As with dreaming, it's a bodily practice, but one that can have only an indirect relation to language and that opens up a path to a different kind of language. "People assume writing is cerebral whereas bodybuilding is material. But they work together." (*HL* 22)

"The body deals with narratives. I don't mean stories. The knee gets hurt and then it gets better." (*LI* 216) Bodybuilding isn't that kind of narrative. It breaks muscle down, makes it fail. While structured by counting off repetitions, the flesh of the body keeps its own time, which appears indirectly as unexpected pain or euphoria. "Method: A muscle's built when and only when its existing form is slowly and radically destroyed. It can be broken down by slowly forcing it to accomplish more than it's able. Then, if and only if the muscle is properly fed with nutrients and sleep, it'll grow back more beautiful than before." (*MM* 112)

Body-work is learning a language through pain. "Because it's about focusing and about consciousness. And it's about focusing through pain. I mean, it's how the bodywork and writing, as you said, is about rhythm. It has a lot to do with the body, writing." (*LI* 116) This writing that the body does on itself, with itself, is writing in the sense that it is temporal, it marks successive moments into flesh. This can be done intentionally. "There's a curl that's very painful to do, and as a bodybuilder you have to learn to get through the pain. I mean, you don't get through it, but you have to learn to just live through it." (LI 117)

There is no "first-hand" account of body-work, only an indirect one. It rejects ordinary language. The gym has its own language game, breathing and counting out repetitions. The repetitions repeat an act up to or beyond the failure of the muscle being exercised. "I must move through failure." (BW 145) Also: "Is the equation between destruction and growth also a formula for art?" (BW 146) Art and bodybuilding break down and refashion material. With body-work, this repeats until the point of final failure, death.

In the end, death rejects all language games, all attempts at linear narrative. The sense of the world is not to be found in the world through language. But in the minimal breath-count language of the bodybuilder's repetition, there is another way that language and the body might come together. Sometimes the body, for no known reason, isn't up for the count. It falls short. "I come upon something, Something I can know because knowledge depends on difference." (BW 149)

Body-work is not really about control: "The body's rich: Who's controlling it? What's the relation between mind and body? I mean, it's like text. When you write, are you controlling a text? Well, I'd say what you're really writing, you're not. You're fucking with it. And I'd say the same thing with bodybuilding when you're going through the pain." (LI 119)

This Acker continues: "Today I was losing stamina, so I had to learn how to work through stamina problems, fatigue. And it's really interesting because you're putting such pressure on your body, learning about all different ways it can fit in. What you do, when you bodybuild, is work to failure. You put a frame around specific muscle groups, and you work each group to failure. Actually, I want to work past failure, which is negative work. And I think you're doing exactly the same thing with the text. . . . To go into the space of wonder." (LI 119)

The material body is a matter of chance and change, of wonder. Sometimes it appears against the repetition of the weights, of the count, of breath, when it fails unexpectedly. As long as we continue to treat the body as disgusting, so long shall we continue to fear our own selves as dangerous others. "Bodybuilding is an obsessive form of meditation. It's about body systems, about aging—estrogen versus testosterone balance—as you get older." (LI 129) It counts against the body's own inscrutable hormonal signaling.

Writing on the page and writing on the body are both practices that are at the same time corporeal and imaginative. An Acker on writing: "Well, a comma's a breath, and a sentence is a thought, and a paragraph is an emotion. . . . You're always working the paragraph against the sentence." (LI 211) Some Ackers found something similar in body-work. "And it became a real crisis for me, because either I had to stop bodybuilding or I had to stop writing because the two are starting to conflict." (LI 115) The writing won.

Hand-jobbing

Solitude is good for dreaming, and for jerking-off. For: "Rubbing the skin or mind into need." (HL 52) Where: "I touch myself again alone I know who I am; I experience strength pulse the muscles between the arms of my back a young virulent athlete. I feel alone and strong." (PE 42)

Rather than assume a world of sensation, without memory, without order, out of which dreams may come—produce it. "I'm going to fuck myself. The nerves muscle around my clit sharply draw in and out, loose and tense, I imagine the clit-muscles I see the clit muscles an inch inside my eyes; an inch below my skin my hand's touching my veins arteries organs should I use a dildo? . . . I feel the clit grow, the skin below the fingers becoming moist. The sensations multiply I can't think of anything else." (PE 72)

Masturbation expels all other thought: "I don't want my brain to hurt, and when my hand is stuck up my cunt, my fingers are full of juices. I want to be in the wild forever and I want to be Heathcliff and I don't care about anything else. See. I'm breaking free." (MM 121)

Masturbation heightens sensation: "While I masturbate, my body says: Here's a rise. The whole surface, ocean, is rippling, a sheet that's metal, wave after wave. . . . Opening up only to *sensitive*. Sensitive is the lover." (*PK* 32) And: "I play with myself, smell the sweat at the pit of my arms, is it sweat, how can I tell what sweat is? I perceive yellow, yellow all around me, outlines of a body. . . . I'm a child, I sense through touch. . . . Open OPEN the nerves roll in cycles I preconceived courses through my body faster and faster in huger and huger rolls until my flesh disintegrates and turns on itself. Like a devouring spider." (*PE* 53–54)

"I'm always at the beginning of desire I can hardly tell when my orgasms rise and fall as if I'm almost coming." (*PE* 51) Masturbation puts the body into a relation with temporality. "Relaxation's opening the field but I don't dare—I'm holding back—open to being a rose, a rose unfolds again and again until the nerves drive the flesh into pure nerves; they are—I'm closing again (becoming rigid)—these are the rhythms of the labyrinth." (*PK* 33)

Not unlike dreams, masturbation is a temporality in which a too-persistent self can disappear. "I was opening and opening to the point that I could touch being pure nerves." (*PK* 32) And: "Then and there, everything disappeared; the world or everything became more sexual." (*PK* 32)

"All I ever do is play with myself. I don't care about politics." (*PE* 200) The play might be the politics, or if not the politics, a twisty country path toward writing otherwise in the world. And so: "Now I touch my cunt I can work." (*PE* 64) The language of the body. "Rewriting while masturbating so I can write, that is see, more clearly." (*ES* 170) Masturbation produces an event with a time of repetition, rising and falling, a sensation without self or memory. Masturbation need not be represented in writing, afterward. Masturbation and writing can happen as part of the same sensation. "What'm I trying to do? My work and my sexuality combine: here the complete sexuality occurs within, is not expressed by, writing." (*PE* 50)

"I live in ecstasy, seeking wisdom." (*PE* 70) Acker's first philosophy produces relations to the body that bypass the self: dreaming, bodybuilding, masturbating. While the roots of the word "masturbation" are obscure, it may in part stem from *manus*, the hand. As a first philosophy, as a first orientation to being in the world, Acker offers a quite special account of the masturbating-and-writing body as that which senses, feels, and thinks the world. "Is sensuality less valuable than rational thought?" (*DQ* 46) "How, exactly, does my body feel pleasure?" (*DQ* 55)

Unlike bodybuilding or dreaming, this hand-writing is ambidextrous: one hand makes strokes of the pen; one hand makes differing strokes of the clit. It is a cure for pessimism. Linear language is a part of it but just a part. Sensations are not merely received but produced. Whole worlds could be imagined otherwise starting from here, from these threads in time. "Where are those who masturbated themselves red and dry every day while fantasizing sexual encounters whose excitements, born of horror and pleasure, knew neither the limits of time nor of space." (*ES* 190)

"My main verb is orgasm in the mythological past tense; in the realm of blackness the mythological's more powerful than the temporal present." (*DQ* 51) Masturbation, and sexuality in general, intensifies the body, cutting it free from the lineage of memory but opening it toward the open weave of myth. "Perhaps come equals know." (*IM* 141)

Orgasm is a *dérive*, rhythmic wandering in a labyrinth rather than a punctuation point, a wandering through a moving field with peaks and lows. "For hours I come and come until there's no difference between coming and reality." (*PE* 49) It is proximate to the dreamworld. "Being able to come, I decided while touching myself, necessitates being able to relax and enter another world. To come is to dream. I don't know how it is for males." (*MM* 43) Straight cis males, perhaps. For trans people of all kinds—it's complicated. But for some, it can be this: "It's all over. The world's stopped. Then, another round of feeling, like a wave, rising under the most recent, retreating wave. Each wave bigger and stronger . . . I'm going to come harder now, in there, no end in sight . . . sailing, each series, starting with a high rise then swoop downwards, each one more violent, direct." (*PK* 38–39)

The body is not always enough for itself. "I prowl like a hungry deserted cat I become aware of my body. I'm not just a mind behind two eyes: I have thoughts in every part of my body all fighting each other all dying to get out. I needed outlets as much as input. I had radios constantly going to drown out the incoming information." (PE 153) This Acker, these Ackers, are in want of an other—and of a second philosophy.

Chapter Two
Second Philosophy

Ackers don't fit in. The phenomenology of the body that is a first philosophy already seems incompatible with home, family, school, and all that. Something is off. This is not a matter of choice. "I can't control this wrongness because by birth I'm wrong." (*IM* 102) Ackers won't belong in the family plot. "Rather than being autistic dumb feelingless ice, I would like the whole apparatus—family and memory—to go to hell." (*ES* 52)

The writing-while-masturbating body or the bodybuilding-and-then-writing body might be that which produces sensations which can be set alongside all other sensations and orient a relation to them. Here this spidery second philosophy moves away from the body in relation to itself or what is at hand and on to what it produces out of its relations to others, when situated in the family, the workplace, and when fucking other people.

"I was so scared I came from an insane family, I stopped writing." (*ES* 18) But not for long. In postwar America, "The nuclear family is now the only reality." (*IM* 79) So let's start with the memory of family—from which all Ackers flee—but not stay there. "Are we always governed by our parents' fucked-up lives?" (*LM* 380) Despite the loopy repeat of the family story across the Acker-text, the answer most Ackers give is no. Expectations of what family can give remain low. "My parents were nevertheless very kind. They never beat me." (*MM* 167)

"My deepest desire was bourgeois." (*MM* 153) Escaping family is also about escaping class. "Kathy is a middle class, though she has no money, American white girl, twenty-nine years of age, no lovers and no prospects of money, who doesn't believe in anyone or anything." (*LM* 5) Most Ackers have bourgeois parents. Rich (but not that rich) Jews, not WASPs, with the worldview of their class. A grandmother character says: "If your mother had invested the 800 shares of IBM I gave her, she would have had a steady income and wouldn't have had to commit suicide." (*HL* 43)

Ackers can move away from a class location in some ways, but it leaves a mark. "I'm born rich and cannot escape my birth (the ways I was told to perceive the world even before I was born. Seeing hearing smelling tasting feeling: all taught how to me.) I want people to wait on me: treat me with respect." (*PE* 85) And: "I was a rich snob, competitive and aggressive." (*MM* 202) And: V: "Existence is horrible." R: "That's an emotion that results from being bourgeois. Living's fun if you have adventures." (*IM* 57)

And so, for this Acker: "He grew up, or rather refused to grow up both totally suspicious and as unformed, as open as a wild animal. This was why Alexander resembled a young fox whose I's are permanently crossed." (*ES* 4) Acker's surname repositioned as a given name. Become and negate his patrimony. Adventure as the refusal of a class inheritance, but adventure as only open to men.

Fathers

"I'm concerned with the father and my mother." (*PA* 90) Variations on the family story occur again and again across the Acker-web. The mother announces: "Your father isn't your real father." (*EU* 167) The real father is absent. "We don't talk about your real father." (*EU* 167) The stepfather is ineffectual. "Daddy, being daddy, needed no one." (*ES* 9) The stepfather doesn't love her, but then neither does she love the stepfather much—usually. "Father was emotionless unless someone managed to penetrate through and touch him." (*MM* 95)

Some teen-Ackers have a boyfriend and the stepfather is jealous. For this one: "My father wants to fuck me, fears his desire which is the only honest part of him, and fears me." (*PE* 43) And also this one: "When I was seventeen, my father tried to fuck me." (*LM* 179) Although for this one: "It's not like he tried to rape me." (*EU* 172) Then for some Ackers, there's a complication: "I've always known that story. What I suddenly remembered or knew is that I sexually desired my adopted father." (*ES* 67)

Whether it's an actual father or not, the power of the father is that which has to be escaped. "While my father was raping me, I learned that I had to do away with myself. . . . As father was making love to me, whenever my consciousness was bad and wandered into the present, I repeated the sacred laws I had just given myself: the laws of silence and of the loss of language. For us, there is no language in the male world." (*MM* 168)

Rather than the hidden God, this is a world of the absent father. "Since I never knew you, every man I fuck is you Daddy." (*PK* 15) The characters that populate the text find the signs and effects of the absent father everywhere, in the form of ownership, power, and control. "My real father was all that is the enemy to humanity." (*ES* 164) Nevertheless, several Ackers still crave this absent father's love, and even his aggression.

Since the Acker-web never knew a real father, any man who fucks her could be him—but never is. In the end, any threads linking her back to fatherhood have to be severed. Lulu to her fathers: "If memories are realities, this world is a prison." (*DQ* 89) Absence of love repeats as absence of self-love. "I can't even love myself because of my father. Tyranny makes only tyranny." (*MM* 161) Fathers beget a world of repetition and sameness, escaped by forgetting, if just for a moment. "I don't know what happened to daddy. I decided to keep on living rather than kill myself." (*ES* 19)

Father is an abstract power that orders and commands, but erases differences in the process, and erases or denies its own desires. An Acker: "I remember desire (my eyes on my father's cock), absence (daddy doesn't exist for me), and all the other feelings, contradictions, which show radical otherness of difference to me. The fight against the patriarchal sexist society is the fight against the refusal to allow contradictions, difference, otherness." (*BW* 59) Fathers: unavoidable, but not to be dwelled upon, or with. Forget their names.

Fathers are an absent presence. "Where and when I grew up, there were no boys, only my mother's mother, my mother, me, and my sister. I've never met my father. My sister and I, especially me, for I was older, weren't allowed anything. I wasn't allowed to be sexual and to perceive my body with my own eyes." (*MM* 32) Sisters are rarely mentioned. Grandmothers function as markers of an inherited class position. An Acker's relation to a mother, a binary relation, forecloses a third term. There's no father, or only an ineffectual father, one who can't stand in for the order of the world outside the family.

"The whole world and consciousness revolve around my mother." (*GE* 14) Which is going to be a problem: "The daughter who does not reject her mother interiorizes prison." (*BW* 69) The binary relation to a mother is an impossible one. "On the one hand, my mother was or is my lover. On the other hand, my mother was a victim in the male-defined society. So if I identify with her, I'm forced to define myself as victim. So how do I deal with this double bind?" (*PA* 90)

The various Ackers usually love their mother but are not loved by her. "Having no husband when she bore me, she resented and continued to resent my existence." (*WP* 303) The mother is present but her love is not. Or worse. Sometimes, a mother is to an Acker as she who lacked the courage to abort. A mother says to an Acker: "I never wanted to have a child. It was a mistake. . . . I wanted to have an abortion, but I was too frightened." (*EU* 166) And yet Ackers are like their mothers. They look alike, sometimes they act the same way, as if an Acker were a clone of a mother, as if the narrative were one of repetition.

This mother can still have an affirmative role. "My image of my mother is the source of my creativity." (*GE* 6) And yet: "I have no idea how to begin to forgive someone much less my mother. I have no idea where to begin: repression's impossible because it's stupid and I'm a materialist." (*GE* 6) The mother is repeated, again and again, across the Acker-web, in variations.

The father is absent from the start; then the mother as well. Relayed as in a dream: "Mommy falls into the sea (my mother's suicide)." (*ES* 25) The death of the mother, usually by suicide, cuts away another thread of selfhood: "I realize that all my life is is endings. Not endings, those are just events; but holes. For instance when my mother died, the 'I' I had always known dropped out. All my history went away. Pretty clothes and gayness amaze me." (GE 64) The family story is continually refused and yet refuses in turn to go away.

"But I don't need my mother's suicide to know putrescent rot when I see it. I have this society." (MM 88) It's not a matter of seeing mommy-daddy-me everywhere, of carrying the memory of them out into the world. It's a matter of going out in the world and then finding the world, in memory, having always been in these mother-and-father figures. How they acted as ciphers for the way gender works, or the way class works.

These Ackers: "I know what abandonment is. If you've been abandoned, you'll always be abandoned: you take your abandonment into you as the only love you can receive. Parents and all other phenomena of the world pass away. . . . It is one form of beauty." (23.08) The family is not what explains the self. "So whose childhood was I now remembering?" (22.41)

Library

"I took out my knife cut out the painted eyes of my ancestral family who were in the gallery. I didn't feel guilty at all." (PE 154) Dysfunctional or ineffectual parents fail to properly imprint the whole social order for which they are supposed to be the mediating figures. "I remained uneducated or wild because I was imprisoned by my mother and had no father. My body was all I had. A a a a I don't know what language is." (MM 10) The father is a fake, a substitute, a stepfather. And as an Acker-daughter says to her mother: "Since you open your body to my unreal father, you're not real and I'm an abortion." (LM 198)

Young Ackers are trapped in a bourgeois household. Being bourgeois, the Acker home contains "this library, which seemed as far as possible from my mother." (MM 197) In the library: "Each book in that bookcase, when I read it, was a world which didn't contain my parents." (DQ 143) And: "I passed out of the human world to my worlds of trees and books." (DQ 142) This being a New York story, there were fewer trees, more books.

Reading is close to the world of dreaming, a vector out of the closeted world. "The kingdom of childhood is the kingdom of lust. Books, by replicating this or any phenomenon, cause perversity." (MM 121) Books are adventures that even girls, trapped in a world of narrow expectations, can enjoy. "I was clever, like a rat, so I came up with another way that I could become a pirate." (BW 158) "Since pirates lived in my books, I ran into the world of books, the only living world I, a girl, could find. I never left that world." (BW 159)

Sexuality is mediated, extending toward Ackers and connecting Ackers to worlds, less from the family romance than from the family library. Memories of an actual family and memories of families from books nest side by side in the Acker-web and have the same standing. If anything, actual Acker memories are a minor part of a field of stories, most of which come from the library. If Ackers have parents, those parents are sometimes books.

Rather than reproducing the family, sex will turn out to be the mechanism for reproducing books. But there might be more than one way to reproduce books, as we shall see later in the third philosophy. "All stories or narratives . . . being stores of revolt, are revolt." (DQ 146) The way out of the house is through the library, into a little urban world that is a kind of living library. "I found a sort of pocket. 'Bohemia.' At that time, there was something called 'Bohemia' and it made a lot of sense." (PA 87) Bohemia, in turn, is the starting point for a third philosophy, of the city.

Books mediate desires that can't be expressed any other way in the context of the family, particularly for a girl. Books are adventure. Books are sexy. Later, reading, like writing, can be combined with masturbation: "First, I took any book and just opened it. I was only going to read a few sentences until I became wet enough for my dildo to slip easily into my cunt." (PK 33) And so: "Every text is a text of desire." (MM 40)

Desire

"The sort of sexual desire that when it moves begins the world started up in me." (EU 22) What impels Ackers out of the family, out even of the library, is desire, which appears as an excess and as a problem: "My deepest desire was bourgeois." (MM 153) There's a tension, then, between the traces an inherited milieu leaves in selves and what another kind of selving beyond that might become. Desire is then also a desire for another kind of desire. "From now on I'm going to decide for myself and live according to my decisions—decisions out of desire." (MM 17) Desire that initiates a world. "That night brought emotions which were ferocious as the winds. I watched the sky and the winds fuck. I needed to fuck and be fucked." (ES 114)

For this Acker, what is desired is not just some other. "The world is my desire." (LM 230) That world is going to be complicated. Because: "I desired exactly that which I couldn't accept." (ES 117) The world, as it is, can't be accepted. "Love plus hate is named desire." (BW 58) Love and hate for the world. They make an inconstant world and inconsistent selves. "Since the I who desired and the eye who perceived had nothing to do with each other and at the same time existed in the same body—mine; I was not possible." (ES 33)

"Once I had fucked, the only thing I wanted was to give myself entirely and absolutely to another person. I didn't and don't know what this desire means other than itself." (MM 14) The moment of desire erases memory and reflection. "Janey can no longer perceive herself wanting. Janey is want." (HL 47) Perhaps writing can be a place where desire takes another form. In writing desire can be felt as a thing apart, both from selves and worlds. "What does my desire look like?" (BW 63) Maybe it is outside of a certain knowingness, a certain schooling. "Desire is innocent." (IM 60) And: "The only thing I desire is innocence." (ES 48) Innocence, or the naïveté with which to wonder.

Desire appears as a relation to some other, although hardly a dependable one. "He is saying that he is the perfect mirror of her real desire and she is making him that way." (GE 40) But as we shall see, the pleasures of this mirroring relation don't extend far beyond the return of the gaze. "Everyone fucks. It's the tease that pleases." (IV 58) This may even be the best part. The moment of the glance that sees the glance that sees another: "Sexual desire is simultaneously eternal and momentary." (BW 20) Fleeting, as the eye and the I diverge.

In the end, desire will point beyond second philosophy, beyond two-ness. There's always a third term: "Desire is the triadic look." (BW 19) Desire might come via the eye, but it is not just the one returning the gaze of the other. Maybe it is the one returning the gaze of the other then looking away, at something or someone else, making desire appear as a lack or gap, or perhaps more as a potential. Desire looks not just to the other but beyond, following the other's gaze. There's an ambivalence to desire, a structural difference or potential.

Sex

An Acker answers some aggressively banal interview questions:

Favorite animal? "Male."

Do you like to travel? "I like to fuck." (BA 20, 22)

An Acker jots down a little ditty:

"Now all I care about is cock / I like it strong / And I like it hot." (22.04)

"If Madame Bovary fucked around, so can I." (LI 90) And: "All I want to do is fuck. Become other people." (23.18) This Acker says with a laugh. "All that I wanted was to fuck and be fucked." (MM 209) And: "The thousands of fucks which turn one into Christ even if one's female and despises him." (22.02) Writing extrudes out of events of sensation; fucking expands the range of such events: "I perceive more clearly during sex." (PK 30) It expands not only sensation but emotion: "Sex, you bring out my emotions." (IM 131) It expands the possibility of sensation not just for an Acker but for the other as well.

Sex makes a difference, and a difference is a knowledge. "Sex's a necessary physical ailment because it changes one." (DQ 154) Sex, along with writing, need not produce more of the same old self. Rather, selves can be created in the time of fucking, or de-created. "My sex fucking is impersonal. My sexuality's impersonal. I'm rapidly losing my identity, the last part of my boredom." (PE 51)

"I destroy either myself or the world whenever we fuck." (MM 48) Sex can create intense situations, which can call into being a self that is the recording of them: "My physical sensations scare me because they confront me with a self when I have no self: sexual touching makes these physical sensations so fierce." (*DQ* 171) And: "Don't you see what you do when you touch flesh. . . . Don't you see? You change the world?" (*IM* 112) Sex can entangle you in something impossible. "We shall define sexuality as that which can't be satisfied and therefore as that which transforms the person." (*GE* 107)

This Acker: "And I see me: sexual slime and disease eaten-up flesh, hairs thick from red crabs." (22.02) On the other side of sex is death. "Sexuality observes its own necessities and these necessities, the necessities of transformations between existence and non-existence, are deeply connected to what is human: joy." (*DP* 21) Although there may be an asymmetry in who gets closest to sex as erasure of being. "You're gonna have to die soon. You'll be like me. You'll be where I now am. Your cockbone will be in my cuntbone." (*GE* 109)

Sex creates its own temporality: "Oh please fuck me for the rest of my life. The rest of my life means fuck me right now. As hard as you can." (*BG* 123) And: "He fucks and fucks her and she comes and comes and so, then, keeps on coming and there is no more time." (*PK* 69) This might be another way of phrasing the relation sex makes between existence and nonexistence. "Right over that black iron railing, the guy and I began to fuck. We are gods." (*EU* 23) As in myth, sex is its own time, that of metamorphosis, and it extends beyond the limits of the human. "Our sexuality isn't human. This is the deepest secret. Being allied to wisdom, it's torn from the material bowels of the flesh." (*IM* 36)

And so, "Like tentacles made of rabbit fur, my legs curled around his stronger, hairier ones. Just as warmth began to seep into my body just below the skin, like milk. I whispered to him that I never want to be without him again. Then my mouth turned around his tongue: I stopped living anything but present time. . . . He answered me, lifted me upward, up above his head, fingers in both cunt and asshole so now I was his vase, he the thorns, and throwing the vase over his shoulder so that it broke on the floor, continued to bring me to orgasm again, fingers moved in a labyrinth of violence. Always this is how I am captured." (*MM* 151)

"Good sex is so rare." (*IV* 64) That is its own special kind of agony. "My sexuality at that time was separate from my real being. For my real being's an ocean in which all beings die and grow. The acceptance of this separation between sexuality and being was an invention of hell." (*MM* 14) And: "We're barely learning what sex could be." (*LI* 181) Because: "Our sexuality comes from repression." (*GE* 109)

This Acker: "Sex exists in the world just to make humans suffer." (23.08) In the Acker-web, uninhibited sexuality is, in the end, not a vector of freedom from family, state, order. Especially not for girls. "Being in prison is being in a cunt. Having any sex in the world is having to have sex with capitalism. What can Janey and Genet do?" (*BG* 135) And: "I don't think humans fuck therefore lovingly relate to each other in equality, whatever that is or means, but out of needs for power and control." (*ES* 54)

Penetration

"While I was passed out, he stuck his cock up my asshole and I came." (*HL* 69) Each kind of sex act produces its own kind of situation. Even if such acts aspire to symmetry, that may be impossible. Just as the eye and I, or sensation and desire, differ, so too the fucker and the fucked. This asymmetry of sex might be just one of the zones in which to think about gender, although in the Acker-text the asymmetries of sex acts can arise in all sorts of ways out of all sorts of bodies. There's no essential diagram of gendered bodies. In that sense all Acker bodies are potentially trans.

A lot of Ackers dwell on the penetrated body. "Come in me, my madness, and since you've already taken me, I beg you with everything that is me to take me." (*BW* 109) There are many Ackers for whom sex is most intense as an act of being-fucked, although there are other Ackers who might dispute this: "There is a basic agreement that the act of kissing is far more explosive than that of fucking." (*GE* 47) There are many detailed descriptions of being-fucked in the Acker-text, where destruction of self, dilation of time, metamorphosis beyond the human, and intensity of orgasm all come together for the penetrated body.

"Once penetrated, the body or garden cannot forget the pleasure that stemmed from its penetration." (*BW* 74) To be fucked is a situation that produces a sensation of the body organized around its penetrability. "Since the body is the first ground of knowledge, my teacher made me take off my clothes. A mouth touched and licked my ass. A finger stuck into my asshole. A dildo thrust into my asshole and a dildo thrust into my cunt. Both dildoes squirted liquid into me which I saw was white. I was so over-the-top excited, I came. The main thing for me was my body's uncontrolled reactions.... My teacher told me it wasn't enough for me to know that my body (me) reacted this way. I had to know more precisely all my complex reactions. Did I feel or react more strongly in my asshole or in my cunt?" (DQ 167)

This Acker: ". . . and she could hear her own noises coming out and lying like animals in her nostrils and mouth, mule noises, and then her body was a drilling machine, she was not animal she was thing, against him against him, I'm a machine I'm a machine I'm out of control, and boom the orgasm just came it was large it made her into it. Come. Like death. The screams didn't come from anyone. She didn't go where this pleasure or perfection led her because she was each sensation totally. The cock began to pump liquid up and down its length into her vagina. Deep in there where there is more sensation than surface feeling, she felt this enter in waves and she, the mucous membranes exactly there, pulsed in complimentary time, come come, it's called coming, she said to herself afterwards, you can't stop it when it happens; you can't do anything about it." (IM 120)

Sex produces a body seamed into time and the world that few other situations produce, and being-fucked is a kind of sex act that produces it with a certain intensity. "There's a definite difference in my physical being or body between when I'm being fucked and I'm not being fucked. How can I say anything when I'm totally uncentralized or not being fucked?" (DQ 56) Being-penetrated creates a node around which every other difference—sensations, selves, genders—can disperse.

In the Acker-field, the one doing the fucking, at least in heterosex situations, occasions only brief remarks. "You become out of control getting into me as much as you can. I'm beyond coming. In a space of consciousness and unconsciousness. Black. No more pain like no more coming. I never knew I could get here. You stop. When cock out of me, I come down enough to start coming. Gradually I stop coming." (BG 125) To be the penetrator is just not that interesting. The penetrator becomes out of control only as much as he can, which apparently is not much, as penetrators like control. Barbarella: "Most men don't like sex. They like being powerful and when you have good sex you lose all power." (GE 110)

The main thing that matters is the anticipation and then the sensation of the being-fucked, about which the fuckers might not even know anything. "As soon as the boxer had come slightly in my mouth, he had said goodbye. I was left alone like an open asshole. I want a cock, a fist up my asshole. I want reality that lies, like everything lies, on the surface of the butcher's shop table where the cuts of meat stink more than they wait." (*HL* 71) The penetrator knows nothing of this. Unless, of course, the penetrator switches.

"In this world, I'm only an object." (*MM* 81) The asymmetry of the fucker and the fucked is a whole low theory of bodily spectrums: male to female, top to bottom, cis to trans. "Human sexual desire is never reciprocal." (*PK* 99) Penetration theory overlaps with a theory of gender but isn't quite that. Supposedly male bodies can be penetrated. "Other times I stick my right hand's third finger in Eddie's asshole. It easily enters. He bucks and looks at me with surprise and openness unusual for him. Openness makes me open." (*DQ* 55–56)

Supposedly female bodies can also penetrate. And it need not always be dicks that penetrate: "His right hand's third finger is sitting in her asshole and his right hand thumb is an inch in her cunt." (*GE* 39) And yet it may be the case that the penetrated know something the penetrators don't, and that many of those in the know will know this in some relation to femininity. "Can the poets speak about what they haven't experienced? Slowly I penetrated her." (*LM* 235)

"This is how the world really is. I screeched. Everyone's penetrating and coming." (*PK* 90) It may only be the penetrated who really come. The asymmetry of penetration becomes a generalized worldview. It is an image of a certain kind of difference, which at first glance is one that is in between the apparent power of the penetrator and the apparent madness of the penetrated. The difference is that it is being-fucked that is a breach of the self. To the being-fucked: "There was no longer any differences between inside and outside." (*PK* 91) Penetrating is a power; being penetrated is—being.

An Acker: "Cock is the action that makes you go mad." (*LM* 234) It makes both penetrator and penetrated go mad in different ways. Penetrators can get delusions of grandeur. "If you can't be it, fuck it." (*MM* 39) Penetrators become an action that imagines itself acting on an object. The penetrated can lose too much of the self and its reasons. "Her legs spread open as she sinks on the bed woom her arms close around those thin shoulders. It feels wonderful. Not weird or sort-of-good or not-really-there. Just straight wonderful. He fucks hard. He likes to fuck. No need thought fucks everything up." (BG 130) It fucks up the relation through its difference.

This is a philosophy of the penetrable body at the moment of penetration: "As the man's cock enters me, every muscle of me begins to shake, every nerve begins to burn and quiver. I'm both liquid and solid. I'm completely pleasure. At this moment. (1) I'm opening enough to contain all identities, things, change everything to energy, a volcano. (2) I'm constant energy and I can never be anything else. (3) I have no emotions; I sense textures of everything against textures; I'm completely part of and aware of the object world. I don't exist." (PE 60) The self is not just breached, but erased, in a moment, in eternity.

The body penetrating is often (but not always) male and the body penetrated is often (but not always) female. It is also possible to map the concepts of body and gender together the other way around: regardless of their anatomy, to penetrate is an act of turning masculine in time; regardless of anatomy, to be penetrated, being-fucked, touches something feminine. Bodies may be cis or trans, male or female, that they may be penetrators or penetrated is a whole other difference, which may or may not map onto or structure the other differences.

"Whenever a man tells me he's a feminist, I tell him I'm a faggot." (LM 310) One ought not to trust any man who thinks he is a feminist who has not welcomed dick in his mouth or ass or ear—and liked it. And on the other hand, the penetrated woman and the penetrated faggot can become interchangeable categories in this second philosophy of the asymmetry of penetration.

Misandry

"I remember that as soon as I've been fucked, like a dog I no longer care about the man who just fucked me who I was madly in love with." (HL 37) It's common for Ackers to love being fucked but not like men much at all. They love men but hate dependence on their penetrators, and search again and again for a way out of this dilemma. "I won't kiss but I get off on sucking the prick of a man I detest. Because I'm penetrating myself." (*HL* 56)

Cisgender heterosexuality, the dominant form of penetrator-penetrated relation, is an asymmetry that is desired as a sexual act but refused as a social one. And as such, a problem: "I didn't know what to do about the useless and, more than useless, virulent and destructive disease named heterosexual sexual love. I've never known." (*ES* 64)

"I totally know what it's like to be regularly fucked by a guy who knows how to control you." (*EU* 155) And so: "Fuck me so I can hate you." (*ES* 42) Men become an impossible desire for those Ackers who are female—as we shall see some of them aren't. Those who are give up too much for the possibility of being penetrated. "Because when I love a man especially when I'm being fucked well I'll do anything for him, otherwise I hate men I don't hate them I just don't want them touching me cause their fingertips burn." (*GE* 91) It's a problem that can't really be solved through compartmentalizing, through treating the sexual as separate from the social. "Part of me, a box, hates men, despises them, I can usually see that box and forget it; now it's exploded. I like to fuck." (*PE* 41)

Those who do the penetrating remain closed to themselves. They act as subjects in the world but they don't react, they don't let the world in much. Various Ackers circle around this problem. This Acker: "I hate men and I don't want their hard world." (*LM* 337) And this one: "It's not that I dislike men—I don't at all, but I dislike the fact that because you're a woman, you can't do things." (*AW* 179)

"It's not women that men fear, it's the . . . how do I say this . . . cessation of the mind/body split/women. Something like women's bodies. Only if I say that, I'm back in dualism." (*IV* 100) Sometimes the problem is men in general: that the closed body of the penetrator can have a kind of power in the world that the opening body of the penetrated cannot. To the penetrator, the penetrated is an object on which, in which, to act. The penetrator is a subject that acts, but that in which he acts is not much to him, maybe nothing. As a social role, that of penetrator tends to domination, acting on objects, not even being able to recognize the penetrated, not brought out of himself by something other. "All the men she has don't recognize her humanity. Kneel down suck off our cocks." (*GE* 44)

"I don't want to ever marry anyone. Especially someone with whom I'm having sex." (*EU* 153) In the eyes of the penetrator, the sexual act of fucking is confused with the social act of owning, with acting on a thing as if it were a commodity, a thing available for satisfying a need or desire. For many Ackers, the problem is that men want to own what they fuck: "Men want young tight fresh girl skin. They want new. They want to own." (*GE* 48)

"Well, hell, sometimes one can't look at some straight men too closely, for the sight causes too much anger." (*IV* 28) And so a male body that is not itself open to dick, at its asshole or elsewhere, is not to be trusted. The penetrator can tend toward treating the penetrable body not just as a thing, but as a disposable thing. He can value that thing but also devalue it, treat it as trash: "As soon as my daughter's dead, she'll be unburiable—no dogs will stick their noses into this cunt—because the stink of rebellion that is named menstrual blood will never leave the skin, even that which is dead." (*MM* 173)

Heterosex is contagion. "My life began when I had gonorrhea." (*ES* 27) But that's not the worst of it. "I'm pregnant. Back to cheapo three dollar herb abortion. Hope it works." (*SW* 54) Where the penetrable body is a cis-female body, cis men are also makers of abortions: "And in those days the men really had all the power, all they did is get these women pregnant." (*LI* 72) A good reason not to trust cis men is that they can not just penetrate but impregnate.

Men who are artists think they can fuck women and also fuck the world. When they fuck the world they themselves can give birth to literature and art. In the Acker-web, men are rather makers of nonlife, both when they fuck women and when they fuck the world. Men are makers of abortions. Whereas for women, abortions enable their return to the world, a transition to agency. With her paper surgical gown as armor, an Acker becomes Don Quixote, and "to Don Quixote having an abortion is a method of becoming a knight and saving the world." (*DQ* 11)

Some Ackers put up with something less than desire as the world. "He's never going to give me what I want but I'll still fuck him." (*HL* 80) Some

Ackers want to change sides, engender themselves otherwise. "I don't want a husband. I want a brother. That's what I want." (*EU* 153) Some Ackers abandon not only men but any of the humanly gendered as objects of desire. "Real men. I'll introduce you to some of my motorcycles. I don't know what sex they are." (*IV* 36) Still others want to abolish an oppressively gendered world. "She had made her decision to survive. To go along with a men's world and then kill it." (*IM* 126)

Rape

There's an additional problem for all those who are penetrated. The penetrator does not just experience his power when he fucks, but also a vulnerability. "They can't get enough fucking. Then they turn on her. They hate her guts because she allowed them to be weak." (*GE* 45) The power of launching into another's body is mixed with an element of exposure, of a subject shown in action to have its weaknesses, including a possibility of failure. There's the danger to the penetrator of a different kind of openness, if not of the body's apertures, then at least to being seen. This can make them dangerous: "And fear is feminine: for women it lies at the heart of heterosexual sex. I don't know whether I believe that. I don't want to believe that." (*GE* 96) But many Ackers do.

There is more than one rapist in the Acker-web. Some of the most extraordinary moments of tension in this writing are when the desires of the penetrated to be taken, to actually be the object, come up against the consequences of being made into objects by the structure of the heterosexual relation. Ackers do not want to be raped. The penetrable body wants something else entirely. But a consequence of the desires of the penetrable body is the vulnerability to being raped, to being taken completely as an object that the subject takes and uses and disposes.

An Acker: "Finally my boyfriend understood . . . that I was leaving him for good; he turned furious; threw me on my stomach on a mattress; couldn't breathe; my asshole looked up at him. He fucked me for a long time in that hole. While he slammed into me I hated him; several minutes passed still fucking me no break; I suddenly notice that I'm feeling pleasure and that I want him to fuck me even more; I started to shake all over the place and come come. As soon as I had felt pleasure, I had begun to feel different emotions about him: I simultaneously liked being fucked this way and hated being raped." (*MM* 169)

Contrast that account of being the body that is raped with this Acker's experience of being violated, and reaction to it: "While the big man was shoving himself into her, the girl lay as stiff as a log and wouldn't allow herself to feel any pleasure because this was the main way her fear would allow her to express anger." (*GE* 87) It ought not need saying that raped bodies don't usually have any connection to pleasure at all. These Ackers are interested in situations where they do, as those highlight the way penetrated bodies make themselves vulnerable to feel the pleasure of being penetrated, which is the same vulnerability that exposes them to unbidden violence.

The rapist is not someone other, some outsider of the social world. He is a consequence of the heterosexual relation as an asymmetrical sexual relation between subject and object. Here is one of those rare Ackers who is at this moment that subject, that rapist: "Later on the rapist thought this: 'Who are the men who rape? They're always asking me this. Who're they? Everyone. Why are you the way you are? They ask. As if I'm a fuckin' freak. As if I'm not human.'" (*IM* 114) The rapist is potentially any man, or rather, any penetrator, anyone who is a subject inserting themselves in another as object.

The possibility of a violation beyond what the penetrated actually wants arrests the whole relation. The penetrated want to be breached, but not broken, want less than what is the full potential of the asymmetry. (We don't want to die.) The penetrator wants more, but in another way. The penetrator wants some share of the experience of getting out of the bounds and bonds of the self. "Perhaps its men who dream of love and women who dream of survival." (*IM* 115) The penetrated is not an object and is not without agency. But sometimes the penetrator cancels and restricts it. There's a lot of female sexual agency in the Acker-web but it is hardly "sex positive" or "empowering."

Consequently: "It's not that I don't enjoy fucking men. It's just that every time a guy's screwed me more than twice, he's thought he could tell me what to do. Since I had to fight the fucker for my own power, my life: I either gave up the fuck or gave up myself. Usually myself because I like fucking so much. Fucked up. I don't want to be fucked up, no more, thank you, sir." (ES 126) To be penetrated is to be centered, to have an axis for sensation in the world. Yet to want to penetrate is a dubious desire, as penetrating is not knowing but owning. To come, and come into the world, as penetrated is to come into the world with one who doesn't come into the world, even if he comes.

This sardonic Acker says: "I don't dislike men. They are, by nature or by societal conditioning, cruel, arrogant, selfish, proud, stupid, stubborn, unwilling to admit their stupidity, willing to be friends only with those people they deem lower than themselves such as women, but they can be taught to be otherwise. They have some good characteristics, though I can't at the moment think what these are." (PE 111) Masculinity (cis, heterosexual) is both desired and rejected, desired and feared. Mostly what it has to offer is dick, although some Ackers find other uses: Romeo: "I will eat you." Juliet: "I'd rather be manipulated." (LM 197) Masculine power kills what it wants. What it wants is not to be confronted by another subject, but to subjugate an object.

And yet, to want to be fucked by them . . . to be caught between fear and want. "In order to touch he had to command. He commanded me; he commanded positions; he invented a world." (ES 92) This is never an unmixed experience. "But if I knew what men were really like, I would never want one. I say this so that I can be more desirable to men." (MM 129)

Lest this all seem too reductive, too based in anatomy, this Acker distinguishes dicks as flesh from dicks as signs: "Not that I give a damn about cocks: it's what they stand for." (MM 131) And yet as bearers of the dick as sign, men are more or less always the same, as the sign of the dick is the same, and is a sign of sameness, in that the dick as that which penetrates an object makes all such objects equivalent. This may have its uses, however. "The first moment a boy put his tongue in my ear, I did something like come. And so I learned that any boy, if he does it in my ear, will do." (MM 207)

To have sex with cis, heterosexual men at all might be a form of masochism. The edge of danger is not incidental, it's what makes men men. This Acker: "I don't call having some young boy between my sheets SEX, I rarely let myself go for young or nice boys because I know I'll get bored. I want the textures of your lives, the complexities set up by betrayals and danger — I like men who hurt me because I don't always see myself, I have my egotism cut up. I love this: I love to be beaten up and hurt and taken for a joy ride. This SEX—what I call SEX—guides my life. I know this Sex of traitors, deviants, scum, and schizophrenics exists. They're the ones I want." (*BG* 129)

A frank view of masculinity at its least charming, as penetrative and potentially violent, might at least forestall disappointment when that potential actually surfaces. "Janey girl still has pretensions. She has to be drained of everything. She has to be disemboweled." (*BG* 11) The Acker-text combines frequent desires for men with a frank dismissal of romantic language about heterosexuality. It's also a theory of living with men that acknowledges only bad options: "I prefer men who hurt to men who want to own me." (*DQ* 57)

At best, this masculinity expresses itself in a language of controlled aggression: "He's whipping me lightly enough so I can feel he likes me." (*DQ* 145) And: "He took a heavy leather belt and whipped me across the back as he fucked me in the ass. It hurt almost too much and I liked it." (*BG* 59) The asymmetry of a sexual relation between penetrating subject and penetrated object may be one of the few things that can touch a world outside fiction and its relentlessly subjective point of view. "Hurt me baby. Show me what love is. The body doesn't lie." (*IM* 6)

Masculinity as something that comes at the body of the other to the point of danger might be a quality that can have its uses if experienced in a controlled way. "I need what you're doing to me because it's only pain and being controlled which're going to cut through my autism." (*IM* 5) Some Ackers want and need this edge of danger. "I'm scared of the unknown and I love it. This is my sexuality." (*IM* 106) "Because for me, desire and pain're the same." (*ES* 32)

Fear and pain in controlled situations, Sado-masochistic situations, s&m situations, might be a practical philosophy of a relation to another within heterosexuality. One that acknowledges the intimacy of this sexuality with the potential for a violence specific to it. "By playing with my blood and shit and death, I'm controlling my life." (ES 51) Heterosexual s&m, being topped by masculinity, becomes the only form in which masculinity can be acknowledged and performed as it actually is, as an asymmetrical relationship. "You who molding me physically by my pleasure at being hurt would have me love you so much that I can't not love you if you don't love me. You force me to love you solely according to your desires." (DQ 158)

A body's longing for pain, like the longing for any other sensation, is an exploitable desire, onto which power and control can latch. Such asymmetries give the lie to talk of equality and sameness, "cause all this stuff about equality not only stinks but makes life very difficult and actually masks some ugly possibilities for violence." (IV 83) s&m is then an alternative fiction to the fiction of equality and sameness, one that is frank about certain desires that the myth of equality cannot countenance. This Acker: "I just get hooked on people telling me what to do." (LI 117) The asymmetries of gender and those of class both traffic in the same feelings. "The minute you know you have to have a boss, you feel fear. Vice versa." (IM 126)

The sexual aesthetic of asymmetry: "I can tell you that a combination of fear that isn't so intense it loses its pleasure and emotional need and physical delight [is] the combination that causes ungovernable exploding reactions in me." (DQ 169) It is different for different Ackers, not to mention even more widely different for other penetrable bodies, as to just how much being accessed by the penetrator, what level of being handled as an object, pushes the penetratrable up against the limits of our own bodies.

Fear saturates time as anticipation of pain. Pain begins as an uncharted territory: "No one, not one of the teachers, had ever mentioned pain. In the history books, in the poetry we read, no one ever tried to tell me what causes pain." (MM 33) Perhaps because, plainly put: "Pain to have a mind." (DQ 52) But it is a pain that is eased by easing into pain. "Pleasure and pain are always fucking." (ES 116) It hurts, but also: "Pain can be interesting." (AW 180) It is perhaps the least explored language of the body. An Acker: "So I make a world in which pain is just one part of a complexity that has multiple, endless names, but which will never be named." (*WP* 304)

Pain, past a certain point, is unbearable; pain, up to that point, could be the bearer of some other things, also unbearable. "Totality or organism is unbearable." (*BW* 22) The theater of S&M as art-work starts from the frank recognition of the asymmetry of any relation between two (or more) humans. It is a time and place set aside, where codes of control, consent, and measure all work from the premise of that difference. S&M recognizes the potential violence inherent in the asymmetries between human bodies. Asymmetry rules out the possibility of an equality based on sameness. But that need not mean complete domination in the form of limitless violence. S&M could be about forms of reciprocity outside of the conceit of an equality and sameness that is simply assumed.

S&M could be a theater of forms that deal with bodies without the absolutes of either total equality or total domination. "I don't know how to talk about a utopian world. We live in this world and there's a lot of suffering. If you learn how to deal with physical pain, maybe you can deal with what's really much greater pain. Now if we're talking about an S&M relationship . . . I think there's a way in which you play with what you most fear in order to learn how to deal with it." (*AW* 180) An art of a measured approach to the penetrable body, one in which the roles are far more diverse and flexible than those of mere cis heterosexual fucking.

"It is necessary to go to as many extremes as possible." (*HL* 41) The body has to be experienced, has to be written, at the limits of its passages into and out of the textual. Yet for most Ackers it is more about the writing than the experiencing. "I have a curiosity about death and pain and power relationships, but I don't have much curiosity about, you know, what kind of bloody ribbon people can allow themselves to be beaten into." (*LI* 118) And so, "I think I'll be a masochist in writing only." (*SW* 46)

Sometimes a more suitable relation to another for the writer is not the fucker and the fucked, or the sadist and the masochist, but the body and the tattooist. The tattooist is an artist who writes directly on the body, penetrating the body with needle and ink. A tattoo "is considered both a defamatory brand and a symbol of a tribe or of a dream." (*ES* 130) Tattooing reverses the relation between body and writing: not writing projecting from the body; writing pierced into the body. A writing most basic and carnal. "That's what tattooing is for me, its myth . . . because the body becomes more text . . . and to ask some artist to do their artwork on your body . . . what trust!" (*HL* 21)

Subjecting the body to the pain of the needle is another version of the body that can choose pain, a kind of power of the penetrated: "Art comes from a gesture of power turned against itself . . . which is what tattooing does, or what women do." (*AW* 179) The drawing at the end of *Empire of the Senseless*, of a knife penetrating the heart of a rose—rose as cunt, rose as asshole—marks the body with its own impossible desire, at the limit of what is possible in this world. The drawing bears the motto: "DISCIPLINE AND ANARCHY." Two of my writer friends have it as a tattoo, a third has another Acker drawing on their flesh. None of them are cis men. For her work to be pricked under the skin seems—fitting.

Affirming a desire for pain, affirming a desire for subjection, even for abjection, negates the powers of the powerful. As if to say: The power you think you have over us, that would compel us, that you expect us to resist—we want it! The masochist isn't compelled to do some other thing to avoid fear and pain, but instead embraces that fear and pain. The masochist demands instead that the situation in which it occurs is one of the masochist's choosing. Otherwise the masochist denies the sadist what he wants.

The sadist's power depends on the masochist responding rationally to a power over the body to avoid pain. These masochistic Ackers abandon reason and embrace pain. An Acker, finally: "And now that we're worthy of the torture through which we've put each other, we can reap the results of that promise we made to the body and soul we created. A promise, a belief, made in madness! Through madness, we've survived." (*IM* 63)

Starting from the asymmetries of power, of men over women, of bosses over workers, S&M dramatizes the desires at work. The masochist, not unlike the writer, controls the scene, and within the scene is the one who bows down and takes what the body wants. Every element of this second philosophy is then available for variation. For instance, pain can be taken out of the heterosexual scene, and can become a pleasure of a different order. For this Acker: "At dawn, two girls got up and walked naked into the ruined garden. Coming to a thick tangle of rose bushes, Farfa leaped through and emerged untouched by the thorns on the other side. And then I jumped, a sweet tearing pain, and landed on hands and knees. I turn the page feeling the rose twist alive in my flesh." (WG 32)

Women

The political is personal: "I've got bad taste when it comes to men." (IV 36) And: "A woman who lives in a patriarchal society can have power, control, and pleasure only when she is hypocritical and deceitful." (BW 69) Viewed from either the personal or the political end of things, cis sucks. And so some Ackers feel like they would prefer to be with women. Although sometimes when they are with women, Ackers behave like men. "Loving a woman is controlling. Whereas, when I make love with a man, I'm the opposite: I'm so physically and mentally open or sensitive, I simultaneously can't bear being touched and come continuously." (DQ 127)

Still, maybe being with other women could be a way out of the double bind of heterosexuality for women: "There are two things they wanted: one was to be able to say 'no' to sex, and one was to be free to say 'yes' to sex." (BW 131) And: "Coming while not being bruised by the hatred of the one who's making you come. You no longer don't have to not exist." (ES 38)

"Even though she appears fem, my student is leading me: I orgasm several times. In this way I learn that, since I can come with a woman, I don't need a man." (MM 135) Masculinity doesn't have a lot to recommend it other than a willingness to penetrate another's body. But even there it is not indispensable: "Her hand enters me her three magic fingers, I love her, we pretend we're communists." (PE 33)

"Female sexuality is not negative." (BW 155) Several Ackers end up in raptures over women who have cunts, for cunts are far more marvelous than dicks: "Hot female flesh on hot female flesh. And it doesn't go anywhere: flesh. Flesh. For the cunt opens and closes, a perpetual motion machine, a scientific wonder, perpetually coming, opening and closing on itself to ecstasy or to nausea—does it, you, ever tire? Roses die faster. Roses die faster than you, you whores in my heart." (ES 141)

Outside the heterosexual relation, the powers of the cunt are more apparent. Janey (still whispering): "This night is opening up, to our thighs, like this cunt which I'm holding in my hand cuntcuntcunt. And we descend, like we're in a tunnel or a cave inside the mind, night is opening all all murderers all you makers of violence come out of your holes. The final Maker of Violence is my thighs, and my bloody fingernails, and the teeth inside my cunt. Please night take over my mind I don't like this poetry." (BG 136)

The rose can be a cunt, or an asshole. Assholes can be cunts too, and can be celebrated as ports of entry into the body. Sometimes, penetrability rather than any particular anatomy may be what makes a girl a girl: "My asshole. I have been told that when my asshole opens, it looks like a rose blooming. Is it true, as Buddhists say, that appearances are deceptive? Answer: my pirates dwell in freedom." (MM 151) There will be pirates to meet later. With these pirates, dick is optional, and openings multiple. While the language is anachronistic, perhaps one could say that there are Ackers who write for trans bodies and not just cis bodies—for trans bodies to come.

A body that opens its mouth, cunt, or asshole is a penetrable body. A body whose skin the tattoo needle punctures is a penetrable body. The difference, and the asymmetry, is not so much gender as penetrability. Likewise, possession of the great symbolic dick need not be anything useful once dicks are denuded of their aura and treated as a practical matter: "We don't need men like God, dumb shit, because we don't need money. We need cocks." (LM 254) As for cocks, you can just strap one on. "No one ever told me you could just walk around with a strap-on, having orgasms." (WD 2) There could be a world in which there is penetration, but without cis masculinity.

Some Ackers discovered this world. Maybe not all of them. "For me, there were no more men left in the world. . . . I stood on the edge of a new world." (PK 23) This world without masculinity is not utopia. A not-cis-male penetrator is still a penetrator, with all of the ambiguities of power that brings. They are also caught up in memory and language just like cis men. There's no idealized feminine essence or fixed anatomy of womanhood here. Genders happen in a field saturated by multiple asymmetries of power: "Women are more dishonest than men because women know how dishonest men are and can't fight back any other way." (*LM* 309) Women—however one defines them—are not inherently always victims. "History also teaches that a clit's like a knife." (*PK* 100) Or a knife not unlike a clit. The ability to break out of treating the other as penetrable, as object, as property—is rare.

In the Acker-text there are at least four genders, four concepts of the body. There may even be a fifth, but let's come back to that. The four more common ones are boys and girls, women and men. These genders are not absolutes. There is, as we shall see, plenty of slippage between them. Nor are they equal or equivalent: "Both girl and woman were the names of nothing." (*BW* 161) As a kind of node or pulse or flux in the mix of genders, girls are a particular fascination, and some Ackers want to be girls among girls. "I know there are girls down here. Who live under the earth. Who put dirt in each other's mouths and take the same out with their lips." (*EU* 20)

Girls are not necessarily pure and powerless. "The viciousness of girls cannot be imagined." (*ES* 266) And: "The sexual thirsts of girls are never satisfied." (*PK* 100) Or maybe it is that Ackers are attracted to particular kinds of girl: "I worshipped the girls who were bad." (*MM* 182) They become a vector out of entanglements with masculinity. "Later I would meet girls who actually were as wild as I thought boys were. Girls carrying cunts who breathed, like those monstrous clams I found on ocean wastes, slime each time they opened, the way I know a heart will if separated from the body: the vulnerability of openness." (*MM* 185) Girls are not necessarily sexually innocent, or innocent in their ruses of power, but they are innocent in their refusal of responsibility. They are not trying to duplicate or replace the power of men. They are trying to escape from it.

Girls can escape together: "The young girl took up one of the hands of her lover . . . and held it. Fingers that trembled while held down in that valley which felt like sand, where the sea began, then explosion after explosion, made the world tremble." (*PK* 43) Ackers implant tender memories of girls, some from books, memories to replace those they have intentionally forgotten, of fathers and husbands, among other things. "What I remember aren't the details of that which happened between girl and girl. After all is gone, what I remember are the colors of Silver's hairs. How the smell of it was the same as its colors." (*ES* 222)

There's a hint of vulnerability and danger with girls that is not quite there with women, which is about something else. "A woman's rising, sexual rising is the rising up of dreams, of writing." (BW 156) Yet there are moments, among women, for another life. And for some although not all Ackers, those are key moments: "Among these women, free yet timorous . . . these exchanges of threats and promises—as if once the slow-thinking male is banished every message from woman to woman is clear and overwhelming—are few in kind and infallible." (GE 115) And: "Women get to know each other by becoming each other." (23.24.9)

With female bodies, with girls or women, another body of sensation might come into being, with or without being penetrated. "At some point without knowing how I get here I get here I have to complete my orgasm I mount her our cunts meet and fit surprisingly for me and easily and I ride her as love is our only way until we begin to peak and need more, and turn around. I can do what I want. I can write more freely make my break to get rid of my damaged mind . . ." (PE 57) Writing too can be nonpenetrative.

"Women's sexuality isn't goal-directed, is all over." (GE 49) There could even be an opening, a being-penetrable without penetrators. "In the midst of my emission, she opens again; each opening opens up; every opening series touches another opening series without entering its territory; there's no confusion anywhere . . . I'm gazing into a world in which sight isn't possible." (PK 115) Not that, like any sex, it need always work or be magical or anything. "She didn't and couldn't get off, either because I was bad at doing exactly what she wanted done to her or because while I was doing those things, the confusion of my emotions was apparent to her. . . . What I can't accept is that I might not have wanted to give her pleasure." (PK 137)

For some Ackers, sex with women can lack an edge of difference but may have other qualities. "Since I didn't want to sleep with women, sleeping with women couldn't endanger me, didn't touch the ranting, raving unknown. A woman, rather than being the unknown, is my mirror. . . . Our desires, repeating each other to infinity, or to the impossibility of infinity like the mirrors in Renaissance paintings, want to keep evolving, rather than die in one orgasm. . . . Whereas a man always rejects: his orgasm is death." (DQ 126)

For other Ackers there's less fear of sex with another of the same gender as becoming the same together, and more interest in becoming different together. "My clit turned into a crawling sea monster, hers likewise, until we were nothing but sea monsters leaving trails of slime. Whoever was 'I' became traces of dust." (MM 46) Here perhaps a fifth concept of the body appears, one whose gender is not even human, and which includes stuffed animals, motorcycles, and sea monsters. Who even knows how many genders there are, or can be?

Engendering

What might be most curious about second philosophy in the Acker-web is that it is a low theory of cis heterosexual fucking but also of its alternatives, and those alternatives modify the language within which bodies can appear. A lot of Ackers acknowledge a desire to be fucked by cis men. They are frank about heterosexual female desire. Yet they insist that masculinity is simply not redeemable, at all. Not through any essential quality or identity, but simply because of what masculinity is made to do and be.

There is a corporeality to this. It is not just a question of narrative, of signs. And yet it is also not a simple question of whether a body has a penis or a vagina. There are many Ackers for whom cis-gendered bodies might not be the norm. Masculinity is that which won't open, which can only be itself by opening another. Masculinity loves nothing other than its own reflection, and treats the other as object not subject. Femininity, reduced to being a object, invaded and consumed, can't be acknowledged as having desires and hence can't be the return of desire that masculine desire acquires. Such might be the forms of narrative inheritance that bodies have to live with and against. A narrative inheritance that is itself something to fuck with. "My hatred of gender . . . a hatred of the expectation that I had to become my womb. My hatred of being defined by the fact that I had a cunt." (AW 177)

If the attributes of masculinity are aggression, possession, and penetration, they are not entirely unique to men. In the Acker-field, masculinity (and femininity) can be distributed unevenly across bodies, or vary from situation to situation. If one wanted to shuck off some of those qualities, men can be, as it were, the scapegoat. Being fucked is a ritual via which the one fucked can transfer residues of their own masculinity onto another. "I need a man because I love men. I love their thick rough skins. I love the ways they totally know about everything so I don't need to know anything. They don't really know everything, but we'll forget about that. They take hold of me; they shove me around; and suddenly my own aggression's off me." (*PE* 199) The aggression of the other, its subjectivity acting on another as an object, also frees the one made an object from its own tendencies.

It is only a temporary fix. Most Ackers at some time or other want also to be freed not just from their own aggression but from the whole binary relation of gender itself. But then: "Has anybody seen gender?" (*BW* 166) What is evoked as a possibility is a connection between corporality and language that can't really be coded in ordinary language, because "we don't know what gender is outside this society." (*IV* 105) And for those who aren't exactly one gender or another: "In order to fuck you have to appear, and neither of us can appear in this society." (*DQ* 130)

Bodies have to navigate an asymmetry congealed into linear language, inherited from memory. It's an impossible relation. And to this Acker, far too limiting: "I always longed after the bodies of boys, but I wanted a girl. I thought I was getting a boy in a girl's body. But no, you loved me too much. That I can't handle. What I really want scares me the most." (*EU* 24) Some Ackers feel more like something masculine: "When I was with you, I was a guy, you never saw the female part." (*IV* 56) Some Ackers don't know what gender they are. "I know what you mean about slipping male/female I never know which one I am." (*IV* 25) And: "We don't even know whether we're male or female. And. But unlike Heathcliff, I can pass for normal." (*MM* 131)

Best then to "turn cocks into water." (*PK* 44) Various Ackers step through different solutions to the asymmetry that still structures and limits the possiblities of the many genders. For one, "pleated black fake-leather pants hide her cocklessness." (*HL* 38) For another, "She could solve this problem only by becoming partly male." (*DQ* 29) And then: "My pussy has a hard orange cock." (*DQ* 95) Some acknowledge their own masculinity: "I'd rather be one of the bad boys than a good girl." (*LI* 220) Some have it thrust upon them. "Feminism, when I grew up, was restrictive. I remember going to them in the early days and saying 'Hi, here's my writing,' and them saying 'You're a man, get out of here.' I just didn't fit at all." (LI 220) Perhaps some of these Ackers are legible now as trans masculine or nonbinary or gender-fluid—to speak a language to which she did not have access. Not that she would have wanted any label.

Becoming partly male is one way to play, although perhaps more as a boy than a man: "This is me: the image. A man's suit. Look at me. I'm a woman who looks like a delicate boy and I'll never change. You can't touch me. I'm impervious. This's the way I'm happy. I'm totally elegant." (DQ 56) A boy but also not a boy: "Even though she had to be a boy because there was nothing else she could be, she wasn't a boy." (DQ 130) Perhaps because "I'm not only not like other females, I'm not like other humans." (DQ 149) Maybe some Ackers are trans, but then maybe a few even transit to fifth genders, to the nonhuman.

Women need not be other to men, or the same as them. There are other concepts of the body, including nonhuman genders. This Acker: "'What the hell do you know!' screams Medusa. Her snakes writhe around nails varnished by the Blood of Jesus Christ. 'I'm your desire's object . . . because I can't be the subject: What you name "love," I name "nothingness." I won't not be: I'll perceive and I'll speak. . . . As long as you men cling to your identity of power-monger or of Jesus Christ, as long as you cling to a dual-istic reality which is a reality molded by power, women will not exist with you. Comradeship is love. Women exist with the deer, the foxes of red-ness, the horses, and the devious cats.'" (DQ 28) And: "Now we're fucking: I don't have any finesse I'm all over you like a raging blonde leopard." (GE 113)

Gender can be locked into the asymmetry of cis heterosex, or it can be protean, like the beginnings, the fun parts, of classical myth. "There's a play with gender. I say 'women' but I'm not even sure." (LI 60) Or, one can allow gender to remain obscure. "I can't get sexual genders straight." (DQ 159) And: "I always get my sexual genders confused." (LM 309) And: "We are neither men nor women." (BW 14) In the Acker-field, bodies can have vari-able or layered or alternating relations to gender. As do their lovers, Ack-ers can come (and come) in all genders. "I won't stop being a tomboy." (PE 9) And: "I get rid of myself as a woman." (PE 25) And: "I became a man and a woman." (PE 49) And: "I'm not always a girl." (ES 220) And: "I'm not happy but at ease only when I'm in drag." (PE 67)

This Acker: "I think I want a wife who has a cock. You understand what I mean. I don't understand why men even try to deal with me like I can ever be a wife, and then bitch at me and hurt me as much as possible cause I'm not a wife. Do you think I'm a wife? (Barbarella giggles.) But when I'm sexually open I totally change and this real femme part comes out." (GE 110) The myth of love as cis heterosexual union looks like a merging of equals but is more the possession of one gender by the other. In its place, the Acker-field starts to write out something more primary, a mythic world where genders remain in flux.

Bodies that are otherwise those of women can have a butch part. "Women are kings. . . . It's like, if you want a cunt, you have a cunt, if you want a cock, you have a cock. . . . If you want to be king, you're king, you know, no-one would ever think of themselves as queens unless they want to be a queen. Queen is like a fag's word anyway." (JE 14) Bodies that are otherwise those of men can have a femme part too. "I'm in love with Peter, a man who is capable of deceiving both sexes. He usually wears the clothes of women. . . . Although Peter is male, I don't regard his gender as a defect." (PE 111) And: "He looked like a girl. He was so aware of his femininity." (DQ 128) This does not redeem masculinity, of course. "In some ways he was like a woman, only in his case he seemed to think that the world revolved around his cock." (PE 239)

Apart from the occasional nonhuman gender, there are often four concepts of gender in the Acker-web: man and woman, girl and boy, and these are sometimes quite malleable and permeable to each other. "He wasn't a man or a boy imitating a woman, but a young girl, for a young girl has no idea neither of sex nor of her own identity. A young girl is not." (DQ 132) And it is possible, pressing against the limits of this language, to be more than one at the same time. "De Franville wasn't a girl, but a cunt. She (He) was so unsure of herself (himself), she (he) fucked everyone she (he) could get her (his) hands on. There were plenty of them. Regardless of sexual gender. At the same time, because she (he) was sexually ambiguous, she (he) looked innocent." (DQ 133)

A mythic world opens in which genders and sexual orientations emerge together, mutate together, differentate together. "Since I could no longer have a man, I would become one. We have such strange ways of fucking these days." (DQ 131) Play within gendered language opens up a more varied space of becoming and encounter. "Obviously, I'm a woman transvestite, who's wildly in love with the most gorgeous fag in town." (PE 113) And: "She was a boy who would never grow up. I shall be a boy too, as soon as I learn my sexuality." (PK 122) And in the end: "I no longer care what my sexuality is." (PK 128)

Out of this indifference within language comes fresh sexual possibilities: "He was sucking an older woman's cunt it was also a cock without changing from a cunt this is a romantic section." (HL 25) And: "She carved away his cock and turned him into a bird." (MM 85) Rather than one all mighty phallus, "I will have cocks everywhere, populating my desolate countryside." (MM 219) And: "Pirate sex began on the date when the liquids began to gush forward. As if when equals because. At the same time, my pirate penis shot out of my body. As it thrust out of my body, it moved into my body. I don't remember where." (PK 114) Sexes and sexualities have a poetics without order, out of order, without property or properties—pirate sex.

"It comes down to the question of whether there are essentially women and men. What would no difference look like?" (LI 220) Many Ackers seek an abolition of gender, but more to open toward their plurality rather than their erasure. "I see this among my students, there's a move in progress, a move away from this world of duality, precisely, from this world defined by two set genders: not everything now has to be coded male or female. This is just the beginning: even those codes, male and female, can be played with. . . . I hope it's moving toward the overthrow of the two-party gender system." (PA 87)

Maybe a gender can be thought along the lines of more than one kind of difference. Maybe genders are never quite coherent things. Most Ackers want to think the corporeality of the gendered body, but not reductively so. The body too has its own poetics. Not only in sex but also in writing, there can be play with the fun bits. "One can't discount the physical. I have friends now who are changing genders, and I know it's very big. I know there are probably mid-genders but, in my experience, there is something about having a womb that can't be discounted. . . . The writer is truly androgynous. The writer is a channeler. In a way, the writer doesn't exist. . . . There is something about having a certain body and maybe that has its imprint on the writing, but there is also the fact that one isn't writing oneself. Although in the transmitting, one is writing a self." (LI 221) In its very otherness, writing can become a passage to transition.

Rather than wanting specific names, categories, roles, or subgroups with whom to identify, sexualities, like selves, might be better without too much naming: "The bear sits on roses with his big tush. . . . But bear doesn't care about squished roses: this is what an orgasm is. When the skin of inside the asshole comes out like a rose. Oh no, I shouldn't be doing this, coming out; asshole skin coming out; it's okay when it's an orgasm. Growly bear, I continued, for I had forgotten where I was, puts dildo in his cunt. Is anyone looking at me? he thinks. If so, does their gaze affect me? . . . The riches of nature and orgasms are so strong, they metamorphose into convulsions. Where the rain of rose petals reigns." (PK 270) The rose of penetrability, involuting over on itself, over and over, perpetually in transition, never arrives at identity: A most tender-point in the Acker-field, the Acker-skin.

Love

Love is the topic where the Acker-text is most turbulent. "Without you I am nothing." (ES 39) Sometimes it's quite classical, this love: "Love is actually the desire I have to become a hermaphrodite." (23.18.2) That could be a merging with another, or becoming both genders in one body, or something else entirely.

Ackers need some other to know they exist, their gaze reflected back in some other's eye. "Love makes time and life." (BW 109) But is love even possible? Love does not just affirm the self, but also impinges upon it. "You can't bear to have anyone love you. You can't bear another person's consciousness." (GE 53)

And yet Ackers can't help themselves. They fall for it. "As soon as Cathy saw me, her heart leaped up like the dog it is. Even though romanticism pretends otherwise." (MM 127) If the Acker-text has a genre, maybe it is an antiromance. "All romanticism is stupid." (IM 45) If sex is hard, love is harder, and maybe impossible. Ackers look for it everywhere.

"Is trust part of love?" (DQ 165) If it is, it might not be possible in this world.

Perhaps the value on which Ackers are most conflicted is love. Given the frank acknowledgement of the carnality of sex, faith in the possibility of love is hard to sustain. Love comes up against the asymmetry of gender. "How can a woman love?" (DQ 9) And: "As soon as a woman loves, she's in danger." (DQ 33)

Perhaps love became impossible under capitalism. Perhaps the narrative form of romance came to prevent rather than celebrate love. "Why have matters changed between men and women? Because today love is a condition of narcissism, because we've been taught possession or materialism rather than possession-less love." (DQ 24) The rise of polyamory might not change that: Love of another is ownership of a property; love of several others is ownership in a timeshare.

For some Ackers, love may no longer be possible. For others, it may never have been possible: "There's no possibility for human love in this world." (DQ 17) A world then beyond redemption. "Perhaps there is an escape from horror through love, but there is no love." (MM 107) And: "she reaffirmed her belief that human love doesn't exist and died." (DQ 36) God is dead, and with it God's love, and now too the romantic love of man, its shadow.

Perhaps love became something else, or was always something else: "When love dies, there's nothing and this world is only horror. Perhaps love has not died. Perhaps there's never been human love. Perhaps all that humans have ever meant by love is control." (MM 105) It may simply be an ideology.

Perhaps love is an alibi for what is inhuman about humans. "Love affairs are when each person can do anything they want and the other person can do anything they want and the other person realizes that the most unbelievable behavior possible is usual." (GE 26) Love could just be exposure to the beastly otherness of the human.

Perhaps love is outside of rational thought anyway: "Love doesn't need human understanding." (DQ 141) Ackers are skeptical arachnids in general: "Is anything ever understood between people?" (HL 106) In the case of love: "Human love occurs only when a human suffers for no reason at all." (DQ 34) In which case there could be no theory of it.

Perhaps love is real but abolishes the self that might know or think or sense it: "I only want the moving toward exaltation, opening toward and becoming other people, the exaltation, then nothing, until it starts again. People are unused to love because they don't go far enough. As far as possible and farther, into their intuited desires. And complete love, apart by nature from 'time,' does not meet complete love where, given consent, anything can happen and there's no such thing as strength or weakness except as masks to be acted out. All forms of love are drag." (PE 58)

Perhaps love is too fictional rather than too real, too much an elaborate form of drag: "But in the past, when I tried to kill off hypocrisy, I destroyed possibilities for love." (MM 26) The lover becomes other to herself. One mask in front of another.

Perhaps love abolishes the self so totally and suddenly that it is actually violence: "Like any beast that's starving right now I leap on any affection and I murder it." (IM 79) And: "I need to love someone who can, by lightly, lightly stroking my flesh, tear open this reality, rip my flesh open until I bleed." (PE 96) But if love is a form of violence, it is a crude one: "The only thing that is possible between us is a car accident." (MM 22)

Far from touching the eternal, love is always chaotic, destabilizing, momentary, multiple. Far from joining in a unity, love is chance and change. "You get in the world, you get your daily life your routine doesn't matter if you're rich poor legal illegal, you begin to believe what doesn't change is real, and love comes along and shows all these unchangeable for ever fixtures to be flimsy paper bits. Love can tear anything to shreds." (BG 125) Love is an annihilating injustice.

Ackers are forever oscillating between solitude and attempts at being with an-other. "Human communion. There's nothing else I want." (PE 62) And what would that communion be? It would be love. "What's love? Love's the unity of friendship and desire." (DQ 46) Yes, "Love's the unity of friendship and desire." (BW 111) Only that might not be possible, for any of the Ackers, for more than the briefest moment.

"Just be my friend." (IV 46) Some Ackers plead. "Please, be my friend." (GE 31) Perhaps the problem is that when love attempts to combine sex with friendship, they prove incompatible: "The rules by which we live: Sex and friendship don't have much to do with each other." (LM 217) And: "Between sex and friendship there seemed to be an impassable gulf that was increasing." (MM 43)

Even friendship, without sex, might be impossible. Even friendship breaches the limits of the self: "The complicity of friendship is pain." (ES 136) Yet in a world without values, even if it is impossible, regard for others remains the only value: "In the long run nothing's important. This is the one sentiment that makes me happy. Please be nice to me." (GE 109)

There are lots and lots of Ackers with whom sex becomes a means to try to find the communion of friendship. "Having sex would make what was outside me like me." (IM 109) But perhaps sex prevents rather than leads to friendship, making love impossible as their synthesis. "I look at my body solely as if it were a web, solely a way of asking people to touch me." (PE 57) And: "My sex operates as a mask for my need for friends." (PE 15) And: "There's no possibility that anyone'll love you any more or that love matters. Because there's no hope of realizing what you want, you're a dead person and you're having sex." (GE 50)

If it ever exists at all, love might be beyond the scope of the limits of the human: "Like death, love is infinite." (DQ 50) Its existence, in its infinity, erases that which attempts to know it. And: "Since I love you, dog . . . my world is only dog, for love by its nature is total. . . . What then . . . is this doggish being? Since I love you and that's all I can do because I love you . . . doggish being, like all being itself, must be love. What is this, you or my sexuality?" (DQ 126) Love is yet another of the gods whose death has to be acknowledged. This one might be a little different. Love may yet exist, but is not accessible to humans, nor to God, who is dead. An unloved love is all that might remain.

Some more limited, mundane love might yet be possible, but outside of gender as given, outside of the inherited forms of myth about them. For love to be possible, sexuality has to be about something else other than a penetration that is an owning of another's body, a body which is then an object only. But even if that love doesn't or can't exist, perhaps it has to be pursued in the negative, in its absence, to make living possible at all: "It's not that she had to have a man: it's that without faith and belief, a human's shit and worse than dead." (DQ 34)

This negative love, one that can't be affirmed, is both dangerous and necessary. "Love destroys common time and reverses subject and object; the verb acts on itself; I'm your mirror; identity's gone because there's no separation between life and death." (DQ 51) Perhaps such a love is only possible outside the asymmetry of gender: "Was it possible that someday—someday—I would hold naked in my arms, and continue to hold and continue to hold, pressed close to my body, a woman on whose femininity and masculine strength I could lean, trusting, whose mettle and daring would place her so high in my esteem that I would long to throw myself at her feet and do as she wished? I dared hardly believe what I was asking. I dared hardly believe myself." (ES 115)

The search for love never ends in the Acker-text, even if love can't come into being, or comes into being only negatively, in its absence. "If I have to love, out of desperation or desperately, I know love only when it's allied with hate." (ES 7) It's the treasure that can't be found, that's not marked on any map, or that is not there where it's marked. "I'm doomed to be in a world to which I don't belong." (DQ 20)

There is no end, in life, to estrangement from others, estrangement from any other world other that one's own. What then is this strange world, in which love doesn't happen? This world that might still be sensed and known in its strangeness. This world whose only reality is one that can't be sensed or known—death—whose absent presence is at the heart of all encounters with the other in the Acker-field's second philosophy.

Death

My Grandmother: "How long does a fuck take?

Phone: "It takes longer than death." (LM 279)

Most Ackers refuse to be morbid. "I won't have this situation I won't I won't I don't care what they say I'm not ready to die I'm not going to." (EU 7) A problem: the denial of the proximity of death. "I remember seeing my father die. . . . His culture had given him no way to deal with death, his own death, so neither his own death nor his own life had any value." (22.52.2) The forgetting that it is internal to us, that "death and life are fucking each other." That anyone could live and write in a world that puts off any life-with-death encounter: "They must be using contraceptives these days." (ES 82)

Here is what to me is Acker's best joke: "In my heart of hearts or cunt I've always known what men want from me. 'Death,' I whispered. My father was inside me and my boss was outside me. They answered me. 'Yes.' I was whispering, . . . 'Death, you're a moralist. Death, you know what's good for other people.'" (ES 59) The boss and the father are makers of death, but are themselves deathless. Some other boss, some other father, can come to stand in the same place.

The boss and the father decide who dies. They make the particulars of who dies seem as if it could have something to do with a right and just order. As if they stood in line in a time that is homogeneous and goes on and on, straight to eternity. That's the language of death of which bosses and fathers approve. "The language by means of which we represent ourselves as judges, as absolute knowers, is not the language of flux, of material, of that which must die. Us." (BW 89) A language of materiality and flux has to be something else than this judgment over life and death which yet knows nothing of it. Yet death itself can only be unknowable. It is the outer limit of a second philosophy, that against which to think but of which thinking's nonknowledge is absolute.

Ackers don't long for death, but they do want to approach it as that which the father and the boss command yet exclude. Maybe there are ways at least to get closer to death without wanting it. Maybe it's a too-slow way to know something of it. Death sets an absolute limit to thought. That of which there is no sensation. "Inasmuch as nothing human is eternal but death, and death is the one thing about which human beings know can't know anything, humans know nothing. They have to fail." (DQ 35) The endless succession of fathers and bosses, each in turn occupying their place as if that place was eternal, know nothing of the only thing that really is eternal, or of the flux of life that refuses their order.

One could psychoanalyze these bosses and fathers: "We recognize the presence of a sadistic component in the sexual instinct. Isn't it possible to believe that this sadism is a death instinct that has been forced to move from the ego to the (always sexual) object?" (MM 74) Or not. It might be more about power than subjectivity. The boss or the father, who inflicts pain and suffering, puts some other in their own place as that which has to die.

Here is a crucial juncture. Ackers who feel for others or for themselves in this situation embrace this sadism, up to a point. Up to the point that it enables a feeling and even a knowledge from proximity to death. Embracing the proximity of death is, strangely enough, release from the fear of it. A fear that power only knows how to exploit. "You're terrified because you place evil and death outside yourself." (*IM* 15) To embrace the death immanent to one's own life is to loosen its death grip.

Looking and feeling toward death is how the body can learn something of what it is: "I always want to test everything to the point of death. Beyond." (*MM* 24) The masochistic body, even more than the sexual body, prolongs the approach toward death in order to feel it as a destiny internal to it. But the masochistic body is still substance, something, and can feel it. "Only death whatever that is is nothing." (*HL* 38) The experience of pain, of submission to control of masochism, orients the body toward death, but also to the falling short of death that is the lot of the body until it actually dies. "I can remember pain but I can't remember death." (*HL* 73)

The world of the bosses and the fathers appears on the one hand as an infinite and eternal one, and on the other as one in which all meaning is finite, its play stopping short at the point of their command. All of this is backward. "Neither we, human, nor art live in a world of finite meaning finitude or are we or art finite in regard to meaning. Identity, fragile, gives way to identity. We and the world are finite only in regard to death." (*BW* 88)

A poetry of and in flux, where identity gives way to identity, might be something like a gender or a sexuality of and in flux, where identity gives way to identity. "Both poetic discourse and sex are processes of transformation. In poetry, silence changes into meaning, meaning into silence. Sex is one movement between life and death. Insofar as we fear death (the loss of identity), both poetry and death are frightening." Instability of meaning or sexuality or gender is scary to the extent that the end of an identity feels like death.

But it could be the opposite. The experience of the end of an identity in sex or art brings out the death that lurks unacknowledged in the world of bosses and fathers. And it shows that they, too, are mortal. Only the flux from whence they came ever remains. Embracing corporeal death and even social death in advance says to power that it too is mortal, that the event it most wants to deny or deflect is already on its way, and that we can be their gravediggers.

This Acker: "Since we had found only the morality of death and actual death in the rich white world and hypocrisy and male chauvinism in the hippy sector, we were looking for life in what the society which we despised considered the kingdoms of disgust and death." (19.11) For some Ackers this takes on a romantic cast, but for others, it's a realm of incremental and formal method.

"Bodybuilding, death and heroism are all related to each other. While the bodybuilder attempts to perfect his body over time, for the process of shaping muscles takes a long time, time inexorably decays then destroys the body. Though the bodybuilder must fail, he keeps on fighting. He uses his knowledge of his inalterable failure and death to carve his heroism." (22.22) And: "To bodybuild is one way to illuminate one's radical differences in the face of that nonhuman equalizer named death." (19.11) The Ackers of the gym are tragic heroes who know their own fatal flaw.

Some Ackers are poets who sing love songs that open their pores toward death as they pour toward death. "If anything I'm what happens after death, which is writing." (BA 19) Death becomes the only absolute other from the point of view of any identity. But it is itself only an instance in a flux that text or sex might embody. Death is the limit point of an Acker's second philosophy. It is the other to a self that cannot be gainsaid. But it is also the weak point of any claim to power. And now this whole civilization is dying, father and bosses and all won't put it back together again.

Chapter Three
Third Philosophy

Cities

"I find it difficult to find people who will accept my alternating hermitage and maniacal falling-in-love. My style forces me to live in San Francisco or New York." (PE 9) The Acker-web spans the grids of cities. Let's move beyond the body and its sensations (first philosophy). Let's move beyond the body's contact with another body (second philosophy). Let's open toward a third philosophy, to theory that comes out of sensations that are of the social, the technical, or the natural.

All of which usually appear in the Acker-text through situations that are urban. "America is so bleak and horrible and endless away from the decaying urban centers." (SW 68) Yet always present, even in cities, are populations of the homeless and the destitute that hover around the fringes of the frame whenever Ackers and cities touch. The city is also an often violent space, a space of masculinity, although as we shall see, not entirely.

"A city in which we can live. What're the materials of this city?" (BW 112) The city can be discovered through wandering its streets without appointments or tasks to accomplish, allowing it to make its own time. A *psychogeography* emerges, of how parts of the city feel, of where one ambience shades into another. It can be a dangerous method, particularly if one appears as female. And so: "I change my women's clothes to men's clothes, roam through the streets of New York." (PE 5)

Psychogeography makes fuzzy maps, finding in actual cities all the "unknown cities . . . each one a labyrinth, a dream, in which streets wound into streets which disappeared in more streets and every street went nowhere." (PK 7) Where "the most expensive clothes store will lie half a block past the bottom of hell, slightly uphill." (MM 163)

In wandering, fresh selves and cities appear. "Myself or any occurrence is a city through which I can wander if I stop judging." (LM 246) Cities wander through Ackers as Ackers wander through cities. The wandering of the city is a step beyond the browsing of the household library. It begins as a path away from family for young Ackers. "The same sabotage of social existence is my constantly walking the city my refusal to be together normal a real person: because I won't be together with my mother. I like this sentence cause it's stupid." (LM 249)

Several actual and imaginary cities appear in the Acker-field, including colonial cities. Although to this Acker all cities are colonial cities: "It's that I see that this distinction that's been made, historically, between the First World and the Third World, has now become a distinction . . . which can occur within an urban center." (LI 49) The Algerian or the Puerto Rican becomes the marker in the metropolitan city, Paris or New York, of the implication in the colonial on which the city depends but disavows.

Most of the cities in the Acker-field are at least in part "that death that is New York." (BW 140) It is the template for all Acker-cities. "New York's a town in which a girl has to learn to think fast." (PE 149) New York is a special place as the city where Ackers move away from the family and discover the city in general as a space of pleasures and dangers. It's an urban space encoded with both general and specific resonances. "When you reside in a city which isn't the city of your childhood, whatever you perceive lacks the resonance of memory." (ES 66)

The city is neither the family writ large nor its cancelation. Rather, the city shows the family as just a piece of itself. "A child loves, but how can a child obey a parent who has no honor? In this city of artists of rapacity, where rats scurry across planks though even the memories of pirates are dead, there's no honor." (MM 94) Neither family nor city is refuge from the other.

Even from the restricted point of view of a run-away bourgeois white girl, an Acker can perceive a city of both desire and pain. "New York City . . . both paradise and end of paradise." (IM 67) One in which more possibilities might have been lost than gained. It is a city in transition: "The white middle class had believed that the mayor was assisting them by means of gentrification and artifying. Now soaring property prices were forcing these classes to become either rich or homeless." (MM 91) This will turn out to be prophetic.

Cities are made of desire. "Stealing was part of the city. Every city is born, continually being born, out of configurations of minds and desires: every city is alive." (PK 83) And yet cities lack love, and in that lack are confusing. "Everyone's totally apart in this city. Everyone is madly cause unsuccessfully trying through success to stave off fear. Is this true? How can I know what's true?" (LM 308)

Still, it is a city most Ackers can't not love, as a possibility. "New York City will become alive again when the people begin to speak to each other again not information but real emotion. A grave is spreading its legs and BEGGING FOR LOVE." (HL 38) The possibilities in the margin that New York failed to nurture might appear elsewhere, for a time. "San Francisco is a little haven in the midst of a really terrifying culture." (LI 126) That too was a temporary condition.

The psychogeography of the city in the Acker-field finds its mythic ambiences through its neglected corners, its hustler zones, its rat-motel basements. "When most people in a city have no money and no source of money, they live without mercy." (PE 241) Bourgeois apartments and prosperous art world enclaves appear to open directly onto spaces of waste and failure. The rats have crawled out of the basement up to the penthouse. It's a city of rats more than people, a kind of collective animal cunning.

All cities become the New York of the seventies, where the dysfunctional margins could no longer be hidden or denied. The city becomes a futureless remnant, or perhaps a premonition of a parasitic and terminal mode of production after capitalism in its heroic and modernizing phase: the city-prison. The Acker-field connects to those "philosophers of the city who know that the city and this way of life is doomed." (PE 111) And: "Just like the sexual—the architectural and philosophical systems of this city collapsed. . . . This collapse of reason rather than theism—the collapse of absolutism—these collapsed bridges are linking the city's concrete chaos to the hills outside the city. In this fantastic landscape, feminism is being born." (*IM* 68) Although as we shall see it is a very distinctive kind of feminism.

Some Ackers connect the fate of the city to a wider perspective. "Perhaps New York City isn't disintegrating. Perhaps one system, that order based on a certain kind of capitalism, is disintegrating while another world, one of tribes, criminal and other, anarchic, is rising out of the rotting streets, sidewalks, bridges." (*BW* 135) A city of lawless power and powerless laws. "It is the city of anarchy, not of anarchists." (*MM* 99)

The city no longer has any project, either for its power, for a counter-power, or the refusal of power. "This new holy city is a reality not only without religion but also without anything to want or seek for: without anything. The city whose first characteristic is, it gives nothing." (*DQ* 41) A city populated entirely by rats and chancers. "And what about the humans? They were all eaten up long ago. They never did know how to survive." (*PE* 228) And: "What had once been a city of renegades . . . had turned into a city of artists." (*MM* 93)

Cities, like bodies, can be penetrated. "There are holes in the city. Not only its concrete and other walls. Everything here is as living as flesh. . . . Over the scrawny footbridges over the filthy freeways over the holes, over the skyscraper roofs, in a sky which burns, the pirate ship of reality is moving out." (*IM* 68) The penetrable city, together with the penetrable body, have to find another mode of existence within this urban unreality. "I want to be mad, not senseless, but angry and beyond memories and reason. I want to be mad. I went further into the city." (*ES* 51)

Sex-work

Besides being a place of wandering freely, the city is a place of *labor*. An Acker cut off from family money is going to have to work. "How can I be free if I'm broke?" (*IM* 24) "'Earn a living' as if we're not already living. . . .'" And: "I try to teach myself politics and philosophical theory but I begin again to starve." (*PE* 11) So there's nothing for it but to work, but as little as possible, as working doesn't solve one's problems. "They always say that money equals safety, though I'm not sure who 'they' are or about whose safety they're speaking." (*ES* 80)

Labor appears as something to avoid or minimize. There's no dignity in labor in the Acker-text. Particularly for girls. "I was a nice shopgirl earning nice money. Nice money doesn't exist. I needed a lot of money. I figured I could sell my body, a resource open to most young women." (PE 143) And so: "I start working a sex show to abolish all poverty and change the world." (PE 140) Three kinds of labor become the activity through which the city most usually appears in the Acker-field: sex-work, art-work, and fame-work.

The last two of these were not really open to girls, which leaves sex-work. "Being a whore beats being a secretary . . . or a wife cause, for the same work, work cause there's no love, only a whore not a wife or secretary gets paid enough she might be able to escape men." (LM 269) Sex-work pays better than non-sex-work, and besides: "A nice girl never does anything for free." (PE 147)

Of the four (or five) genders, sex-work is connected to the gender of *the girl*. "QUESTION: Why do women become whores? My answer: It's not women, it's girls. Girls also freely fuck men and murder. It's our American way. Question: Why do girls become whores? Answer: A lot of girls do it for a while. The ones who don't for a while, just die." (IM 99) Which could be either actual or social death. The girl is something that appears where two events intersect: powerlessness in the world and desirability, particularly to men. The girl—cis or trans—is an event at that nexus.

If it's men who have money and power, then, a girl who "doesn't have money has to get money out of a man." (LM 337) She might not have to do much besides work on creating the spectacle of sex. "Understand: a girl can make a good living without having to turn tricks." (PE 146) But such work is hardly glamorous and has its dangers. "I didn't know if I was going to make money or get raped. I didn't have any choice." (PE 144)

Sex-work is the girl making a spectacle of herself: "With the creeps males chauvinists rednecks pukes John Birchers worse liberals murderers we get in the audience it's a strong show they don't want to see anything but dead cunt they make everything dead with their eyes. . . . I come out dance strip do hard spreads no expression 10 seconds each held still to Ike and Tina Turner's NO RESPECT dance at the end sadism hands on the hip as they clap." (HL 30)

Instances of community are rare in the Acker-web, but among sex-workers an Acker finds one: "Here, the women don't need feminism to allow them to curl around each other like cats, or to put their heads on each other's shoulders for consolation, or to hold hands. The women support each other, not because they are sisters, for we're all brothers and sisters and yet we torture each other in perhaps unaccountable ways, but because suffering, each one's particular problems, runs through all of their flesh like air can run through a window screen in the full heat of a drowsing summer. They smell each other's cunts and hate men." (IM 117) And so: "The hint that it was possible to live in a community . . . saved me from despair and nihilism." (MM 14)

This Acker: "When I was a stripper and did performances—I almost change personality, it's a really strong experience. And it's all right except that I don't do it that easily, it's too strong an experience." (LI 14) An experience that changes an Acker's perspective. "I hate men because I've had to be a semi-prostitute." (PE 31) The heterosexual relation is already, for girls, one of danger. Putting it on a cash basis provides an income but hardly improves things: "All the shits cared about was my cunt they moved as I moved so they wouldn't miss a glimpse light meat." (HL 31) The spectacle of the girl is not the girl: "The last time I got on stage for the first ten minutes I felt I wasn't me." (HL 25)

Writing, like any art, can't just come from the pure pleasure of sensation. Many Ackers are materialists, and want to make manifest writing's means of production. The situation of a writer will shape the writing. If the writer has to work, work will shape it, one way or another. "She learns from history that purity comes from lies or impurity: historical example: after Mme. De Tournon lived with a poet who made her support him by working dirty movies and in a sex show, she swore she hated men. She would always be a lesbian, even though she wasn't sure she physically liked fucking women as much as men, so she could devote herself to her art." (GE 80)

An Acker: "I took the expensive clothes I bought with the money I earned off my body so that men could photograph me." (ES 63) Even the more basic forms of sex-work are the making of a luxury product, and an Acker doing a bit of sex-work can indulge a taste for other luxury products: "Always luxury before necessity." (SW 38) The labor point of view for the sex worker is a particular one, as it can also lead to a rare glimpse of the self as product. "It's possible to perceive yourself just as you'd perceive anything else. . . . This is how strippers perceive their bodies." (ES 27)

Another Acker: "Oh sex sex sex and time to work." (SW 116) Meaning: sex outside of the commodity, and the real work of writing. Sex-work enables writing by offering more free time, but ends up changing both writing and fucking. "And the sex show really didn't make you feel very nice about sex." (LI 71) Sex-work dispels some of the aura around heterosexuality. Sex can be commodified like anything else, and became one of the prime drivers of commodification.

In the Acker-web, sex is neither romantic nor liberation, but nor is it exclusively a domain of power. Rather, sex becomes a practice about which to ask political and aesthetic questions. An Acker: "I was now living two lives or in two societies: a society of sex shows and forty-second street and one of poets." (19.03) The art, politics, and Acker's low theory might come as much from one of these worlds as the other.

"Prostitution's supporting everyone these days." (PE 222) Rather than being some sort of exception, what if sex-work was something like the norm for what work is becoming? In a city like New York in the twenty-first century, it seems anachronistic to think of the industrial worker as the model. But then it also seems to miss a lot to think of some kind of cognitive worker as the model when so much of what's required at work, particularly from female workers, is emotional and even erotic performances. Along with wages for housework or wages for Facebook, how about wages for sex-work for all? "Women are whores now. I think women every time they fuck no matter who they fuck should get paid." (HL 45)

Art-work

"Working as a stripper is a very high form if you want to take it like that. . . . I mean it's gorgeous and a real art unto itself. . . . I could never be a good one." (LI 23) Art-work versus sex-work functions something like a class distinction. "Almost every living artist who keeps on doing art has family money or at least one helpful sex partner." (GE 77) Artist is an ambiguous class category, still with some residue of the marginal outsider left over from modernism, but really art is on the way to becoming just a business making bespoke commodities for a ruling class again. "All of my artist friends were starving before they landed in their middle-class mother's wombs." (GE 28) Art-work is a world of privileged pets. And for a certain class of art-dude, immunity: "Famous artists murder their wives and go scot-free." (IM 20)

Ackers don't do sex-work for long, and do not really do art-work: "I was never an artist." (LI 75) But they do know something about art, having been in its milieu. Most Ackers have a materialist approach to actual art-work. "I don't really know what art is. I know what an art context is." (LI 24) Most Ackers see art-work as a peculiar thing, but one still shaped by relations of class and gender. "Whenever someone, the literati, the professors, declare that there is such a thing as 'total ornament,' that 'art is pure,' what they are saying is that the rich own culture, discourse, and probably the world. If this seems like a non sequitur, you figure it out." (BW 4)

"Why's a Cubist painting, if it is, better art than a Vivienne Westwood dress?" (DQ 47) Art-work is a man's world. The forms that matter are the forms that obsess them. "On no side, from no perspective, do women and men mutually see each other or mutually act with each other. Art, also, is fetishism." (DQ 94) In the city, an array of art, like an array of women, appears as a spectacular world of things. Both the aesthetic and the sexual relation are burdened by the weight of the commodity as a world of dead things.

Nevertheless, art is—or was—an index to the viability of the city. "What is it . . . to be an artist? Where is the value that will keep this life in hell going?" (DDH) "You're losing possibility. What art is to me is partly the opening of possibilities." (LI 57) The class basis of the art context is changing, and art-work is changing form. "The middle class who served as the backbone of the art world is becoming conscious of its own demise: people are realizing they can no longer afford mortgages on their homes . . . nor can they afford to send their children to college; decent medical care is a luxury; homelessness the specter in front of their eyes. The once staunch middle-classes do not have the leisure to attend poetry readings." (AD 7)

This is what was or could have been: "Choosing to be an artist means living against this world. Why would anyone choose to be an artist? Cripples didn't choose to be crippled." (*LM* 195) What could have been is an art that could still touch an outside. "What matters to me? Art. Art equal to sex." (*LM* 218) An art that capitalism could not quite assimilate: "You don't understand what art is cause you're scared of your wildness." (*DQ* 45) "I thought, in those golden days when poverty was noble and the United States was rich, art is our way, our true Western religion." (*BW* 83) That is what, to most Ackers, is being lost in their time.

This Acker: "In those times art, for me, the highest of all possible existences, wasn't so much what one did but how one chose to live." (19.03) That art is passing. "Art is being totally marginalized to the point of extinction." (*AD* 7) In its place, something different, still called art, an aspect of what art always was too, perhaps. "Art was simply stock in a certain stock market." (*BW* 86) "Art is increasingly confined to a world of whimsy, an amusing stock market for the rich." (*BW* 41) "Cowboys and financiers run the old art world and that world gave birth, as its artists, to cowboys and financiers." (*AD* 9)

How to make art other to that of "the golden cowboys of art" and their world? (23.01) That might call on different aesthetic tactics: "The artist doesn't need to find out the limits of his or her medium, to 'make it new'; the artist, though politically and socially powerless, must find the ways for all of our survival." (*BW* 11) "All that does not concern intention is simply prettiness, that prettiness is, above all, despicable." (*BW* 83) The concept of the work, if it is not to be just an idea in the artist's head, is the laboring body of the artist, but that aspect of it that does its best to keep something from being stripped from it, and made into a commodity, that pretty thing.

"If, in any society that seems psychotic, art is questionable (I mean the word *questionable* in every possible sense): what can art criticism be?" (23.01) "The art-world or the world of non-materialism is becoming materialistic therefore the society's dead." (*LM* 216) Art is fully subsumed into that to which it was once a partial exception. "The people talk either about how they earn their money or who's becoming more famous. . . . Since the only ideas are for sale, none are mentioned. A few women appear to maintain the surface that sex is still possible." (*GE* 122–23)

An Acker who appears in porno films notes: "The only difference between the artists I fuck and the studs in the movies is that I can talk to the studs in the movies." (PE 196) Art-work is a way to survive that may have some advantages over sex-work, but it is mostly available only to men, and there's a trade-off between possible means of survival and the shutting down of friendship and love.

And yet art is not without possibility. Even while subordinated to the commodity form, art retains the lingering possibility of bringing formlessness into this fallen world. "The law increasingly seems to be regarding art (the body) as the actualization, not quite of chaos, but as the organic incorporation of chaos and death into life, as the violent overcoming of the society-chaos dualism." (BW 35)

Fame-work

Still, art-work offers the possibility of avoiding wage labor, or at least minimizing it. "I must give people art that demands very little attention and takes almost nothing for me to do." (LM 252) But to make that pay, one has to be famous. As writing from the late twentieth century, the Acker-field is quite canny about the necessities of spectacular labor of a kind that has become commonplace in the twenty-first. "The main characteristic of my American life is fame. Everyone wants media fame that is total isolation. For Americans, human identity has to be being against the world." (LM 312)

"I'm part of this culture that doesn't want me. . . . We're hustling, we're doing the two-step, the dances of those who've been historically ousted (i.e., the good-as-dead), because we're trying to survive. Our only survival card is FAME and the other side of the card, the pretty picture, is HOMELESS-NESS." (IV 48) In the city as it is coming to be, "There is only appearance and disappearance, those people who appear in the media and those people who have disappeared from the possibility of any sort of home." (BW 5) And so: "It's part of a writer's life you just never know if you're about to be homeless or rich." (IV 46)

"I want to be rich and famous; no, I want to be able to talk with people without having them put me down." (PE 20) With a modicum of fame: "I'm able to do the work I want and have the men I respect discuss my and their work among each other and with me. I care about the economic aspect as much as I care about my fucking with men. I often sleep with my women friends." (PE 14) Not unlike sex-work, fame-work is a put-on that might generate enough to live on, without too much work, to make free time.

Avoiding work calls for being supported either by a patron or a public, to create some semblance of autonomy. "She craved my love as she craved her friends' and the public's love only so she could do what she wanted and evade the responsibility." (GE 58) Fame opens up ways of working less but fucking more: "How are you ever going to get famous and get fucked?" (PE 189) Although it may not always work. "I think I'm getting famous but no good boyfriends." (SW 166)

A horde of leather-jacket-Ackers will become branded as: "Antigone on a motorcycle." (ES 165) Still, it's demanding. "I have to work as hard as possible to make up for my lack of beauty and charm." (PE 101) There's a crafting of appearances, a theater of the body. And yet: "I can't bear seeing what I've become." (IV 49)

What many Ackers think they have become: "To my mind I was in a little cage in the zoo that instead of 'monkey' said 'female American radical.' So whenever they wanted the female American radical to comment on anything, to make a token appearance, they'd pull me out of the cage and give me some money. It was quite lucrative, I must say." (LI 205)

Capitalism

Being "a bit of a rebel Marxist" (MP 12), most Ackers are critics of capitalism. Sometimes, capital appears in the Acker-text as eternal capitalism, self-same and ever expanding. "I am giving an accurate picture of God: A despot who needs a constant increase of His Power in order to survive. *God equals capitalism.*" (ES 45) Far from being an obsolete challenge to a dead god, the sacrilegious quality of the Acker-text becomes a contemporary tactic, but only when it goes after the most contemporary alibis of the sacred, aiming for the will to power that wields those alibis as sock puppets.

Capitalism is defined by the law of value. Even sex workers and art workers (if they have no private income) have to sell their labor to survive. They sell their capacity to work to the owners of capital, in exchange for a wage which represents only a part of the total value of their work. The difference between the total value of what labor produces and the sum workers actually receive is the measure of exploitation.

Those are the basics, but Ackers wander off and explore some other consequences of the imposition of this rationality in which all labor can be reduced to calculable quantities. "In the modern period, exchange value has come to dominate society; all qualities have been and are reduced to quantitative equivalences. This process inheres in the concept of reason." (DQ 72) Reason itself becomes suspect as organized domination.

What could be outside the law of value, its generalized workhouse clock time? Perhaps the body is not entirely subsumed and made exchangeable: "The sensuality of your fleshs' our only made value." (LM 391) Maybe what's real is not the time of exchange value at all, but something more intimate, corporeal: "Now there are two times: no time and slow time. No time isn't the capitalist's substitution of commodities for values, as you say it is; no time is loneliness and the absence of love. The other time, slow time, is touching someone." (LM 291) There's a connection between the absence of love and commodification. The latter reduces everything, including bodies, selves, to sameness, and love can't endure in sameness. If love exists at all it is in its impossible, negative relation to human differences. Love is impossible, is absolute, eternal—approachable only in the negative, but within the time of capital not approachable at all.

The body is not easily extractable from commodified sameness. "By buying (eating) I'm bought (eaten). I am the commodity. The commodity buys me." (LM 301) The body is formed in the image of the marketplace: "I see that education is one means by which this economic class system becomes incorporated in the body as personal rules. The world outside me that's human seems to be formed by economics, hierarchy and class." (MM 12) And: "In any society based on class, humiliation is one method by which political power is transformed into social or personal relationships." (DDH)

Sexuality becomes a means of redirecting desire from immediate, sensual time to the fetish of its appearance, of which sex-work becomes the model form. An Acker: "These businessmen have to discover products that obvious necessity sells. Sex is such a product. Just get rid of the puritanism sweetheart your parents spoonfed you in between materialism which the sexual revolution did thanks to free love and hippies sex is a terrific hook. Sexual desire is a naturally fluctuating phenomena. The sex product presents a naturally expanding market. Now capitalists are doing everything they can to bring world sexual desire to an unbearable edge." (HL 42)

The illusory rationality of commodified time meets the simulated orderliness of desires as genre marketing: "The magazines were arranged in categories of kinds of sexual activity. It's possible to name everything and to destroy the world." (IM 123) Materialism, in the sense of acquisitiveness, seeing the worth only of things as measured in the marketplace, becomes the law. A law that negates the possibility of love as incommensurable, qualitative difference, that subjects it to merely exchangeable, measurable difference. "Does capitalism which must be based on materialism or the absence of values stink?" (LM 219) It actually stinks.

Still, sometimes there are Ackers who want to hold on to the possibility of another life, one that makes use values rather than exchange values, one that makes itself, together with others, without exploitation, as directly lived bodily pleasure and play. "Is use value a post-capitalistic construction? The value of this life is what I make or do. I live in absolute loneliness. What's the value of this life which is painful if it's not what I make or do in the world?" (LM 301)

Seen from the point of view of sex-work, art-work, and fame-work, capitalism might be mutating into something else. A mode of production in which these three forms of labor are not unproductive margins but centers of extraction, not so much of surplus value but of surplus desire. The extraction of surplus desire becomes the main business of the city. Art, sex, and beauty come exclusively under the compulsion to extort value. "If the society, still fearing all chaos, suddenly stops marginalizing these realms, of dreams, of non-procreative sexuality, and art, and begins viewing these activities as part of its own domain, it will begin trying to control, then censor, then criminalize these phenomena." (BW 35) The law of desire subject to the law of value comes with its own police.

The modern world may have stepped through more than one mode of production. "Gone are the glorious days of sailing when white men, by marketing slaves, ruled the entire earth." (ES 71) The kind of industrial capitalism that grew out of and supplanted the slave mode of production may be passing as well, at least at the leading edge. "There is a new group of predators in the world." (BW vii)

Post-capitalism has two senses in the Acker-web. One is the revolutionary possibility of life without exploitation, but the other is that exploitation itself might have changed form. This might then still be a world with a ruling class extracting a surplus out of dominated classes, including labor as traditionally understood, but which might also have added some other means of domination to its arsenal.

"You never recognize an end when it's happening." (IM 111) But from the vantage point of New York, London, and San Francisco, Ackers witnessed this strange post-capitalism emerge as it extended the commodity form into aesthetics and information but in the process modified the commodity form itself. "I saw New York becoming more and more a fiction about what happens to capitalism, and the art world as a real illustration of what was taking place." (LI 29) Ackers witnessed, from the epicenters of its power, a quiet but violent transition: "My reality, between post-industrial and computerization." (LM 313)

Some Ackers were warily curious about the internet, this other web. "Imagine a scenario of all the services becoming like AOL." (RC 52) Which is what post-capitalism seems to have become since Acker's death. "It's not a machine to me. It's more like a living mind. . . . Sometimes I feel like it's a mind eating me. . . . I have to be careful it doesn't devour me. I imagine the computer getting fatter and fatter and not allowing me to dream ever again and sucking out my thoughts." (RC 54)

When asked to list her five favorite websites, an Acker lists five imaginary ones instead. Site one: type out a dream. "As soon as you do this, the dream starts to take place. Note that we cannot interpret dreams. Rather, dreams interpret us." (22.45) Site two: you make art, words appear as if out of your head, instructions to draw the worst thing that ever happened to you. "If you don't do this, you'll never be an artist and you'll have to go back to being a bank official or a real estate agent." (22.45) Site three: you travel back through causes and change the future. You lose yourself. Site four: It's a mirror. "Everything that exists glides up before your eyes." (22.45) Site five: It's you. "I have no idea where it is nor if you can get there. Maybe you're back at the beginning." (22.45) This is an accurate map of the what internet media turned into in post-capitalism.

For some Ackers, post-capitalism is in its own self-identity endless, self-same, but with new appearances. "The multinationals along with their computers have changed and are changing reality. Viewed as organisms, they've attained immortality via biochips." (ES 83) Commodification as control seizes hold not just of labor but of everything. "Capitalism needs new territory or fresh blood." (ES 33) It has infiltrated all of the domains of the sacred and subordinated them to itself. "Since an emotion's an announcement of value, in this society of the death (of values) emotions moved liked zombies through humans." (MM 14)

Some other Ackers detect a strange mutation in the mode of production, features that are no less about exploitation but might work in strange ways, or display odd "post-capitalist money-powers." (DQ 71) The art world, for instance, becomes a prototype for some kind of political economy of information. "I call these years THE BOHEMIA OF FINANCE (that's what I called the art world . . .)." (PE 148) The art world no longer sells handmade things. It sells unique concepts—intellectual property. "The rules of commodity have destroyed the imagination. Here the only art allowed is made by post-capitalism rules." (DDH)

The quantitative information that is money and the qualitative information that is aesthetics meet in some peculiar way. "Her gown is Chanel, not Claude Montana nor Jean-Paul Gaultier. Money, not being Marxist, is worshipping humanity, as it should." (DQ 84) That's a particularly curious sentence. A human who is caught up in fetishism sees only the dance of money and things, but a more critical human might see beyond the thing to the labor that made it. Uncritical money, like the uncritical human, is fetishistic, but what it makes a fetish is not the commodity but the human. All it can see now is humans exchanging things that are brands, that are qualitative information. It can't see labor and production, the material world, either.

Mr. Fuckface: "You see, we own the language." (*BG* 136) A provisional theory of this wrinkle in the old mode of exploitation is to conceive it as adding to the separation between use and exchange values a separation between the signified and signifier aspects of the sign. The signifier, like exchange value, is a kind of exchangeable equivalence, a formal sameness. The signified, or meaning, is—like use value—something intimate, corporeal, and unquantifiable. Factory labor produces use values. This other labor of fame-work or sex-work or art-work produces signifieds. Just as capitalism forces the material product of labor into the sameness of exchange value, post-capitalism forces the informational product of fame work, sex-work, and art-work into the sameness of the signifier. Exchange values meet in the market as quantitative sameness; signifieds meet in the market as qualitative sameness.

Exchange value converts the qualities of the active body into extractable and measurable products. It turns substance into commodity. "Products are out of date. No one can afford to buy anyway." (*HL* 76) Post-capitalism adds the extraction of the value of signifieds: emotions, sensations, desires, and concepts, through the capture and ownership of signifiers. They are our feelings, lusts, needs; but owned and controlled now through their brands, copyrights, patents—through signifieds produced and distributed digitally, and that become the property of a new kind of ruling class.

This post-capitalism commodifies information rather than things. And: "Since the only reality of phenomena is symbolic, the world's most controllable by those who can best manipulate these symbolic relations. Semiotics is a useful model to the post-capitalists." (*LM* 293) The Marxian critique of political economy has to move on to the critique of structural linguistics, and in both cases, ask the same question: Who made that which appears on the market as mere thing?

"Theory: The separations between signifiers and signifieds are widening. . . . The powers of post-capitalism are determining the increasing of these separations. Post-capitalists' general strategy right now is to render language (all that which signifies) abstract therefore easily manipulable. For example: money. Another example is commodity value. . . . In the case of language and of economy the signified and the actual objects have no value don't exist or else have only whatever values those who control the signifiers assign them. Language is making me sick. Unless I destroy

the relations between language and their signifieds that is their control."
(*LM* 300–301)

Rather than anomalies, outlaws, outliers to capitalism, the artist becomes the prototype of those subjects from whom post-capitalism extracts value in the form of surplus information. Money as information about quantity wants aesthetics as information about quality. It wants artists, but it makes artists over entirely as what they always were at least in part: hustlers—whores. "Imagination was both a dead business and the only business left to the dead." (*ES* 35)

How then to dissent within post-capitalism? It might call into existence a labor point of view specific to its leading forms of labor, with unexpected oppositional worldviews. This Acker: "In the era in which men searched for and lived according to absolutes and women didn't exist—only their sexual organs—the pirates were renegades. When businessmen and artists came into power, in accordance with the necessities of late capitalism, men's desires for absolutes stopped. Became nostalgia and romance. The history of the century can be seen as defined by the struggle between a model of, or desire for, an absolute reality and a model, or recognition, of reality as indeterminate." (*MM* 108) To think and feel and act, in and against post-capitalism might be the work and play of different historical agents with their own historical awareness, unlike those of previous labor movements.

History

Here is an Acker-text image of the ruling class. "Mr. Knockwurst: 'Every night Sahih tells me my workers play these records of screams and to amuse themselves instead of sleeping they knife each other. Is that what we call language?' (no answer.) 'They're all Janeys. They're all perverts, transsexuals, criminals and women. We'll have to think of a plan to exterminate them and get a new breed of workers.'" (*BG* 136)

An Acker: "Excuse these remnants of Marxism." (23.01) On the other side of the signifier, and of the ruling class that would own and control it, is pulsating, quivering, amorphous, amoral flesh. But now that value can be extracted from it in the form of the signifier, unruly signifieds and the bodies that spawn them have to not only be whipped into line but whipped into a frenzy of the production of ever new signifiers.

How did it come to this? "All that she knew was that the world, totality was terror." (ES 79) Where control by men and control by capital overlap is in a kind of *thanaticism*, not so much the death drive as a universal but a death power—Thanatos—that is rather more specific. "The rich who have suicided in life are taking us, the whole human world, as if they love us, into death." (ES 72) And: "Soon there was nowhere left to set on fire." (ES 85)

"Who dies for love now? Who questions reality through suffering and madness?" (IM 50) Some Ackers react to the accelerated violence of post-capitalism with a nihilistic withdrawal. "I'm not fucking anymore cause sex is a prison. It's become a support of this post-capitalist system like art." (HL 41) And: "I want—because it's my ugliness, my lack of femininity, my wounded body, earned minute by minute that is all that is left to speak—I want you to be without hope." (BG 139) And: "I used to complain that the world isn't fair. Now I don't think the world isn't fair. I don't think." (GE 30)

"Depression meaning the poor person perceives fewer and fewer possibilities." (BG 57) Some Ackers stray into an existential nihilism. "Humans are packs of wild dogs. When they speak, their teeth are new razor blades. Their institutions are crimson chain saws." (ES 135) Irony is used sparingly in the Acker-field: "There is always a reason for nihilism." (ES 110) The problem with this is that "so long as you're dwelling in the reactive you're really reinforcing the society that you hate." (HL 17) And: "I will not descend into the night, for that romanticism is a disease."

Other Ackers see spaces of possibility even in the post-capitalist take-over of emotional, affective, libidinal, and conceptual life, although the problem with its colonization of intimate information is the separation of the world of information from the world of the tangible. "Perhaps this society is living out its dying in its ruins. But I would have no way of knowing this." (ES 63)

There's a clearing of the field, a dispensing with old beliefs and counter-beliefs from obsolete worlds: "To prove that there was nothing to be believed; nothing to be loved, and nothing worth living for; but everything to be hated, in the wide world." (GE 72) A devaluation of all that power might prop up as a value, until: "The whole rotten world come down and break." (*ES* 211)

"If history does make us . . . if those who are older than us formed us, you're a walking disease." (*ES* 69) Among the various faiths that have died in the Acker-field—god, man, art—maybe none weigh heavier than the death of history. And: "I had been taught that through rationality humans can know and control otherness, our histories and environments." (*MM* 54) But maybe that was just another delusion. "History is moving however it's moving, apart from what we think is right and wrong." (*PA* 87) And: "If there's a history of human progress, men have made it up." (*ES* 259)

"The era of art and business, or capitalism in its finality, is the era of anarchy." (*MM* 101) Anarchy but not that of anarchists. Both the subjective and objective worlds become enmeshed in a volatile temporality. Objective time, or rather historical time, can no longer be conceived as having origins, destiny, laws of motion.

No one can speak for history any more with unmarked authority. "How can your reasons or so-called rationality be separate from you? And if your reasons're you, there's only desire and will. Therefore there's no morality in the twentieth century: there's only ambition." (*LM* 326)

History can be sensed instead as an ever-changing possibility space whose contours are only touched when actualized. "The problem now is that theory dependent on absolute models can't account for temporal change. What is given in human history and through human history is not the determined sequence of the determined, but the emergence of radical otherness, immanent creation, nontrivial novelty." (*IM* 52)

There's no consistent and self-same subject that can be the author of theory from on high, and who could survey history, discover its hidden concept, and announce its destiny. "Since all acts, including expressive acts, are inter-dependent, paradise cannot be an absolute. Theory doesn't work." (*ES* 113) Instead, post-capitalism appears as: "The world beyond time. The bloody outline of a head on every desk in the world. The bloody outline of alienated work. The bloody outline of fetuses. There's no more need to imagine. Blood is dripping down our fingertips while we're living dreams." (*DQ* 122) What might be possible still is a low theory from within contingent time, as the concept produced out of the work and play of those marginal to post-capitalism's extraction of value from all forms of desire in the form of information.

Politics

While clearly heretical in relation to the political economic theories of capitalism current in the late twentieth century, the Acker-field does not drift back toward mere liberalism, in either aesthetics or politics. "It was the era of democracy in which the state of the art was the art of the state." (*MM* 97) It does not abandon history in the name of some version of Cold War Americana. "Daddy, you want to know about politics? I'll tell you about politics. The United States' overrunning El Salvador and Nicaragua." (*LM* 380)

In a sly way, this Acker acknowledges the violence within the American prison-state itself: "But like most Americans, I keep pretending that horror is taking place outside America's shores." (*MM* 103) For: "This is what liberalism is. Hypocrisy." (*LM* 215) Because for this Acker: "America. Death. If you're anything but Death, you're the masses of exiles." (*ES* 163) It is the fine principles of American liberalism that everyday violence refutes in practice. Rather than resort to lofty principles, some Ackers go to a kind of *basic* materialism, not of things but of formless, useless waste. "Society's progress to totalitarianism arose and keeps arising from its refusal to be shit." (*MM* 128) These Ackers go toward what is ejected, excluded, denied.

That there is an irrational side to the spectacle of American presidential politics strikes each generation as a novelty. "For a nation which proclaims itself free and democratic is in reality directed by a few hundred imbeciles, if that many, who fear the consequences of the intelligence of others far more than their own stupidity." (*IM* 75)

The more political Ackers start not so much from the intellectual leftist currents of their time, but from something more basic. For instance, from that brief experience of sex-work. "The 42nd st experience made me learn about street politics. . . . You see people from the bottom up, and sexual behavior, especially sex minus relationship." (*LI* 73)

Most of the sources of political energy for Ackers are American. "Aboli-tionism; feminism; utopianism; vegetarianism; etc. The secret history of the United States." (BW 127) These are currents which are of interest not so much as confrontations with power as refusals of it. "Law is the basis of so-ciety. Identity is the only law." (BW 58) The struggle is not to replace one law, one identity, with another, but to escape them. And it continues. "Queer politics is not identity politics. . . . But I'm not sure that everyone agrees what queer means, nor have we yet examined its relation to class." (PA 88)

"How can I escape this unbearable political reality?" (MM 205) Not that there's any hope, but there might be some tactics in accelerating rather than resisting the devaluation of all values if all values that are available are those of a corrupt ruling class. This Acker addresses them: "You are dead. Your kind is over with. The loss of memory that you taught the me-dia and their consumers has turned back on you, as all policies turn back on their policy-makers. A double oblivion. For dream is that which is most sacred in human and/or beast." (MM 215) The nihilism of post-capitalism is, strangely enough, a space of possibility.

"It is true that our racist, sexist, classist mores have to change or we will all kill all of us." (ES 154) And so, "The only practical attitude now toward the United States and toward the history it has made is to destroy it all. That is exactly what I've tried to do. Here was the beginning of language. My language." (MM 196)

It's a dangerous tactic:

"Marxist Feminist: 'But how can I tell the difference between the real and what isn't real that is, for our purposes, between their disgusting weapons and our good weapons?'

Situationalist With Italian Accent: 'You can't.'" (LM 270)

Post-capitalism secretes its own form of state, with tendencies toward the imposition of the tactics learned in colonial wars on formerly imperial populations. Such a state wants no longer to be loved but feared and, at the same time, lusted after. State violence becomes an object of fascination and desire. "May one fact remain to form human memory: since a state is just a mask that secretes and shelters the power relations behind it, every state is fetishized or sexually desirable." (MM 181)

"And what of race?" (BW 85) The revolutions that recur in the Acker-text are anticolonial ones, from the Haitian revolution to twentieth-century African independence struggles, in Algeria and elsewhere. The struggle is always one not only of defeating white imperial power but also not ending up doubling and duplicating it.

Confronting the violence of the state with a counterviolence has not proven successful in the overdeveloped world, and indeed the desire for it is suspect. "All the acts of terrorism, all the outrages which have struck and which strike the imagination of humans, have been and are either OF-FENSIVE or DEFENSIVE. If they are offensive, for a long time experience has shown that they will fail. Only desperate or deluded people resort to offensive terrorism. If they are defensive acts, experience has shown that these acts can be somewhat successful. Such success, however, can be only momentary and precarious. It is always and only the State (or Society) which resorts to defensive terrorism, either because it is in some grave so-cial crisis or because it fears its destruction."[1] (IM 70)

Many Ackers are suspicious of countering the spectacle of charismatic, if demented, power with forms of spectacular counterpower. Leaders won't deliver salvation: "We do not need authorities but we do need informa-tion." (MM 124) Information tactics might take the place of what had for-merly been imagined as a cultural politics. But what if there is neither cul-ture nor politics? At least as these domains were traditionally understood, as superstructures raised up over, and directing, an infrastructure of cap-italist exploitation: "The dominant classes' ideological structures, obvi-ously, determine whether or not they'll continue to be dominated." (ES 125) Perhaps that basic social form no longer holds now that post-capitalism relies on extracting signifiers from bodies as much as on extracting labor from bodies.

"Up until the 1970s the ancient world, the world which is daily life and thinking and loving existed—but it was swept away." (LM 175) The appearances of a culture and a polity remain, but not the substance. To the extent that the shell of a culture still exists, it is no longer a site of contestation. The long march through the superstructures ended in defeat. "The perception based on culture is a drug, a necessity for sociopolitical control." (ES 36) And: "Culture is that which falsifies." (LM 191) Culture is now only a means of control.

The consensus illusion of culture knows something is up, and scapegoats have to be found. In "the newspapers therefore everybody blames the lumpen-proletariat." (LM 297) In the United States of the twenty-first century, there's a remarkable degree of agreement about this. The liberal columnists blame the rural redneck whites for not voting Democrat. The illiberal columnists blame the urban nonwhite masses for not voting Republican. Whatever it is, it's always the fault of the relatively powerless.

"There's no more education, no more culture—if culture depends on a commonly understood history—and perhaps no more middle class in the United States. There's War." (MM 29) Formerly colonial strategies of domination have come home to roost. But this war isn't just one of outright violence. It is also an information war. "The war is now at least partially a language war. What else is writing (now) about?" (BA 23) "War, you mirror of our sexuality." (ES 26)

This loops right back to the tactics of the Acker-field's first philosophy. It began by dispensing with the individual subject as coherent owner of its own self, with a memory and a destiny. The same tactic applies in the social-technical field of a third philosophy as in the phenomenological field of a first philosophy. "But what if I isn't the subject, but the object? If the subject-object dichotomy is here the inappropriate model? (Note: the war is now, further than the body or sensible fact, on the language level.) I don't mean. I am meant. That's ridiculous. There's no meaning. Is meaning a post-capitalist invention?" (LM 301)

Meaning—the signified—is that which post-capitalism exploits through the commodification of information in the form of the signifier, stripped of all its referential context, the bodies that felt and fucked and lived it. Post-capitalism harvests desires, feelings, sensations, meanings—and pays for them in mere signage. It offers for sale signifiers that it insists still attract and excite the body, albeit in a reduced and distorted way. The sign becomes a fetish, shorn of the sweat and tears and cries of its making.

A culture extracted from, and alienated from the body, obsessed with death, and yet unprepared for it. American culture is a death cult. "I remember seeing my father die. . . . His culture had given him no way to deal with death, his own death, so neither his own death nor his own life had any value." (22.52.2) And: "In American culture there's not much difference between a thing and the representation of a thing, between death and the representation of death." (22.52.2) Even a pandemic can become a mere sign of itself, subject to disbelief and dispute.

And so the tactic has to be a refusal of this dead current and debased currency of meaning. "The sub-programme altered certain core custodial commands so that she could retrieve the code. The code said: GET RID OF MEANING. YOUR MIND IS A NIGHTMARE THAT HAS BEEN EATING YOU. NOW EAT YOUR MIND." (ES 38) "End all representations which exist for purposes other than enjoyment." (ES 95) Take back the signifier from the information-commodity form.

"I'm no longer interested in being defined, positively or negatively, by a culture I think's sick." (IM 24) In any case: "The only culture that ever causes trouble is amoral." (DQ 21) And so: "Go take your shit to the grave. That's what I say. I'll tell you something, tonight when night comes, I'm going to crawl into your houses, and in your dreams where you have no power, I'll make you steal and whore. I'll turn you around." (BG 133)

Would it be possible to belong together, in a culture, that is not based on the policing of identities? Could a culture come together not around an image of what it is but images of what else it could become? "Culture is one way by which a community attempts to bring its past up out of senselessness and to find in dream and imagination possibilities for action." (BW 4) What a culture might have in common is not an ideal of what it means to itself, but rather the material means out of which meaning is made. "Language, any language including verbal and visual ones, supposes a community." (*BW* 17) To do language-work is already to really belong through the difference it makes.

Agency

"But what did I have left? Is a former victim the owner of no thing?" (*ES* 85) If there's a collective agency in the Acker-field, it is those who don't own capital but who also don't exactly do wage labor, either. Some are successful and honored, and get to call themselves artists. Many are not. They come in a few types that are hard to put names to, as they are never at home in any name. They are the tip of the melting iceberg of the homelessness of the world. "All of us girls have been dead for so long. But we're not going to be any more." (*PK* 114) Those a dead empire ostracizes through social death might be the last ones left alive.

"Romanticism *is* the world. Why? Because there's got to be something. There has to be something for we who are and know we're homeless." (*HL* 58) While skeptical of the romantic in several other senses, most Ackers hold on to this: the agency of the displaced, the marginal, the recalcitrant and—through them—the possibility of the world. Possibility alone is not enough, however. "Every possibility doesn't become actual fact. So knowing is separate from acting in the common world." (*DQ* 54)

These displaced ones all too often find no possibilities in the world. This sensibility in part looks back to a persistent sense of aesthetic or poetic rebellion and its foils. "I saw my friends in that brothel destroyed by madness starving hysterical naked dragging themselves through the whitey's streets at dawn looking for an angry fix I saw myself fucked-up nothing purposeless collaborating over and over again with those I hated old collaborating with my own death—all of us collaborating with Death." (*ES* 145)

The margin of possibility may have become very slight. Not only the effort of labor but the effort of feelings, sensations, pleasures, pains, concepts— information—are all within the post-capitalist commodity form and modify that form. "The realm of the outlaw has become redefined: today the wild places which excite the most profound thinkers are conceptual. Flesh unto flesh." (*ES* 140) And: "Now there's no possibility of revolting successfully on a technological or social level. The successful revolt is us; mind and body." (*LM* 300) To refuse even part of corporeal existence to the commodity form, "you have to become a criminal or a pervert." (*HL* 34) At least in the eyes of the ruling class.

For some of us it's not a choice. "I didn't choose to be the freak I was born to be." (*LM* 278) Some of those freaks who were called queers decided to wear that name with pride. So if we can be queers then why not also be whores? How about some *whore pride*? To celebrate queerness is often a way to avoid talking about labor or the sale of the sensual, fascinating, or erotic body. To celebrate whores is to connect the deviant body back to its place in the mode of production. "We need to do more than be whores and masturbate." (*PK* 56)

In the Acker-web there might be a lot of ways to be a whore. It might and might not mean *sex worker*. Whoring might include a lot of other transactions, including those of artists. It might sometimes be undertaken in situations of violence and duress, but not always. The key quality is the struggle to become and remain a free agent, not becoming anyone's possession: "A whore goes from man to man; she's no man's girl." (*GE* 116) The rebellion of the whores: "We got rid of our johns, now our dreams don't mean anything." (*PK* 54) To be neither owned nor rented, by anyone. To extract the body from the commodification of its surfaces and signs. But what then, dream realized, can one become?

The whore might be a more promising kind of being in the world of post-capitalism than the artist. It is still mostly men who get to be artists, or at least to become independent through art-work. Artists deal in too compromised a form of agency: "Revolutionaries hiding from the maws of the police which are the maws of the rich by pretending they're interested only in pleasure." (*PE* 111) The artist might have been privileged but marginal to capitalism, whereas in post-capitalism they become more integral to a commodity form that absorbs information out of the not-quite-laboring activities of bodies. In post-capitalism, the artist is a far less interesting social type than the sex worker.

Not kin but kith to the whores are the punk boys. "To be kissed by a punk boy was to be drawn to insanity or toward death. The last of the race of white men." (*PK* 41) Several Ackers try to unpick the way narrative writing generates race, but not with as much insight as when they unpick how narrative makes genders. "The whites make death because they separate death and life." (ES 75) Most Ackers try to be race traitors, but whiteness is hard to escape. At least, punk boys only count as such if they try to escape from both masculinity and whiteness—and not as some noble achievement but as a minimal condition for coming into being. They benefit from openness to tutelage: "The whores explained to the saints that they were voyaging to the end of the night." (PK 41)

Another ambivalent figure, who appears more often than the punk, is the pirate. "As long as I can remember, I have wanted to be a pirate." (ES 20) In imagination at least, there was a time when: "Pirates sailed the shark-wondrous seas." (EU 164) "And to be a pirate—that's kind of like the dumb myth of freedom; go make your own laws and control our own ship." (LI 61) "Today there are no more pirates therefore I can't be a pirate." (ES 26) The pirate is an amoral agent of the imagination, homeless and lawless. The pirate crosses the boundaries between worlds, and is also to some extent an historical figure. "The pirates knew, if not all of them consciously, that the civilizations and cultures that they were invading economically depended on the enslavement of other civilizations and cultures. Pirates took prisoners, didn't make slaves." (MM 109)

Pirate and whore form mythic couplings and doublings. "The pirates loved women who were sexual and dangerous. We live by the images of those we decide are heroes and gods. As the empire, whatever empire, had decayed, the manner of life irrevocably became exile. The prostitutes drove mad the pirates, caught, like insects in webs, in their own thwarted ambitions and longings for somewhere else. . . . The pirates worshipped the whores in abandoned submission." (MM 112)

Pirates escape the laws even of gender. "Pirates aren't always either male or female." (PK 112) As we'll see later, their bodies might be dysphoric about this. Here's one of my favorite Ackers again: "Pirate sex began on the date when the liquids began to gush forward. As if *when* equals *because*. At the same time, my pirate penis shot out of my body. As it thrust out of my body, it moved into my body. I don't remember where." (PK 114) Pirate sexuality is outside of identity, outside of the concept of gender, outside the commodity form: "On dreams and actions in pirates: Their rotten souls burn in their bowels. They only go for pleasure. For them alone, you see, naked bodies dance. Unseizable, soft, ethereal, shadowy: the gush of cunts in action." (MM 109)

Not being enclosed in identities, pirate-whores in revolt neither have subjectivity nor are they objects made over by commodification. They refuse to have all of the value extracted from their bodies in the form of signifiers severed from signifieds. "For the first time, I was seeing the pirate girls in their true colors. Black and red. They wore their insides on their outsides, blood smeared all over the surfaces. When opened, the heart's blood turns black." (ES 265)

Punks, whores, pirates: one can become another, or is more than one at once. And all can be sailors. "In order to see, I have to touch or be what I see. For this reason, seers are sailors. "A writer's one type of sailor, a person without human relationships." (HL 51) "When seers become artists, they become pirates. This's about identity." (MM 101) Identities don't have to disappear, they just become transitive, temporary. This is not the romanticism of accelerated annihilation. Rather, in sailing through situations, selves happen as effects, not unlike foam crests on waves, up and under, up and under again.

Sailors are not bound within any territory or home. They come into existence in the difference between times and spaces. "Sailors set out on perilous journeys just so they can see in actuality cities they have only imagined." (ES 118) And: "A sailor is a man keeps on approaching the limits of what is desirable." (MM 13) There are sailors of actual seas, but one has to be a man to do that, and then there are sailors of textual seas. "Since ANY PLACE BUT HERE is the motto of all sailors, I decided I was a sailor." (ES 156)

Perhaps the sea was central rather than peripheral to the actual history of capitalism. From whaling to slaving, the sailor was caught up in commodification at its most naked. Sailors are free agents to most Ackers, although in actuality many were pressed labor. Ackers who are mythic sailors set off on an imaginary sea, an open plain along which to flee. "I always wanted to be a sailor. . . . Sailors leave anarchy in their drunken wake. . . . A sailor is a human who has traded poverty for the riches of imaginative reality. . . . A sailor has a lover in every port and doesn't know how to love. Heart upon heart sits tattooed on every sailor's ass. Though the sailor longs for home, her or his real love is change. . . . No roses grow on sailor's graves." (ES 113)

Anarchy is a suitably indefinable term in the Acker-web, being both that which escapes order but also order that imposes itself as sheer power in post-capitalism. The imaginary sea becomes a calenture across which to flee post-capitalism. Sexuality, the city, and writing can be the oceans within which sailors wander. Or maybe even the body as it is supposed to be organized is a thing to flee. "Let your cunt come outside your body and crawl, like a snail, along the flesh. Slither down your legs until there are trails of blood over the skin. Blood has this unmistakable smell. Then the cunt will travel, a sailor, to foreign lands. Will rub itself like a dog, smell, and be fucked." (*MM* 59)

Girls

The spidery swarm of rebellious nonsubjects and nonidentities can include artists, punks, whores, pirates, sailors, and some not discussed here such as knights and poets. And then there are the lawless, fatherless girls, whose possible being-together was first glimpsed backstage once at a sex show. "I can't keep up with these Girls. My generation, spoon-fed Marx and Hegel, thought we could change the world by altering what was out there—the political and economic configurations, all that seemed to make history. Emotions and personal—especially sexual—relationships were for girls, because girls were unimportant." (*LI* 187) But for this Acker: "I am bored with discussing the fearful actions of the patriarchy." (19.11)

Girls are, among other things, objects that power perceives as a thing to desire. As if they had no subjectivity. Rather than claiming to be subjects, girls in the Acker-web escape into unknowability, as far as power's gaze is concerned. Their bodies may be penetrable, and that is the function assigned them as objects, but otherwise they can choose not to be known at all. The girl too is not an identity but an event, something produced by chance and fluid time. Lulu: "You can't change me cause there's nothing to change. I've never been." (*DQ* 78)

In the language of identity, the girl has never been. She is the empty slot in a language defined by others. But there might be other ways girls can be in language. "Is it possible that the girl can find her actual body, and so what gender might be, in language? In a letter that, not yet language, has no discernable meaning?" (*BW* 164) In the absence in language, where the girl isn't, could be many other possibilities. "I suspect that the body . . . might not be co-equivalent with materiality, that my body might be deeply connected to, if not be, language. But what is this language? This language which is not constructed on hierarchical subject-object relations?" (BW 166)

There might be many kinds of girls, which is a problem, as sometimes they want nothing to do with each other. Their selective visibility to men can bring with it a too selective awareness of each other. "Girls have to accept girls who aren't like them." (ES 264) A girl is a node of attraction but also of vulnerability, whose actions are constrained by others' desires and violence—by men's desires and violence. Their vulnerability is their agency. Their possibility is in refusing the legitimacy of any agency that it not at least in part girl.

To be a girl in the world is fearful but also a fearsome thing to be: "Doctor, I'm not paranoid. I'm a girl." (IM 138) Girls enter masculine identities, penetrate them, through the senses, through the projection of their own penetrability. And so men, always anxious about their own openings, want not just to fuck them but to hurt them and kill them. Men react badly to their vulnerability to their own desire for the girl and take it out on the girl. Girls' only power is in their amorality and ability to exploit their own desirability: "In reality, the girl was desperate to fuck and scared to fuck because fucking was how she earned money and got power." (IM 140)

A girl might be better off refusing to have sexual relations with anyone living. "Motorcycles? My relation to motorcycles. Well, I'm a girl. And there's this big hot throbbing thing between my legs, whenever I want him/her, and he/she's mine and won't reject me like humans have the habit of doing." (IV 31) Maybe a motorcycle, or any technical thing, is outside the spectrum of human genders and has other ones. Maybe girls would rather be gendered in relation to those inhuman genders.

The girl said: "You understand that it's only with the highest form of feeling (whatever that is) and not because we hate you that we're going to take our ease in your homes and mansions, your innermost sanctuaries, we're going to sleep in your beds (you want us to anyway) on your unbloodstained mattresses on the sheets on which you fuck your wives. We want to feed on your flesh. We want—we're going to reproduce only girls by ourselves in the midst of your leftover cockhair, in your armpits, in whatever beards you have. We're going to sniff your emissions and must while we're penetrating (with our fingers) your ears, nostrils, and eye sockets. To ensure that you'll never again know sleep. . . . In the future, we'll never conceal anything about ourselves (unlike you) because our only purpose here is the marking of history, your history. As if we haven't. Because you said that we hadn't." (*MM* 51) A manifesto for—let's call it—*femmunism*.

Revolution

I want to break my habit of refusing to refer Acker back to precursors, to lineage, just once. I want to name one lineage that's not often perceived as part of her provenance. It's the postindependence African novel. It's her connection to this particular version of postcolonial literature, one that appears on her horizon mostly in her years in London. I'm not a well-situated reader to explore this. I want to leave the Acker-text open at this node as an offering for readers to come who might be.

This Acker: "So it's hard to talk about my experience politically in the United States; it's maybe not more than here, but to me, there it's so much about black and white. . . . Anyway, there's this series of Heinemann books which are incredible and I would go through them. Collett's of London used to have a whole series, and I'd go there to get books, and I pick up all of the Heinemann series, and there's some amazing writers in there. There's Ouologuem's *Bound to Violence*, and he was actually exiled. There's a writer called Armah . . . I think *Why Are We So Blest*? was the one that most influenced me. . . . [Cyprian] Ekwensi. Again, he was solving problems for me about how to be surprised, how to write something that's not dogmatic, how to be political." (*LI* 31)

And this Acker: "In *Bound to Violence*, Yambo Ouologuem (Heinemann 1971) joins historical facts to passional and imaginative truths. So much of our education is the process of separating our reasoning faculties from our emotive and imagining ones. Ouologuem is of the greatest kinds of writer, a healer of the wounds of a faulty society has made." (22.35) This interest connects to those of other Ackers in Black and anticolonial revolutions, from Haiti to Algeria. The wounds of faulty societies are those that revolutions replicate rather than overthrow. Her interest here is in writers who know themselves to be implicated, in and against revolutions, who write in and against the crucial moment of restoration, where power resumes its old habits in new livery.[2] Where the new power turns against its marginal figures, much as the old one had before it.

This Acker: "To what extent to do we remain obligated to a world even when our presence is no longer desired in that world?" (BW 102) Artists, poets, punks, whores, knights, pirates, sailors, girls: makers of the sense and sign and heat of their own bodies. But who find the signs they emit captured and owned and used against them. And that's at best. That's when their bodies and minds are not violated and gas-lit and punished and imprisoned. So: "Why're we asslicking the rich's asses?" (DQ 123) It's time for "a revolution of whores, a revolution defined by all methods that exist as distant, as far as possible, from profit." (PK 30) It's time to declare: "I won't accept that this world must be pain: A future only of torment is no future for anyone." (DQ 163) A revolution that has to be made, over and over, even in and against those that succeeded.

"1968 is over. 1981 is over. Future is between my legs ha ha." (LM 290) There are a lot of revolutions in the Acker-web. It is not obsessed with nostalgia for the Eurocentric myth of Paris in 1968. Revolutions happen all the time, but mostly against colonialism, as Ackers come to know from attention to African writers. "Suddenly the people in this city were free. They were free to experiment." (ES 13) Revolutions attempt "the only thing in the world that's worth beginning: the end of the world." (PK 27) But they are always caught in a bind. "Intention: escape this horror as I know it and am made by it." (PE 136) How can revolutions avoid becoming the law they oppose? "When all that's known is sick the unknown has to look better." (ES 33) Until that too becomes part of the known.

Revolution within and against post-capitalism can't ignore how intimate commodification has become, how close it presses its exchange-value carving knives into the flesh. "Is liberation or revolution a revolution when it hasn't removed from the faces and bodies the dead skin that makes them ugly? There's still dead blood from your knife on one of my cunt lips." (IM 46) The dead skin of dead time, commodity time, of the death-in-life of having the information stripped from our bodies and sold back to us, masks the possibility of other lives, other cities.

Some Ackers dream of a libidinal revolution. "If we lived in a society without bosses, we'd be fucking all the time. We wouldn't have to be images. Cunt special. We could fuck every artist in the world." *(PE 201)* And: "Soon this world will be nothing but pleasure, the worlds in which we live and are nothing but desires for more and more intense joy." *(PK 32)* And for some: "Love's the only revolution, the only way I can escape this society's controls." *(PE 195)*

Others are skeptical. Even a brief experience of sex-work and of the so-called sexual revolution as it was practiced (mostly for the benefit of cis men) in the late twentieth century rather cools an Acker's ardor for it. It can't be as imagined by penetrators, as the availability of the world to their dicks. Those dicks can now be detachable, interchangeable, or optional: a sexual politics in which dicks aren't central. "In the future, I will be the sun, because that is what my legs are spread around." *(PK 116)*

Some Ackers have a more destructive character, but hold on to the fragmentary potentials that the negations of this world hide in their shadows: "Revolutions or liberations aim—obscurely—at discovering (rediscovering) a laughing insolence goaded by past unhappiness, goaded by the systems and men responsible for unhappiness and shame. A laughing insolence which realizes that, freed from shame, human growth is easy. This is why this obvious destruction veils a hidden glory." *(IM 45)*

There are many Ackers who start to dream of revolution not from the events of pleasure but of pain. "I am a masochist. This is a real revolution." *(GE 52)* "Masochism is now rebellion." *(DQ 158)* "Masochism is only political rebellion." *(ES 58)* "Freedom was the individual embracement of non-sexual masochism." *(DQ 118)* Because: "Pain is only pain and eradicates all pretense." *(DQ 140)* Masochism is not just kink or a pathology: "Each time I slice the blade through my wrist I'm finally able to act out war. You call it masochism because you're trying to keep your power over me, but you're not going to anymore." *(LM 300)* The masochist takes over the assigning of control over the body and makes a gift of it, which like all gifts, entails on the part of the recipient certain obligations. The masochist may be bound in rope but the sadist is bound in obligations.

And yet there's no attempt to make the sexuality of whores, pirates, and perverts something respectable, each with its own flag and T-shirt. The goal is not queer citizenship in the existing state through legitimizing its various identities. Rather, as the mad captain says: "Valiant beasts; because your sexuality does not partake of this human sexuality . . . I will now lead you in a fight to death or to life against the religious white men and against all of the alienation that their religious image-making or control brings to humans." (*DQ* 178) Being inside the enclosure is not the objective.

It will be a revolution of the penetrable, or perhaps of the reversible, of surfaces that can open but also swell to fill corresponding voids. It will be a revolution against ownership by that which gives away ownership of itself. It will be a refusal of the penetrated to be just the voided object for dick to fill: "They said it was a hole, but it was impossible for her to think of any part of herself as a hole. Only as squishy and vulnerable flesh, for flesh is thicker than skin. She was wet up there. When she thrust three of her fingers in there, she felt taken." (*IM* 140) For those of us who know we are holes, whether cis or trans, gay or straight, or none of the above, we can learn to top each other—and ourselves.

Holes

The penetrable are not nothing, not voids for their master's voice or dick. "I see his cock enter me, slide into me like it belongs in my slimy walls, I tighten my muscles I tighten them around the cock, jiggling, thrusting upward, thousands of tiny fingers on the cock, fingers and burning tongues." (*PE* 100) They—we—are not the other, the lack, the supplement, the second-sex organ. "I can feel your cock moving inside my skin skin I can begin to come the muscles of my cunt begin to move around your cock my muscles free themselves swirl to the tip of my clit out through my legs the center of my stomach new newer muscles vibrate I'm beginning to come I don't know you." (*PE* 7) The penetrated body comes to know itself, not its penetrator. The hole, which is not nothing, not a void or absence, comes into its own.

We don't *need* their dicks, even if we *want* them, sometimes. To want to be fucked need not be to want all that comes with it. In the post-capitalist world, the hole without the dick is labor without capital. It is also art-work or sex-work without the extraction of surplus information. It is a refusal of all the dick signals and being dicked by signals shorn of the writhing, pullulating, concentrating bodies that make them.

It's the revolution of the girls who are willing; willing to give up themselves to each other, who no longer need to be recognized or taken. "The more I try to describe myself, the more I find a hole." (MM 22) One does not have to say yes to power and become its void, even if that's how it usually works: "He made her a hole. He blasted into her." (HL 38) In any case, maybe the other side of the penetration of the hole by the dick is the active surrounding of the dick.

Any-body can void itself, although how, and how easily, may vary. "All of him wants only one thing: to be opened up." (IM 13) "A hole of the body, which every man but not woman . . . has to make, is the abyss of the mouth. . . . Today, all that's interior is becoming exterior and this is what I call revolution, and those humans who are holes are the leaders of this revolution." (PK 20) The mad quest of those with inverse or inverted lances: "To become a knight, one must be completely hole-y." (DQ 13)

The holes need not be the obvious ones: cunts, asses, mouths. The ears and nose are holes. "For me, every area of my skin was an orifice; therefore, each part of the body could do and did everything to mine." (PK 22) The body is penetrable everywhere. And what's at the bottom of the hole is not nothing. Nor is it the essence of the self, some private property of the soul. "'I' is not an interior affair." (MM 211) Rather than the I, all interiority, the eye: which looks out, and in looking out can be looked into.

The penetrable might also, at the same time, penetrate, opening while being opened, rather than remaining closed while being opened. This Acker: "I saw myself wearing a strap-on with the cock that wasn't in my cunt fucking the writer of this I saw that I didn't want to come through my new cock before he did I saw right at that moment before he was about to come, he screamed 'Hold my prick' the second his head was in my right palm, the prick shot into that hand so then I could come I totally let loose am letting loose for am simultaneously at the edge of pissing and of coming I saw this is what the writer called *coming in him*." (23.24.8–9) Who knows? I might even have been that writer, although I am surely not the only one it could be.

The revolution of the penetrable is not just about bodies. The body of the city, also: "The pipes, fallopian tubes unfucked, unmaintained, wriggled, broke, burst open, upwards, rose up through all the materials above them."

(*MM* 91) And: "Water pipes burst through the streets' concrete. Through these holes. Through holes in the flesh, the faces of the dead stare at the living. . . . Through human guilt, we can see the living." (*MM* 106) And: "The landscape is full of holes, something to do with what should be the heart of a country." (*IM* 115)

There's a risk in any will to revolution. There's a risk in opening up the body beyond its restricted repertoire. "If we teach these champagne emotions are worth noticing, we're destroying the social bonds people need to live." (*GE* 122) But maybe it's the chance of another life against the certainty of slow death. A death not just of bodies but also cities, even of nature itself.

"Either this is a time for total despair or it's a time of madness. It's ridiculous to think that mad people will succeed where intellectuals, unions, Wobblies, etc, didn't. I think they will." (*BG* 127) All the old gods die in the Acker-web. After the death of god comes the death of man, of imagination, of art, of love, of desire, of history. The good order won't result from making anything else sacred in the absence of god. Instead, only an experimental living with disorder.

A revolution of wild gone girls. In the footsteps of the "nameless, the pirates of yesteryear." (*MM* 95) It is a nihilist vision of revolution. The stripping bare of bodies and values reveals a world without aura, justice, or order. It becomes instead a world of violence and chance. The violence has to be felt, has to be known, so it can be deflected. That's the particular role of masochism, as a way of refusing to pass violence on to some other body, the way a certain kind of radical feminism ended up deflecting the violence it won't acknowledge onto trans women.

There's a connection between the acceptance of masochism among Ackers, their skepticism as to whether the body can even be known without careful and experimental study, and my hunch that, had she lived, she would have continued to be generous in making space in her texts for trans people such as me—a question I'll take up by way of a conclusion. Her revolution was not for the restoration of any identity. Not for their adding of ever more identities to an official list. It is a revolution to unleash the generative, generous capacity of non-identity—for anyone and everyone.

This Acker: "Today a certain part of the feminist canon argues that men are essentially different from women. Women, perhaps because they can have babies, are gentle, patient, nurturing, non-aggressive, non-violent. Whereas men make war and are irrationally violent and self-serving. The same feminists argue that bodybuilding is an unnatural sport for women because the women who bodybuild only want to be men. Perhaps it is time for a reappraisal of what it is to be female." (22.22) The hole in your body could be the wound of a muscle worked past failure.

The revolutionary path passes through the abnegation of identities, even, eventually, of marginal ones. Nihilism acknowledges a world of violence but also of chance. The god of history is dead. Noise and disorder won't be resolved at the end of history. But then neither is it entirely a world as an iron cage, enclosed in ever more perfect surveillance and rational- ization. If there's chance, there's still no hope, but there's a chance. An Acker: "To be beautiful is to be a seashell, so open that all the oceans and the fluids of the earth, of the body, are heard through you. Openness so open that it turns itself inside out and makes a snail-shaped labyrinth that leads to the future." (23.08) A hole that fills itself with the plenitude of its own nothingness.

Fiction

"We Have Proven That Communication Is Impossible." (*GE* 27) Communi- cation only creates fictions: the fiction of the object as a separate thing, the fiction of the self that can know and own the object, the fiction of a reliable means of relating object and subject, the fiction of the fluctuating fortunes of objects and subjects being resolved somewhere or some time, the fiction of a measurable and calculable time within which objects or subjects are self-same.

The Acker-field is a sequence of books about—no, not about. They are not about anything. They don't mean, they do. What do they do? Get rid of the self. Among other things. For writer but also reader. If you let them in. You have to want it to fuck you. It happens when there's a hole. Rather than say *one reads*, one could say that *one is booked*. A body can be booked a bit like the way it can be fucked. A body uses its agency to give access to itself to another. A body lets go of its boundedness, its self, its selfishness, and through opening to sensation disappears into the turbulent real.

Being booked might be different to reading just as being fucked is different to fucking. "The only way is to annihilate all that's been written. That can be done only through writing. Such destruction leaves all that is essential intact. Resembling the processes of time, such destruction allows only the traces of death to persist. I'm a dead person." (*MM* 123) Such a reduction expels meaning from the text and subjectivity from the body at once.

The risk, the challenge, is to go even further into the devaluation of all values. "My language is my irrationality. Desire burns up all the old dead language morality. I'm not interested in truth." (*LM* 215) The feeling of being in a post-truth world really accelerated in the twenty-first century. The transgressors of official pieties, of which Acker might be a celebrated example, are made scapegoats for a phenomenon that they had the audacity to expose. The stripping of information from bodies, a new kind of commodification, casts all anchored truths to the winds. If there's a cause for that, it is post-capitalism, not Kathy Acker or other transgressors of respectable literary form.

An Acker: "And the men—well, there seems to be some sort of crisis; the men seem to be absolutely *floundering* about." (*AW* 179) The panic attack of feeling exposed to information without meaning, stripped from its bodies and situations, caused a stampede among those who cling tight to their tattered rags of identity: whiteness, masculinity, petit-bourgeois exclusion. They went looking for ways to circle the fictional wagons, close the gates, and amp up streams of actual and symbolic violence to keep identity afloat on the rising tides.

"I'd like to say that everything I do, every way I've seemed to feel, however I've seemed to grasp at you, are war tactics." (*BG* 127) Tactics can change. The war has a new contour. This tactic might seem a little out of date: "For any revolution to succeed nowadays, the media liberals and those in power have to experience the revolt as childish irresponsible alienated and defeatist; it must remain marginal and, as for meaning, ambiguous." (*LM* 299) Media liberals and those in power are no longer quite the same thing. Even if media liberals and those in power both profit by amping up attack-information directed at each other.

During the rising tide of reaction, it might be tempting to throw in one's lot with the media liberals, if there is such a thing. But they are no friend to that revolting class of whores, pirates, punks, sailors, and autonomous girls that post-capitalism pokes, with its social media prompts, to gin up commodified desire. A revolting class quickly put in its place if it confronts the ruling class head on. A ruling class for whom America is really a one-party state which, with typical American largesse, has two parties. If that's the contours of it, then to appear childish and unthreatening seems like a survival tactic worth recalling from past information wars. Dwell in the void of the noise.

How to be a writer who actually writes for their own times and not as if the nineteenth century machinery of the novel still had a world with which to engage? Ackers are nearly all prose writers. Their sentences are regular, logical sentences, artless at first glance but often constructed with a minimalist elegance. Rather than break the sentence, they break the expectation of what the sentence is supposed to do—be a container for hidden reservoirs of meaning unique to the author's mind.

This Acker: "Language is more important than meaning. Don't make anything out of broken-up syntax cause you're looking to make meaning where nonsense will. Of course nonsense isn't only nonsense. I'll say again that writing isn't just writing, it's a meeting of writing and living the way existence is the meeting of mental and material or language of idea and sign." (LM 246) The chosen tactic is prose fiction, not poetry.

"I tell you truly: right now fiction's the method of revolution." (LM 271) Rather than shore up some other identity against hegemonic whiteness, masculinity, and petit-bourgeois privilege, strip the last charms from identity itself. It's a war tactic of disenchantment: "As soon as we all stop being enchanted . . . human love'll again be possible." (DQ 102) And then: "It's the end of the world. There are no more eyes." (PK 71)

Some Ackers: "What I have always hated about the bourgeois story is that it closes down. I don't use the bourgeois story-line because the real content of that novel is the property structure of reality. It's about ownership. That isn't my world-reality. My world isn't about ownership. In my world people don't even remember their names, they aren't sure of their sexuality, they aren't sure if they can define their genders. That's the way you feel in the mythical stories. You don't know quite why they act the way they act, and they don't care. . . . The reader doesn't own the character." (*HL* 51)

The Acker-text is not a career of novels. "Everything in the novel exists for the sake of meaning. Like hippy acid rock. All this meaning is evil. I want to go back to those first English novels . . . novels based on jokes or just that are." (*LM* 317) The plot of the bourgeois novel is the marriage of sexuality with property. Sexuality is enabled by, or confined by, property. Acker books are marketed as novels, but it's no fun to read them as such. They are caught in an ambivalent space, as all art-work is, between work and property, signified and signifier. These days they get some terrible Amazon reviews from readers who want them to mean something.

The Acker-work is more a texture of fictions: "I write in the dizziness that seizes that which is fed up with language and attempts to escape through it: the abyss named *fiction*. For I can only be concerned with the imaginary when I discuss reality or women." (*MM* 80) Rather than a women's writing that tries to inhabit the old forms, it's a refusal of it, and a refusal then also of those forms that would confine what *woman* can mean by insisting that it be a kind of subject that means things.

The Acker-fiction doesn't ask you to figure out what lies beyond the signifier any further than the level of what the words denote. Sure, you can read into them, into their connotations. Maybe it's impossible not to. You can guess at what might be the referents to which the signs refer in the world. But you don't have to read into it too much. You can look at the page and see writing, see a form of language, see what it does. What it did to you.

There might be a language on the other side of that language, glimpsed in a gasp or sigh of masturbation or bodybuilding. But actualized by pressing even further into the fiction of language. "Any statement beginning 'I know that . . . ' characterizes a certain game. Once I understand the game, I understand what's being said. The statement 'I know that . . . ' doesn't have to do with knowing. Compare 'I know I am scared' to 'Help!' What's this language that knows? 'Help!' Language describes reality. Do I mean to describe when I cry out? A cry is language turning in on its own identity, its signifier-signified relation. 'To of for by' isn't a cry or language-destroying-itself. The language has to be recognizably destroying itself."

(*LM* 313) Fiction is a texture made up of what expresses itself out of this body in particular but articulated through any self whatever.

Détournement

Some Ackers calls their way of writing, among other things, a "slash and gash method." (*LW* 60) They calls it copying, meshing, mushing, mashing, glopping, hacking, messing, rewriting, appropriating. (*DDH*) One could also call it *détournement*: to take an existing text on a detour, to bring it into play with other texts, to copy faithlessly, fixing a few things along the way. This writing is a kind of art-work, a product of the body, but of a body that will do its best not to have its concepts, feelings, memories stripped of it and made into property. A body that does not claim to create out of pure spirit, like a god.

"Does 'make' mean 'create'?" (*BW* 9) Maybe not. The author as creator is pretending to be a god, if a minor one. "I suspect the ideology of creativity started when the bourgeoisie . . . made a capitalistic marketplace for books." (*BW* 9) Maybe this is just an illusion whose purpose is to justify ownership of what is really common to all—language. "Nobody really owns nothing. Dead men don't fuck." (*BW* 10)

Who got to be owners of the works they created? Men did, mostly. "Only the incredible egotism that resulted from the belief in phallic centrism could have come up with the notion of creativity. Of course, a woman is the muse. If she were to open her mouth, she would blast the notion of poetic creativity apart." (*BW* 10) In the writing business, women got to be muses, then secretaries. Neither of which pays as well as sex-work. Then, when the business figured out that most book-buyers were women, there were women writers. Who became bourgeois writers in bourgeois forms.

Language understood as something nobody owns is a different language with which to write than a language a writer will claim to create and own. This Acker: "Now I'll never again have to make up a bourgeois novel. Didn't." (*DDH*) Instead: "I have become interested in languages which I cannot *make up*, which I cannot *create* or even *create in*: I have become interested in languages which I can only come upon (as I disappear), a pirate upon buried treasure." (*BW* 166) The writer, doing a kind of art-work, is caught up in the inconsistencies of communication, at least as post-capitalism shapes it. Language can circulate almost for free, and certainly in ways that can't readily be commodified. Or, at least, it could. A revolutionary writer is on the side of the free intercourse of signs and bodies.

Sometimes Acker calls her art-working methods deconstruction. "To copy down, to appropriate, to deconstruct other texts is to break down those perceptual habits the culture doesn't want to be broken. Deconstruction demands not so much plagiarism as breaking into copyright law." (DDH) Let's call it, rather, détournement, which highlights the way this writing rubs up against the property question, the question that for Marx was the key to critical agency.

"People tell me that so-and-so is putting my work on the net without permission, but that's cool. It's a compliment they are reading it. If it's out in the world, you use it. Life doesn't have copyright written all over it." (RC 54) This was before post-capitalism figured out how to extract not just surplus labor but also surplus information out of our desire to share, out of our will to commune. Some Ackers saw what was coming, though. "If it is at this historical moment difficult for a writer to make a living by depending on copyright, in the future it may prove impossible for all but the very, very few." (BW 101) And anyway: "The literary industry depends upon copyright. But not literature." (BW 103) What matters to literature might be outside the bourgeois book trade, in part or whole.

And yet a writer is also a whore, renting or selling a capacity of the body, allowing what's signified to be separated from what's intimately felt. Selling the signs of life. Most Ackers simply refuse to authorize the text as the creation, and thus the property, of a unique and whole and singular body, even as they rely on a property form that takes that for granted. "If I had to be totally honest I would say that what I'm doing is breach of copyright—it's not, because I change words—but so what? I mean we're playing a game, we earn our money out of the stupid law but we hate it because we know that's a jive. What else can we do? That's one of the basic contradictions of living in capitalism." (LI 95)

To be revolutionary it might not be enough that writing is as outside the commodity form as is possible. The undoing of the commodity form might need to enter the body of the text in a certain way as well, in writing that refuses the stripping of signs from bodies, signifiers from signifieds, where those stripped signifiers become the property of the reader and a receptacle for the reader to insert their own meanings. The book, not unlike the girl, might instead be multiply penetrable, readable many ways, and yet opaque to the claim of the penetrator, or reader, to mastery over it. Which is why I make no claim to have mastered the body of the Acker-text, just to have put this other textual body alongside it for a little while, so that they might touch.

"Please be my friend," she said. I wasn't a good friend. I try to be a better friend, in writing. These Ackers: "Once more we need to see what writing is. We need to step away from all the business. We need to step to the personal. . . . We need to remember friends, that we write deeply out of friendship, that we write to our friends. We need to regain some of the energy, as writers and as readers, that people have on the internet when for the first time they email, when they discover that they can write anything, even to a stranger, even the most personal of matters. When they discover that strangers can communicate to each other." (BW 103)

This was before post-capitalism learned to extract its surplus out of our desire for friendship, inflame it into noise and bitterness, and extract even more surplus information out of the rancor. The goal might remain, however: a writing-and-reading between bodies rather than subjects, a selving rather than a (non)communication between selves. Here there's a stability that runs through from that Acker who, as The Black Tarantula, made serial works sent as gifts by mail in the seventies and that other, later Acker experimenting with collaborative writing under assumed names in the internet in the nineties, back when it was still, in several senses, free.

Rather than filling the post-capitalist internet's information-extraction forms with mere content, let's make and unmake form otherwise. "The desire to play, to make literary structures that play into and in unknown or unknowable realms, those of chance and death and the lack of language, is the desire to live in a world that is open and dangerous, that is limitless. To play, then, both in structure and in content, is to desire to live in wonder." (TK 18)

Ackers desire a formally challenging writing, but not one that you need three MFAs to write and two PhDs to read. And so it will draw on the communal stock of everyday forms that give readers pleasure. This Acker: "Good literature was read by an elite diminishing in size and cultural strength. Decided to use or to write both good literature and schlock. To mix them up in terms of content and formally, offending everyone. Writing in which all kinds of writing mingled seemed, not immoral, but amoral, even to the masses." (*DDH*) The Acker-web spans genres as well as genders, refusing to let them have defining properties. The Acker-flow always returns to the senseless, formlessness nothing that destabilizes signifiers, that strips them of sense, of properties. Where: there is no privatized language.

Myth

"Authors make up stories; no one person invents myths." (*BW* 32) The very last of the Ackers were voyaging toward a renewal of myth when cancer sank the lifeboat. There were a lot of Ackers who were fascinated by myth, however. It's a stable obsession. Sometimes they wrote new ones with new selvings, the myth of the sailor by the sailor, and so on. Sometimes, they rewrote the old ones.

A young Acker rewrites Aristophanes's *The Poet and the Women*: "The women (I see the women as a group of roaring dykes: dykes versus drag-queens; what an image of the present!) who are reality want to kill the poet Euripides. Euripides uses a fantasy, gets his father in law in drag which is a totally wonderful fantasy human and wonderfully funny to stop the women from condemning him. He uses fantasy to attack. Then a total drag-dance occurs: the women are fooled by the fantasy, another drag queen comes in and stops the fantasy, and now the father in law's in a mess. So far Aristophanes has played off the fantasy-reality war by showing fantasy as funny but low, the father in law is a lousy woman, and then the father in law's wonderful speech about being a woman! Very tacky, even sleazy, to use current slang. But then: Euripides has to rescue his father in law using high camp, not low camp, grand tragic speeches, all those disguises. . . . This is the other side of drag, homosexuality-fantasy . . . the only place where poetry exists (no wonder Plato loved Aristophanes). Can the poet enchant the women into his world so they will return his father in law. . . . Everything ends with the DANCE: (last speech of the play), this has all been fantasy (that frame) and now go home, may the goddesses the women of fantasy believe our enchantments." (23.18.3)

Myth, where language, gender, desire and the real are all in play. Myth, where, as we shall see, narrative is most plastic. Let's end, or almost end, with a myth that for us Westerners, even those who don't want to be home there, consider a kind of key for any lock.

Oedipus: "I am the biggest shit in the world. I murdered my father and raped and effectively killed my mother. All righteous people should murder me. Someone please touch me. Physically touch this mentally diseased flesh. I'd do anything for a hug. There's no end to, because there's no escape from, my being-pain. . . . Please just love me a little. I'm so lonely, traveling from foreign land to foreign land. I don't know what a family is. All other human beings have families. Since I killed mine off, I don't have a family. . . . Who am I? Therefore: what is there to believe in? How hard it is to live with consciousness. (There must be consciousness.) Please touch me, my leader, just once. Just give me a hug and I'll never ask you again."

Leader: "No. I am not going to touch you. I don't want you. Neither are you allowed to rest in the myth of how disgusting or bad you are, for you know the particulars of why you're disgusting. You know consciousness."

Oedipus: "I'd rather be physically hurt than know consciousness or myself. Myself is total pain." (DQ 147)

Oedipus penetrated his own mother with his dick and his own father with his sword, but all he really wants is to be touched. This Oedipus is a self that is trapped in memory, and as a self that is produced by memory, produced by guilt. Oedipus wants out of this prison house of self-centering language, this language that produces a self in its gender, in its role, in its family romance. This Oedipus wants a love that annihilates subjectivity, that will affirm its own loss, its own pain, even its crimes. To which narrative responds by making him pay.

"Myths make actuality, that's what myths do." (MM 19) But could there be another kind of myth? A kind of myth about gods who are slippery verbs rather than proper nouns? A writing outside of the information-commodity form might take some cues from writing that, while hardly free from domination, was at least made within a different mode of production.

Maybe fiction could look more like the myth than the novel, with its relentless need to enclose the subjectivity of novelist, character, and reader as self-same, consistent, rational yet with emotional sympathies, each in possession of itself and all it can acquire. Maybe a fiction whose subject isn't man, but the Gods: "The Gods are those who infinitely desire to become other people and so, suffer endlessly." (*PE* 67) These gods are not dead, these gods of the formless, lawless, mutating world in which language is just one kind of difference.

Gods and humans and other monsters form a continuum. "What is it to be human? A girl, Leda, fucked a swan, had bestial sex. Subsequently she gave birth to Clytemnestra who murdered her first husband. Afterwards Clytemnestra gave birth to Orestes. Bestiality, husband murder, patricide, incest." (*IM* 77) Hardly a noble world, this world of slave-owners.

Many late Ackers want another kind of myth, a myth after the novel. "You don't quite know what the world is, you're in a strange world. The early Greek stories were all about strange worlds. . . . You're allowed to just move, you're allowed to wander. It's like travelling. I've always envied men this and I can never travel being a woman. I always wanted to be a sailor, that's what I really love." (*HL* 23)

Perhaps there could be a myth of the body as an event in the world. A world which makes differences, chancy, without a fixed point to anchor meaning. With only one horizon, which means nothing at all: death. "Swimming through an ocean is feeling pleasure. If the only event I can know is death, that is dream or myth, dream and myth must be the only knowing I have. What, then, is this ocean?" (*ES* 55) The ocean, perhaps, is possibility, not so much a throw of the dice as the dice perpetually in mid-air, not quite landed, not yet snakes' eyes.

Nature

A very prescient Acker: "If the greenhouse effect increases, won't more people become frightened? Won't they have to effect radical change? It is clear, not only to feminists, that the male commitment to hierarchical power has harmed not only men's relations to women and women's to men, but also the human relation to nature. The world is starting to burn." (MP 12)

The decisions post-capitalism makes could destroy the earth before anyone figures out the mode of revolution specific to it. It has already destroyed the exteriority of a nature that is the ground of romantic yearning. "Since natural is now unnatural and unnatural is natural, those who love can't know. How should I know what to do?" (BW 110) Some Ackers don't want to abandon all of the romantic strategies, however. "Romanticism *is* the world. Why? Because there's got to be something. There has to be something for we who are and know we're homeless." (HL 58)

This Acker: "Either the law of the state is the highest standard for human life and coincides with the divine government of the universe, or else I have to live either in eternal chaos away from human laws or find some certainty outside human law in eternal order of nature, or do both." (23.18) Ackers do all of those things: and, and, and. But the order is just a moment of the chaos.

What is now a post-capitalist rationality is a reason unto death. This is how it thinks: "When the world ends, there'll be no more air. That's why it's important to pollute the air now. Before it's too late." (DQ 81) This rationality seems to be madness. "Why are humans beings still rational, that is, making nuclear bombs polluting inventing DNA etc.? Because they don't see the absolute degradation and poverty around their flesh because if they did, they would be in such horror they would have to throw away their minds and want to become, at any price, only part-humans." (DQ 71) The human too might be a god that is dead.

The last god, the last dead god, might be nature. It's a hard word to do without, as it means so many contradictory things. The nature that is dead might in the first instance be the one that appears as separate to man, a thing apart, that man can penetrate and order and control. A control which, paradoxically, also then considers itself natural. "In this century what we know as 'natural' our conquerors have invented as their identities and use as tools to control us." (LM 326)

This decisive, controlling rationality has its quirks. Man is separate from and in control of nature, but despite being separate from nature his control is natural. Which would make him part of what he controls. Or maybe he only controls, and considers really natural in the sense of penetrable and controllable, a nature that is female. And so on, not unlike a bad myth. A perplexed Acker: "I'm confused. On the one hand, I'm human just like my husband; on the other hand I'm unnatural because I'm female. Females are those beings who only want revenge. My humanity has tempered infinite revenge into caused revenge or ambition. Irrationality, Animalism, and Night: own me. Since I can't know, I don't want clinging to my thoughts fucking up my mind." (LM 326) It which it might make more sense to think: "Nature is female because, as is the case with women, she does not exist." (BW 70)

Nature means contradictory things, which complicates language that tries to separate nature from not-nature. "Does horror come from Nature?" (MM 108) It remains an open question, a hole in thought, even if "our natures are deeply animal." (IM 38) And: "There's no way out of nature." (LM 328) And: "If you wish to strive for peace of mind and pleasure, believe. If you wish to find out the truth, inquire. The truth of human nature, or partial truths, could be abhorrent and ugly." (IM 49)

Nature is not one thing, a thing apart, to be contemplated by an owner. "I understand that 'naturalness' depends on my perception or on who I am." (LM 227) Nature plays in an ambivalent way with gender. If there's to be nature and not-nature, it is only a matter of time before the genders align one way or the other with that other binary. "All that's so-called 'natural' is neurotic. I'll tell you what's really natural: sex . . . (He doesn't fuck any more cause he has so many political responsibilities.) . . . holocausts, murders, any extraordinary events, peoples'-fingers-getting-cut-off, sexualities that make people crazy always: these're natural." (LM 334) The natural is rejected or ejected from orderly concepts, even concepts of nature.

"What is this thing: human? What is the measure of human?" (LM 303) The natural and the human are contradictory, temporary, inconsistent things. Power considers itself reasonable and its reasons natural. Yet what power controls is an inert nature without reason. An unnatural nature controls a natural not-nature. And yet these might still be things with which to form tactics. "But: we're still human. Human because we keep battling against all these horrors, the horrors caused and not caused by us." (ES 69)

Rather than being the anchor of meaning, maybe nature is that which always confuses it. Language itself might be in nature, but any use of language about nature remains outside of it. "The girl is thinking that most people are saying the human world is ending. . . . This landscape without any given meaning is as present as any statement such as the world is about to end." (*LM* 199)

The problem is not one of misreading nature, but of thinking that a reading discloses meaning at all. Reading as interpreting is a claim to mastery. Perhaps it is rather that: "We are the failures on, not the governors of, this earth." (*HL* 55) A failure, also, to be human. A failure that is maybe inevitable or maybe just one that reflects on who got to attempt it: "She never wanted to be a master." (*PK* 39) But she doesn't claim possession of some alternative knowledge of nature, either.

Perhaps there could be a nature not of the dominators but of the masochists: "He showed me how to insert a razor blade into my wrists just for fun. Not for any other reason. Thus, I learned how to approach and understand nature, how to make gargantuan red flowers, like roses blooming, drops of blood, so full and dripping the earth under them, my body, shook for hours afterwards. During those afterhours, I fantasized my blood pouring outwards. This was relief that there were no decisions left." (*ES* 9–10) Perhaps the human is that inconstant thing, one part of which decided to dominate nature, and ended up producing the greenhouse effect, climate change, so that it would in the end have few or no decisions left to it at all.

Afterword
Dysphoric

Kathy occasioned two panic attacks. One was in Karlsruhe, Germany. Matias Viegener, her executor, had invited me to a symposium on Acker's work.[1] He gave me plenty of lead time, so I could think about what I would say. I thought I should read all of her books. I was on leave at the time, so this was possible. As it happened, it was the year I finally came out as trans and went on hormones. A messy year. Held together in part by becoming entangled in the Acker-web, or maybe becoming its kleptoparasite.

By the time the symposium came around, I had a draft of this whole book. And yet in Karlsruhe, anxiety got to me. There were people there who had known Kathy much better, as well as real scholars of Acker's work. Due to some unforeseen events, I ended up being bumped into the concluding slot of the day. I could barely breathe.

I thought about going back to my hotel room for a break, but it was too far. There were low, flat, padded ottomans up the back of the venue, like upholstered lily pads. Everyone was at the bar or outside smoking, so it was quiet back there. I took my coat and curled up in a ball under it on one of the lily pads, trying to be invisible. Trying to breathe.

It went fine in the end, I guess.

The second panic attack was at the Trans | Acker symposium at The New School. In a manic moment I committed myself to organizing this, raised the money for it, invited the speakers, and then on the eve felt completely overwhelmed. Two of the invited guests—Juliana Huxtable and Grace Lavery—couldn't make it, and that added to the swell of panic. Good thing I had the very capable Kato Trieu working with me. Right before the event, I left Kato to do the last bits of preparation, fled to the all-gender toilet, locked myself in a stall, just trying to breathe.

It all worked out just fine.

I want to conclude this book by working through what I gleaned from some of the other Trans | Acker presenters, including what I imagine the two who could not come might have said.[2] In a moment when Acker is becoming a sort-of canonical American writer, I want to push her back in the direction of, in every sense, a minor literature—*trans lit*: the writing of and by and for trans people.[3] Or rather: writing among those for whom being cis gendered is not their state, their homeland, their family, their fantasy.

One of the things that caught my attention while writing this book was the range of anthologies in which Acker has appeared.[4] She has been grouped with selections of writers and writing that are downtown, transgressive, postmodern, cyberpunk, feminist, conceptual, revolutionary, new narrative, queer, sexworkers, and so on. I think this plurality of contexts is a tribute to the quality of the work. So I want to end by suggesting a beginning: of including Acker within the space of trans writing. Not to trap her there, but rather as an instance of how the Acker-web might connect to others consigned to being minor and marginal.

Although my own memories of Kathy hint at a relation to gender that in the broader sense seems to me trans, my memory, as we have seen, is unreliable. As I remember it: Kathy told me about seeing a doctor about having a mastectomy because of not wanting to have breasts any more. The doctor refused to consider it as there was nothing—at the time—medically wrong them. The breast cancer, at the time, undetected. Did Kathy really tell me this? And if so, why?

Acker wouldn't be the first American author, in or near the modernist canon, who one could imagine as closet trans. The most surprising example is surely Ernest Hemingway. Valerie Rohy points out the curious instances in his biography and his texts.[5] But in the end it's much less interesting to project trans-ness onto the writer than to ask, with Rohy, what a *transgender reading* might be, independent of such claims.

Rohy's trans reading does not try to diagnose the writer. Trans people have enough problems with experts trying to categorize us. Rather, Rohy is attentive to how gender norms structure both writing and reading, in a way that may be not unlike the way that gender norms structure heterosexuality. It's more interesting to treat the text as negotiating the structure of gender than to try to out the author as either cis or trans. I won't insist that Acker was trans, but I do want to ask why she is *assumed* to be cis, and how that presumption shapes her reception.

From a trans reading, the Acker-text does have moments in which trans-femme characters break with what Emma Heaney sees as the trans-femme's chronic position in modernist literature.[6] The trans-femme character is an artifact of psychiatry, psychoanalysis, and sexology, all determining, through clinical means of dubious reliability, that she is a *type*. That type then appears in the modernist novel as an avatar of the pleasures and dangers of the *new woman* who emerges out of changes in the social and political structures of gender in modernity itself. In modernist literature, and after it in queer theory, the trans-feminine is not someone in particular; she is an avatar of somebody's theory about cis people's fascinations and horrors about gender and sexuality.[7]

The trans character in modern Western literature, trans-femme or more occasionally trans-masc, usually appears somewhere in a grid of cis attention, within a *cis gaze*, if you will.[8] I think of this as a matrix governed by two axes. One is a continuum from envy to pity; the other, from lust to disgust. The cis-lit that offers locations outside that matrix of attention within which to read trans-ness are few. Acker is one of them. She makes room for us—several rooms, as we'll see. A whole imaginary hotel's worth of room. My intuition, both in writing *Philosophy for Spiders* and in convening the Trans | Acker symposium, was that it was worth checking in and checking out these possibilities.

The New School event went off swimmingly, thanks to dear Kato, while I managed to keep it together as hostess from opening remarks to the after-conference dinner at the hotel where we'd stashed the out-of-town guests. Over the starters, I could see out of the corner of my eye a trans woman who had tagged along from the symposium and joined us for dinner flirting with Kato, while another who had also tagged along flirted with me.

All in all it went even better than planned. I went home, alone, exhausted, with that girl's number, and slept for fourteen hours.

Kathy appeared again in a dream that night or that morning. Or so I imagine. I wrote it down, but I can't read my writing. She became illegible. Maybe she just came to say goodbye. Maybe—what I hope—is that she is taking an interest now in the trans literary futures that are some of the possibilities engendered by her own work.[9] That we might have her absence to guide us.

Roz Kaveney: "Six months later, I dreamed I was at a party and Kathy was there and we talked—she was wearing a brown leopard-skin print sleeveless shirt I knew quite well and a violently yellow pair of plush velvet leopard-skin print trousers that I had never seen before. After a bit, I thought of something. 'Kathy, you're dead,' I said. 'Sure,' she said, ' but you didn't think that was going to stop me, did you?'"[10]

To wrap things up, I want to put *Philosophy for Spiders* in the context of the web of other trans readers and writers that I was trying to weave for Acker, and for myself, at Trans | Acker. This is what I gleaned from that event that speaks to this book, although sometimes aslant to it.

Kato Trieu reads the pirate body within the Acker-text as the *dysphoric body*.[11] This body might not know what it is, only that it isn't in the gendered category imposed upon it and demanded of it. The dysphoric body is a hard one to know. It feels unreasonable, unknowable, unseen. What it wants to be is absent. It doesn't make sense in reference to the self-evident codes of cis-gender difference. It wants to come into being through its own self-related differences. At best, it can come to be through wonder.

The dysphoric pirate body calls for a language that is something other than mimetic. Language has to describe a body that is not. This Acker finds this body through experiments and observations on its self-related differences, by forgetting what in her head is what language says it ought to and must be. This Acker finds another language, a mythic language of the body, of its metamorphosis.

What might be done with the dysphoric body is to be found through certain practices. The practice of masturbation. Or the practice of masochism, not as theater but as a phenomenology of what lies on the other side of what a body can bear.[12] Or (for the trans-masc-inclined body) the practice of being the one who is fucked—but where that one is a boy, not a girl or woman. Or (again maybe a trans-masc thing) the practice of bodybuilding, which articulates the body not in relation to those standard tropes of gender in the novel, or in cis life—of birth and reproduction—but in relation to death.

Here lies a body which, out of practices in and on its various aspects, might locate itself outside of cis-gender. It's not the cis or trans body as something that is given, or even as something achieved. It's the dysphoric body, felt as what it does, as a body which, whether it transitions between normative genders or not, transitions outside of the institutional order of gender and its reasons. The Acker-web's pirate bodies are those of a free yet malleable gender itself.

Kay Gabriel talked about the *plasticity* of Acker's sentences, how they enable a plasticity of narrative.[13] They circle so often around childhood and adolescence. Acker characters refuse to grow up. There's no passage from possibility to decision to maturity. Things go sideways rather than rise or fall. Acker childhoods are do-overs, variations on it, over and over. Not unlike those of trans people. The I that greets us from the text has no commitment to consistency or subjective coherence. For trans writers, that could be an I that frees us from the consistent scripts of the self we prepare to get doctors to recognize us in their categories.

The Acker-text offers two other resources for trans writing. One is its interest in the body at work in and against the commodity form. The other is that bodies and commodities are nearly always in an urban setting. Any trans literature to come has to deal centrally with the necessity of sex-work for many trans people, particularly trans women.[14] And that trans lives in the city are fraught ones, at some remove from the myth of the city as harboring bohemian frolics.[15] The plastic sentence, wandering narrative, nonsubjective I, all playing in and against the commodification of the body, in the post-bohemian city, might all be elements of a trans lit to come.[16]

Marquis Bey spoke of Acker's trans *locutions*, her nonnormative ways of writing, as a trans relation to language.[17] Something that recurs across the Acker-web are various hatreds of gender, experienced and understood as a regime to coerce bodies into identities with, among other things, consistent narratives.

Acker *bodies* language, says Bey, using the poetics of Black English to deploy a polyvalent term, meaning both to give language to the body but also to take it down, to kill it. Acker writes from edges where language and body meet, or don't. She makes language for neither normativity nor its counteridentities. This is not writing that's all that helpful for trans identity. But it might be for a trans-ness that would rather be somewhere else than where cis normativity locates us as its other, to be looked upon with lust/disgust and/or pity/envy.

Torrey Peters spoke of the cult of the *sad literary trans woman*.[18] Starting with Imogen Binnie's 2013 novel *Nevada*—which name-checks Acker—there's been a distinctive, mostly North American trans writing that eschews the narrative arc of upward and onward that is characteristic of trans autobiographies written for cis people.[19] This iteration of a trans counterliterature was an important achievement, but might have its own traps.[20]

Sad literary trans girl novels fit the tradition of the novel as a cultural form meant to cultivate a kind of subjectivity. It's a form that is focused on domestic matters and observes details of behavior as clues to character. Moral values attach to qualities of mind. Authority rests on both the intensity and the self-awareness of feeling—particularly that of women.[21]

In its modern form, this kind of novel sometimes treats ugly feelings as particularly authoritative, even if they do not speak well of a character's destiny and reveal nothing so much as her lack of agency.[22] The sad literary cis woman—most often young, white, attractive—is destroyed by her own suffering. Sadness becomes a mark of powerlessness but also of refinement. Peters picks up on a further turn in this tradition, in contemporary novels where cis women characters still hurt, but shift away from wounded affect.[23] These characters are numb, clever, jaded, or sarcastic, and steer clear of self-pity.

In trans girl lit, this later turn has not quite happened. The girls are still sad. Why? For the outmoded femme glamour of it. Or because we are still denied access to so much of womanhood. Or because trans girls, once you've known a few, often do live lives that are fucking sad. In more literary terms, mainly because the intensity of such an affect conveys femme authority, which is the key to this novelistic tradition as a cultural institution.

Some Ackers are that sad literary woman, trading on her feminine authority or, in a more French-femme theory mode, on *abjection*.[24] But many Ackers are ironic, playful, or detached about it. She can be read in a trans key in her flitting between these possibilities. The Acker-text is available to trans reading in the sense of trans as fluid, hybrid, labile—that sense of trans-ness close to queerness.[25]

I wonder how useful that version of Acker, or of trans-ness, is for trans lit, given that for many of us the intractability of our desire to be the gender we need is not something fluid at all. Nor are our bodies as plastic as we would like. Changing them is difficult and the process quite boring. Shoving a needle in your ass every week quickly becomes routine.

Nor is everyday language particular malleable, as I reflect when correcting the receptionist at my trans health clinic who has called me sir for the third time. Reading the Acker-text as invoking the dysphoric body seems promising, however, as a writing of that from which many (although not all) kinds of trans-ness might arise, and which subtends any of the linguistic or corporeal strategies for working it.

There might be other ways that the Acker-text might open the door to other textual spaces, beyond both the conventional upward-curving narrative of the conventional trans memoir and the desultory drift of the sad literary trans woman. In Peters's own case, I take her ambition to be to install trans themes, trans characters, fully and self-consciously into the bourgeois novel.[26] So that there could be novels in which trans characters get to do at least some of the things cis characters do, and have their own feelings about it. Acker then offers a key to open rooms in trans lit beyond the sad literary trans girl, without returning her to the conventions of the trans memoir.

Grace Lavery wants to free a certain kind of realist fiction from the claim that it is bourgeois.[27] She is interested in realism not as mimesis but as a practice of self-care. Realist fiction models a reflection on feelings about one's actions that can cut away beautiful and damaging fantasies and reconcile the reader to a deeper sense of well-being, of growing in and despite an ugly world. Although, to me, this realism's happy ending, where the possible is the desirable, could be nothing but bourgeois.

And yet as Peters points out, post-*Nevada* trans lit doesn't offer a whole lot by way of templates for self-care beyond the bare minimum of survival. They are about poverty, trauma, addiction, the loss of loved ones. Their more jolly moods are loneliness, anxiety, and panic. In that sense, bourgeois realism remains aspirational. Perhaps we have a right to attain it before we can join the critique of it.

Lavery draws on Janet Mock's *Redefining Realness*.[28] Rather than realness as the fantasy of passing as cis, this realness is coming to terms with the dysphoric body as it is. The dysphoric body is not the queer body, whose transgressions of gender norms can be enacted in utopian movements of drag, parody, or provocation.[29] The dysphoric body painfully wrought into some livable shape has to pass through the streets and inhabit the mundane moments of everyday life. The language of this piratical body remains inscrutable, even to itself, other than through the groping articulations of its own differences.

What would make for a wonderful trans literature would be for it to explore all of the formal devices, generic conventions, devil's bargains with the culture industry, and kinds of readership-formation that are open to it. Here I think Acker is useful again, even in relation to realist fiction. As Gabriel says, the Acker-text is studded with refusals to grow up. And, one might add, replete with fantasies, and not just of surmounting the dysphoric body.

The fantastic and the ordinary are both equally real in the Acker-text. There's ugly feelings about the ugly world, but never a reconciliation to it. A trans reading of the Acker-text can find the dysphoric, pirate body, but it isn't necessarily a queer one. Its hatred of gender is a permanent condition. The Acker-text can be romantic, antirealist, but it points to other possibilities besides those played out in this same skein by queer theory.[30]

Juliana Huxtable writes, sometimes in prose which, as with the Acker-text, breathes with the techniques of poetry. I'd like to offer her the same courtesy I offered to Acker in not reducing her to her sources, although the benefit of highlighting which of Acker's gifts she accepts is to see then also, by contrast, what Huxtable adds.

In her book *Mucus in My Pineal Gland*, Huxtable writes from within the city where bohemia went extinct.[31] The Huxtable-text is fully from within the mesh of its post-capitalist accumulation strategies, where art-work, fame-work, and sex-work are sources of affect, image, and gesture to be turned into intellectual property. She, too, is a New Yorker of her time.

Her texts extrude out of a digital dream space in which desire no longer negates the object it lacks.[32] Want gorges on the images that flood it. And yet the collapse of desire and lack into want and excess doesn't succeed in eroding the old class, race, or gender codes, just in making them presets. The transubstantiation of the commodity form from the ownership of things to the ownership of information seems still to have plenty of ways of classifying and enslaving bodies, and much the same bodies.

Huxtable goes where Acker could not: into the spiraling out of race and gender braided together, out of the same history.[33] Like Acker, one of her sources for détournement is porn, but where Acker hesitates, and as a white girl rightly so, Huxtable plunges in to the genre of race-play, where top and bottom, male and female, domme and sub interact also with that other differentiating code of American desire: white and Black. The technics of internet porn chops and screws the nightmare codes of American power into the memes that spooge over the limit of attention, a surface without gap or lack made entirely of what had formerly been America's *latent destiny*.

The discovery of a sexuality is always mediated. Maybe the discovery of one's sex is too.[34] Maybe even the apparent self-relation of the dysphoric body requires an outside that is not a human gender. Maybe technics is a third gender that distributes bodies into the other two (or not). The dysphoric body isn't unique in relation to the third gender of technics, but it highlights the role of that technics for all bodies, of any sex or gender.[35]

The Acker-text already understands the uses of porn technics for the dysphoric body. The transsexual body is nowhere more legible than in porn, where at least our bodies exist, are wanted, fuckable, even have agency. Porn is the genre where the cis gaze hovers over lust more than disgust and envy more than pity. Huxtable mines that quadrant of the cis gaze for material in a way that's sometimes absent in most other strands of trans lit.[36]

As we check out of the dream hotel to which Acker led us, checking the drawers to make sure we don't leave anything we want to remember behind, I'm clutching these notes for a trans reading and writing after Acker. A low theory after Acker seems to me particularly well adapted to the needs and desires of the dysphoric body, a category that maybe overlaps a lot with the trans body but is not ever identical to it.[37]

The Acker-text has been a lot of things. Looking back over the forty years'–worth of anthologies in which her work has appeared, it has offered gifts to many vital cultural moments. Her first philosophy of the body brackets off received ideas about it to the extent that such a thing is possible and produces a sensory record of it that assumes as little as possible, particularly about gender. Her second philosophy of relation, otherness, and desire brings no baggage from the first about the essential body and yet is fiercely attached to the body's materiality. This then broadens out into a third philosophy of all that which triangulates a body's relation to an-other, from the body's commodification of itself as fame, art, sex, to the transformations of the city that morphs, not so much into the social factory as into the social studio for extracting sense from bodies.

There's enough in the Acker-web, among other things, to dispense with the practice of taking trans-ness as an anomaly that explains cis lives. The Acker-text undoes the default understanding of the body as always already gendered. It's not the only place that happens, but it might be the one that expands that intuition the furthest. Into a philosophy for spiders, where the spiders are us. After my stay at the Acker-hotel, I've not had any more panic attacks. I'm breathing steady. I'm out, weaving with words. Here at the end of the world. There's Janeys everywhere. Some of us trans.

Acknowledgments

I'm especially grateful to Matias Viegener, executor of the Kathy Acker estate. We met when he asked my permission to publish my email correspondence with Kathy. I was reluctant at first, but, instinctually and immediately, I trusted Matias's judgment. All these years later those emails can still cause me a very particular kind of pain. I'm glad they are out in the world. Not least because their existence led to invitations to talk about Kathy's work, which made me study it deeply and properly.

Thanks to everyone at the Badischer Kunstverein for inviting me to the symposium Kathy Acker: Get Rid of Meaning. Thanks to *The Brooklyn Rail* for giving me space to write about the exhibition that went with that symposium. Thanks to everyone at e-flux for inviting me to contribute to the feminisms issue of *e-flux journal*. A piece of the first part of this book appeared in *Cordite Review* as "Kathy Acker and the Viewing Room," and so my thanks to the editors there as well.

I wrote this book while on sabbatical from The New School in 2018, and I am grateful to that institution for that time. I taught Kathy Acker to my undergraduate students in the Eugene Lang College division of The New School, and I hope Kathy and I did not terrify them too much. I'm always thankful that I have such wonderful Lang students in my life. Thanks to Macushla Robinson for research assistance.

Thanks to the keepers of the Kathy Acker papers at the David M. Rubenstein Rare Book & Manuscript Library at Duke University; to Daniel Schulz, who catalogued Kathy's personal library at the University of Cologne; and to Hanjo Berressem for allowing me to spend some alone time with her books.

Thanks to everyone at Duke University Press: to Ken Wissoker for whisking this book off to external readers, who gave encouraging and thoughtful reports. To Joshua Tranen and Jessica Ryan and everyone else involved in the making of the book.

There is a lot of fine scholarship on Kathy already. The book that spoke to me personally as well as professionally is the one by Douglas A. Martin. I met Douglas in the summer of 2018 over dinner in upstate New York, basically to ask his blessing to write this book. I am so thankful that he so generously gave it.

In 2019 I organized a symposium called Trans | Acker where I invited some of my favorite transgender writers to discuss her work. My thanks to the brothers, sisters, and others who came and shared their trans Acker readings with me, including Torrey Peters, Marquis Bey, Megan Milks, Kay Gabriel, Jackie Ess, Eli Erlich, and especially to the late Kato Trieu, who ran the event.

I miss Kato so much. Learned so much from him. As one does with one's students when study is real and vital and necessary to living our lives at all. This book would be nothing without the study we did on Acker together. The three of us: Kathy, Kato and me, put up against the wall by gender. This book laid to rest what Kathy's death meant to me but is now only the beginning of what Kato's death means to me. Your pain is over, fearless man.

Notes

Part I. The City of Memory

1. Martine Sciolino, "Confessions of a Kleptoparasite," *Review of Contemporary Fiction* 9, no. 3 (1989): 63.

2. On interpretation, see Alexander Galloway's contribution to *Excommunication* (Chicago: University of Chicago Press, 2013).

3. Patrick Greaney, "Insinuation: Détournement as Gendered Repetition," *South Atlantic Quarterly* 110 (1) (2011): 75–88, 84.

4. Tom McCarthy, "Kathy Acker's Infidel Heteroglossia," in *Typewriters, Bombs, Jellyfish: Essays* (New York: New York Review Books, 2017), 257.

5. The three books I found most useful: Georgina Colby, *Kathy Acker: Writing the Impossible* (Edinburgh: Edinburgh University Press, 2016); Chris Kraus, *After Kathy Acker* (Los Angeles: Semiotext(e), 2015); Douglas A. Martin, *Acker* (New York: Nightboat, 2017).

6. Vanessa Place, "Afterword," in *I'll Drown My Book: Conceptual Writing by Women*, ed. Caroline Bergvall et al. (Los Angeles: Les Figues Press, 2012), 445.

7. Ashley Crawford and Ray Edgar, eds., *Transit Lounge* (Melbourne: Craftsman's House, 1998).

8. Noel King, "Kathy Acker on the Loose," *Meanjin* 55, no. 2 (1996): 338.

9. Justine Ettler, *The River Ophelia* (Sydney: Picador Australia, 1995). The copy Justine gave Kathy is in Kathy's library in Cologne.

10. Dodie Bellamy, "Digging through Kathy Acker's Stuff," in *When the Sick Rule the World* (Los Angeles: Semiotext(e), 2015), 127.

11. Amy Scholder, "Editor's Note," in *Essential Acker*, ed. Amy Scholder and Dennis Cooper (New York: Grove Press, 2002), xiii.

12. Danielle Talbot, "Blood, Grunge and Literature," *The Age*, August 4, 1995.

13. Eileen Myles, *Inferno: A Poet's Novel* (New York: O/R Books, 2010), 156.

14. Pam Brown, "1995," in *Home by Dark* (Bristol: Shearsman Books, 2013), 34.

15. She told me she was a little afraid of Linda Dement, although they were collaborating at the time of Acker's death. See George Alexander, "Linda Dement's Eurydice," *Art Monthly*, April 2002.

16. Andrew Kohut et al., *Americans Going Online* (Washington, DC: Pew Research Center, 1995).

17. Matthew Kirschenbaum, *Track Changes: A Literary History of Word Processing* (Cambridge, MA: Harvard University Press, 2016).

18. Fred Turner, *From Counterculture to Cyberculture* (Chicago: University of Chicago Press, 2008); Julian Dibbell, *My Tiny Life: Crime and Passion in a Virtual World* (New York: Holt, 1999).

19. Rosie Cross, "Acker Online," in *Transit Lounge*, ed. Ashley Crawford and Ray Edgar (Melbourne: Craftsman's House, 1998), 51.

20. Kathy Acker and McKenzie Wark, *I'm Very into You: Correspondence 1995–1996* (Los Angeles: Semiotext(e), 2015).

21. David Velasco, "Natural's Not in It," review of *I'm Very into You: Correspondence 1995–1996* by Kathy Acker and McKenzie Wark, *Bookforum* 24, no. 4 (December 2017).

22. Lynne Tillman, "Selective Memory," *Review of Contemporary Fiction* 9, no. 3 (Fall 1989): 68.

23. Joseph Needham, *Science and Civilization in China, Vol. 2.* (Cambridge: Cambridge University Press, 1969), 189.

24. Amy Wendling, *Karl Marx on Technology and Alienation* (London: Palgrave Macmillan, 2011), 166–67.

25. Avital Ronell, "Kathy Goes to Hell," in *Lust for Life: On the Writings of Kathy Acker*, ed. Amy Scholder, Carla Harryman, and Avital Ronell (New York: Verso, 2006), 20.

26. Matias Viegener, *The Assassination of Kathy Acker*, Guillotine Series no. 13 (New York: Guillotine Series, 2018), 32–33.

27. Sianne Ngai, *Our Aesthetic Categories: Zany, Cute, Interesting* (Cambridge, MA: Harvard University Press, 2015).

28. Gary Indiana, *Rent Boy* (New York: High Risk Books, 1994), 91. The Sandy character is clearly a portrait of Kathy. See (*IV* 39).

29. Jonathan Kemp, "Kathy Acker's Houseboy," *Minor Literature[s]*, April 2019.

30. Bellamy, "Digging," 131.

31. Jacques Derrida, *Dissemination* (Chicago: University of Chicago Press, 1983).

32. McKenzie Wark, "The Virtual Sensoria," presented at ISEA95: Sixth International Symposium on Electronic Art, September 17–24, 1995, Montreal, Quebec.

33. Kraus, *After Kathy Acker*, 34.

34. GE 68, LM 256, EU 179.

35. Peter Wollen and Mel Freilicher both give Sutton Place as Acker's home address in their memorial pieces. Wollen places it on the Upper West Side, which connects Kathy to the psychogeography of the city in a different and interesting way.

36. Sarah Schulman, "Realizing They're Gone," in *Gentrification of the Mind* (Berkeley: University of California Press, 2011), 75.

37. Mel Freilicher, "One or Two Things That I Know About Kathy Acker," in *The Encyclopedia of Rebels* (San Diego, CA: City Works Press, 2013), 97.

38. Guy Hocquenghem, *The Screwball Asses* (Los Angeles: Semiotext(e), 2010), 11, 15. Kathy's library contained another of his books, *Love in Relief* (New York: Seahorse Press, 1986).

39. Kate Zambreno, "New York City, Summer 2013," *Icon*, ed. Amy Scholder (New York: Feminist Press at CUNY, 2014), 232.

40. Acker and Wark, *I'm Very into You*, 115. The détourned text is from Italo Calvino, "Cities and Signs 2," in *Invisible Cities* (San Diego, CA: Harcourt Brace, 1974), 19.

41. Charles Shaar Murray, "Kathy Acker Remembered," *Tha Kulcha*, accessed July 30, 2020, http://charlesshaarmurray.com/journalism/tha-kulcha/kathy-acker-remembered/.

42. Neil Bartlett and Robin Whitmore, *The Seven Sacraments of Nicholas Poussin* (London: Artangel, 1998), 43.

43. Leslie Dick, "Seventeen Paragraphs on Kathy Acker," in Scholder, Harryman, and Ronell, *Lust for Life*, 112.

44. Umberto Eco, *The Name of the Rose* (San Diego, CA: Harcourt Brace, 1983). The edition Kathy had in her library.

45. Julian Brimmers, "Kathy Acker's Library," *Paris Review* 225 (Summer 2018).

46. Steven Shaviro, "Kathy Acker," in *Doom Patrols* (New York: Serpent's Tail, 1997), 83–84.

47. Linda Stupart, *Virus* (London: Arcadia Missa, 2016): 110.

Part II. Chapter 3. Third Philosophy

1. Since the source for this détournement is obscure and touches on my own previous research, I'll give it: Gianfranco Sanguinetti, *On Terrorism and the State* (London: B. M. Chronos, 1982), 57. Sanguinetti was the last member of the Situationist International.

2. See for example, Ayi Kwei Armah, *Why Are We So Blest?* (London: Heinemann, 1972); Cybrian Ekwensi, *Beautiful Feathers* (London: Heinemann, 1971); Yambo Ouologuem, *Bound to Violence* (London: Heinemann, 1971). The latter, interestingly, like Acker practiced détournement and was caught up in a scandal for plagiarizing a bit of Graham Greene. He explains his methods in Christopher Wise, ed., *A Yambo Ouologuem Reader: The Duty of Violence, a Black Ghostwriter's Letter to France, and the Thousand and One Bibles of Sex* (Trenton, NJ: Africa World Press, 2008). About fifteen of the volumes of the Heinemann African Library series can still be found in the Kathy Acker library in Cologne.

Afterword

1. For an account of that event, co-curated by Anja Casser and Matias Viegener, see McKenzie Wark, "Kathy Acker: Get Rid of Meaning," *Brooklyn Rail*, February 2019, brooklynrail.org/2019/02/artseen/Kathy-Acker-Get-Rid -of-Meaning.

2. I've left out Megan Milks, who contributed a reading, part of a work in progress that will end up in her forthcoming novel, so I'll let you go and find that for yourself in her preferred version. But see also Megan Milks, "Janey and Genet in Tangier," in *Kathy Acker and Transnationalism*, ed. P. Mackay and K. Nichol (Newcastle, UK: Cambridge Scholars Publishing, 2009), 91–114.

3. On trans lit in prose, see McKenzie Wark, "Girls Like Us," *The White Review*, December 2020. Accessed January 14, 2021. https://www.thewhitereview .org/feature/girls-like-us/.

4. See the list I've included in the reference section that follows.

5. Valerie Rohy, "Hemingway, Literalism and Transgender Reading," *Twentieth Century Literature* 57, no. 2 (Summer 2011): 148–179.

6. Emma Heaney, *The New Woman: Literary Modernism, Queer Theory, and the Trans Feminine Allegory* (Evanston, IL: Northwestern University Press, 2017).

7. See also Jay Prosser, *Second Skins* (New York: Columbia University Press, 1998).

8. Em McAvan, "Rhetorics of Disgust and Indeterminacy in Transphobic Acts of Violence," in *Homofiles: Theory, Sexuality and Graduate Study*, ed. Jes Battis (Lanham, MD: Lexington Books, 2011).

9. When she was alive, Acker had encouraged trans writer Roz Kavaney, whose novel about trans sex workers in Chicago she read in manuscript. It was published as *Tiny Pieces of Skull* (London: Team Angelica Publishing, 2015).

10. Roz Kaveney, "Just Because Cathexys Showed an Interest." Roz Kaveney's LiveJournal, June 23, 2007. Accessed July 30, 2020. https://rozk.livejournal.com /158882.html.

11. K. K. Trieu, "Building the Pirate Body," *Transgender Studies Quarterly* 7, no. 3 (August 2020): 499–507.

12. See also Kevin Floyd, "Deconstructing Masochism in Kathy Acker's *Blood and Guts in High School*," in *Critical Studies on the Feminist Subject*, ed. Gionana Covi (Trento, Italy: Dipartimento di scienze filologiche e storiche, 1997); and Arthur F. Redding, "Bruises, Roses: Masochism and the Writing of Kathy Acker," *Contemporary Literature* 35, no. 2 (1994): 281–304.

13. Kay Gabriel, "Nothing Until It Is Made Actual, or Acker versus Growing Up," *Transgender Studies Quarterly* 7, no. 3 (August 2020): 489–498.

14. See Red Jordan Arobateau, *The Big Change* (Oakland, CA: Red Jordan Press, 1976); Toni Newman, *I Rise: The Transformation of Toni Newman* (Middletown, DE: SPI Productions, 2020).

15. See for example, Iván Monalisa Ojeda, *Never, Ever Ever, Coming Down* (Brooklyn, NY: Sangría Publishers, 2016).

16. Or in some ways is already here. See T. Fleischmann, *Time Is the Thing a Body Moves Through* (Minneapolis, MN: Coffeehouse Press, 2019); Porpentine Heartscape, *Psycho Nymph Exile* (London: Arcadia Missa, 2017); and Kay Gabriel's own *A Queen in Bucks County* (New York: Nightboat, 2022). My own autofiction book *Reverse Cowgirl* (Los Angeles: Semiotext(e), 2020) aspired to be read in this company.

17. Marquis Bey, "Cutting Up Words: Kathy Acker's Trans Locutions," *Transgender Studies Quarterly* 7, no. 3 (August 2020): 479–488.

18. Drawing on Leslie Jamison, "The Cult of the Literary Sad Woman," *New York Times*, November 7, 2019.

19. Imogen Binnie, *Nevada* (New York: Topside Press, 2013). Other examples could include: Sybil Lamb, *I've Got a Time Bomb* (New York: Topside Press, 2015); Casey Plett, *A Safe Girl To Love* (New York: Topside Press, 2014); Casey Plett, *Little Fish* (Vancouver, BC: Arsenal Pulp Press, 2015); Kai Cheng Thom, *Fierce Femmes and Notorious Liars* (Montreal: Metonymy Press, 2016); Jia Qing Wilson-Yang, *Small Beauty* (Montreal: Metonymy Press, 2018); Hazel Jane Plante, *Little Blue Encyclopedia (for Vivian)* (Montreal: Metonymy Press, 2019); Hannah Baer, *Trans Girl Suicide Museum* (Los Angeles: Hesse Press, 2019); as well as the early self-published novellas of Torrey Peters.

20. On the need for a trans counterliterature, see the classic statement by Sandy Stone, "The Empire Strikes Back: A Posttranssexual Manifesto," in *The Transgender Studies Reader*, ed. Susan Stryker and Stephen Whittle (New York: Routledge, 2006), 221–236.

21. Here Peters is drawing on Nancy Armstrong, *Desire and Domestic Fiction: A Political History of the Novel* (New York: Oxford University Press, 1990).

22. Sianne Ngai, *Ugly Feelings* (Cambridge, MA: Harvard University Press, 2007).

23. Here Peters follows Leslie Jamison, "Grand Unified Theory of Female Pain," *Virginia Quarterly Review* 90, no. 2 (Spring 2014).

24. Hanjo Berressem, "Body-Wound-Writing," *American Studies* 43, no. 3 (January 1999): 393–441.

25. See, for example, Jack Halberstam, *In a Queer Time and Place: Transgender Bodies, Subcultural Lives* (New York: NYU Press, 2005).

26. An ambition achieved: see Torrey Peters, *Detransition, Baby: A Novel* (New York: One World, 2021).

27. Grace Lavery, "Trans Realism," *Critical Inquiry* 46 (Summer 2020): 719–444.

28. Janet Mock, *Redefining Realness* (New York: Simon and Schuster, 2014).

29. José Esteban Muñoz, *Cruising Utopia* (New York: NYU Press, 2009). I'm thinking in particular of the fine chapter on Kevin Aviance.

30. On moving beyond the Acker of queer theory, see Claire Finch, "Kathy Acker's Dildos: Literary Prosthetics and Textual Unmaking," *Gender Forum* 74 (2019): 55–80.

31. Juliana Huxtable, *Mucus in My Pineal Gland* (New York: Capricious, 2017).

32. See Jodi Dean on the decline in symbolic efficiency: Jodi Dean, *Blog Theory: Feedback and Capture in the Circuits of Drive* (Cambridge, UK: Polity Press, 2010).

33. C. Riley Snorton, *Black on Both Sides: A Racial History of Trans Identity* (Minneapolis: University of Minnesota Press, 2017).

34. See Paul B. Preciado, *Testo Junkie* (New York: Feminist Press at CUNY, 2013)—another text which, incidentally, name-checks Acker.

35. Paul B. Preciado, *Testo Junkie* (New York: Femminist Press at CUNY, 2013).

36. Although see Andrea Long Chu, *Females* (New York: Verso Books, 2019) and Torrey Peters's self-published novellas *The Masker* and *Glamour Boutique* for other strategies for using trans porn in trans writing.

37. The trans body need not be dysphoric; the dysphoric body need not be trans. As I was finishing page proofs for this book, I read this: "To this day, I am not really sure what she saw in me, or why she valued my friendship. But I think her liking for me might have something to do with . . . what could be called (in contemporary terms) my mild gender dysphoria: my failure to adequately perform straight masculinity, even as I am unable to imagine myself in any other terms." It's from Steven Shaviro, "Remembering Kathy Acker," in *Kathy Acker in Seattle*, ed. Daniel Schulz (Seattle: Misfit Lit, 2020), 76. Which makes me wonder which other of Kathy's assigned male at birth lovers might have been dysphoric, or even trans. I can think of at least one. But let's not invade the bodies of others with our suppositions.

Reading List

One. The Acker-Text

Papers

All material from the Acker papers at Duke University are cited by file box, then folder, then page number, if there is one. Hence (23.24.8–9) is from box 23, file 24, at pages 8–9.

Books

BG   Acker, Kathy. *Blood and Guts in High School*. New York: Grove Press, 2017.
BW   Acker, Kathy. *Bodies of Work: Essays*. London: Serpent's Tail, 1997.
DQ   Acker, Kathy. *Don Quixote*. New York: Grove Press, 1986.
ES   Acker, Kathy. *Empire of the Senseless*. New York: Grove Press, 2018.
EU   Acker, Kathy. *Eurydice in the Underworld*. London: Arcadia Books, 1997.
GE   Acker, Kathy. *Great Expectations*. New York: Grove Press, 1982.
HL   Acker, Kathy. *Hannibal Lecter, My Father*. Edited by Sylvère Lotringer. New York: Semiotext(e), 1991.
IM   Acker, Kathy. *In Memoriam to Identity*. New York: Grove Press, 1998.
LM   Acker, Kathy. *Literal Madness*. New York: Grove Press, 2018.
MM   Acker, Kathy. *My Mother: Demonology*. New York: Grove Press, 2000.
PE   Acker, Kathy. *Portrait of an Eye*. New York: Grove Press, 1998.
PK   Acker, Kathy. *Pussy, King of the Pirates*. New York: Grove Press, 1996.

Interviews

AW   Acker, Kathy. "Interview with Andrea Juno." In *Angry Women,* edited by V. Vale and Andrea Juno, 177–85. San Francisco, CA: Re/Search, 1991.
BA   Acker, Kathy. "Interview with Mark Magill." In *BOMB: The Author Interviews*, edited by Betsy Sussler, 51–78. New York: Soho Press, 2014.

BB   Bratton, Benjamin. "Conversation with Kathy Acker." _SPEED_ 1, no. 1 (1994). Accessed August 3, 2020. http://nideffer.net/proj/_SPEED_/1.1 /acker.html.

JE   Ettler, Justine. "Kathy Acker, King of the Pussies." *Rolling Stone Australia*, November 1995, 24–25.

LI   Scholder, Amy, and Douglas A. Martin, eds. *Kathy Acker: The Last Interview*. Brooklyn, NY: Melville House, 2018.

NK   King, Noel. "Kathy Acker on the Loose." *Meanjin* 55, no. 2 (1996): 334–39.

RC   Cross, Rosie. "Acker Online." In *Transit Lounge*, edited by Ashley Crawford and Ray Edgar, 43–44. Melbourne: Craftsman's House, 1997.

WD   Sirius, R. U. "Kathy Acker: Where Does She Get Off?" *Io*, 1997. Accessed August 3, 2020. http://www.altx.com/io/acker.html.

Occasional Texts

AD   Acker, Kathy. "After the End of the Artworld." In *The Multimedia Text: Art and Design Profile No. 45*, edited by Nicholas Zurbrugg, 7–9. London: Art and Design, 1995.

DDH   Acker, Kathy. "Dead Doll Humility." *Postmodern Culture* 1, no. 1 (September 1990). Accessed July 30, 2020. http://pmc.iath.virginia.edu/text-only /issue.990/acker.990.

IV   Acker, Kathy, and McKenzie Wark. *I'm Very into You: Correspondence 1995–1996*. Los Angeles: Semiotext(e), 2015.

LJ   Acker, Kathy. *Homage to Leroi Jones and Other Early Works*. Edited by Gabrielle Kappes. New York: CUNY Poetics Document Initiative, 2015.

MP   Acker, Kathy. "Manpower." *New Statesman*, June 2, 1989, 12.

NW   Acker, Kathy. "Notes in Writing: From the Life of Baudelaire." *L=A=N=G=U=A=G=E*, nos. 9–10 (October 1979): 1–3.

PA   Acker, Kathy. "Paragraphs." *Journal of the Midwest Modern Languages Association* 28, no. 1 (Spring 1995): 87–92.

SW   Acker, Kathy, and Paul Buck. *Spread Wide*. Paris: Éditions Dis Voir, 2004.

TK   Acker, Kathy. "The Killers." In *Biting the Error: Writers Explore Narrative*, edited by Mary Burger, Robert Glück, Camille Roy, and Gail Scott, 14–18. Toronto: Coach House Books, 2004.

WP   Acker, Kathy. "Writing Praxis." In *Conjunctions*, 21 (1993): 304–5.

Two. Secondary Texts

Acker in Australia

Brown, Pam. "1995." In *Home by Dark*, 34. Bristol, UK: Shearsman Books, 2013.

Ettler, Justine. "Kathy Acker, King of the Pussies." *Rolling Stone Australia*, November 1995.

Ettler, Justine. "When I Met Kathy Acker." *M/C Journal* 21, no. 5 (2018). Accessed July 30, 2020. https://doi.org/10.5204/mcj.1483.

King, Noel. "Kathy Acker on the Loose." *Meanjin* 55, no. 2 (1996): 334–39.

Talbot, Danielle. "Pleasure and Pain in Acker's World." *The Age*, July 26, 1995, 21.

Talbot, Danielle. "Blood, Grunge and Literature." *The Age*, August 4, 1995, 17.

Acker by Other Writers

Bellamy, Dodie. "Digging through Kathy Acker's Stuff." In *When the Sick Rule the World*, 124–50. Los Angeles: Semiotext(e), 2015.

Boone, Bruce. "Kathy Acker's Great Expectations." In *Dismembered: Poems, Stories, and Essays*, 145–52. New York: Nightboat Books, 2020.

Freilicher, Mel. "One or Two Things That I Know about Kathy Acker." In *The Encyclopedia of Rebels*, 93–104. San Diego, CA: City Works Press, 2013.

Hegemann, Helene. *Axolotl Roadkill*. London: Corsair, 2012

Home, Stewart. *69 Things to Do with a Dead Princess*. Edinburgh: Canongate, 2003.

Indiana, Gary. *Rent Boy*. New York: High Risk Books, 1994.

Kaveney, Roz. "Just Because Cathexys Showed an Interest." Roz Kaveney's LiveJournal, June 23, 2007. Accessed July 30, 2020. https://rozk.livejournal.com/158882.html.

Kemp, Jonathan. "Kathy Acker's Houseboy." *Minor Literature[s]*, April 25, 2019.

Kruger, Barbara. "You No Wanna Dadda." *ZG* (Breakdown Issue), 1983.

Laing, Olivia. *Crudo*. London: Picador, 2018.

McCarthy, Tom. "Kathy Acker's Infidel Heteroglossia." In *Typewriters, Bombs, Jellyfish: Essays*, 255–74. New York: New York Review Books, 2017.

Myles, Eileen. *Inferno: A Poet's Novel*. New York: O/R Books, 2010.

Place, Vanessa. "Afterword." In *I'll Drown My Book: Conceptual Writing by Women*, edited by Caroline Bergvall, Laynie Browne, Teresa Carmody, and Vanessa Place, 445–47. Los Angeles: Les Figues Press, 2012.

Schulman, Sarah. "Realizing They"re Gone." In *Gentrification of the Mind*, 53–81. Berkeley: University of California Press, 2017.

Shaviro, Steven. "Kathy Acker." In *Doom Patrols*, 82–90. New York: Serpent's Tail, 1997.

Stupart, Linda. "Kathy's Body." In *The Bodies That Remain*, edited by Emmy Beber, 225–30. Goleta, CA: Punctum Books, 2018.

Stupart, Linda. *Virus*. London: Arcadia Missa, 2016.

Tillman, Lynne. "Selective Memory." *Review of Contemporary Fiction* 9, no. 3 (Fall 1989): 68–70.

David Velasco, "Natural's Not in It," *Bookforum* 24, no. 4 (December 2017).

Viegener, Matias. *The Assassination of Kathy Acker*. Guillotine Series no. 13. New York: Guillotine Series, 2018.

Viegener, Matias. *2500 Random Things About Me*. Los Angeles: Les Figues Press, 2012.

Zambreno, Kate. "New York City, Summer 2013." In *Icon*, edited by Amy Scholder, 221–44 New York: Feminist Press at CUNY, 2014.

Edited Volumes on Acker

Gajoux, Justin, and Sebastian Jailaud, eds. *Acker 1971–1975*. Paris: Éditions Ismael, 2019.

Hardin, Michael, ed. *Devouring Institutions: The Life and Work of Kathy Acker*. San Diego, CA: Hyperbole Books, 2004.

Scholder, Amy, Carla Harryman, and Avital Ronell, eds. *Lust for Life: On the Writings of Kathy Acker*. New York: Verso Books, 2006.

Schulz, David, ed. *Kathy Acker in Seattle*. Seattle: Misfit Lit, 2020.

Monographs on Acker

Borowska, Emilia. *The Politics of Kathy Acker: Revolution and the Avant-Garde*. Edinburgh: Edinburgh University Press, 2019.

Colby, Georgina. *Kathy Acker: Writing the Impossible*. Edinburgh: Edinburgh University Press, 2016.

Dew, Spencer. *Learning for Revolution: The Work of Kathy Acker*. San Diego, CA: Hyperbole Books, 2011.

Henderson, Margaret. *Kathy Acker: Punk Writer*. London: Routledge, 2020.

Kraus, Chris. *After Kathy Acker*. Los Angeles: Semiotext(e), 2015.

Martin, Douglas A. *Acker*. New York: Nightboat, 2017.

Other Monographs

Berry, Ellen. *Women's Experimental Writing*. London: Bloomsbury, 2016.

Campbell, Marion. *Poetic Revolutionaries: Intertextuality and Subversion*. Amsterdam: Rodopi, 2014.

Greaney, Patrick. *Quotational Practices: Repeating the Future in Contemporary Art*. Minneapolis: University of Minnesota Press, 2014.

Irr, Caren. *Pink Pirates: Contemporary American Women Writers and Copyright*. Iowa City: University of Iowa Press, 2010.

Marczewska, Kaja. *This Is Not a Copy: Writing at the Iterative Turn*. London: Bloomsbury, 2018.

Mookerjee, Robin. *Transgressive Fiction: The New Satiric Tradition*. London: Palgrave Macmillan, 2013.

Moran, Joe. *Star Authors*. London: Pluto Press, 2000.

Pritchard, Nicola. *Tactical Readings*. Lewisburg, PA: Bucknell University Press, 2002.

Siegle, Robert. *Suburban Ambush: Downtown Writing and the Fiction of Insurgency*. Baltimore, MD: Johns Hopkins University Press, 1989.

Tabbi, Joseph. *Postmodern Sublime: Technology and American Writing from Mailer to Cyberpunk*. Ithaca, NY: Cornell University Press, 1996.

Vichnar, David. *Subtexts: Essays on Fiction*. Prague: Litteraria Pragnesia, 2015.

Yuknavich, Lidia. *Allegories of Violence*. New York: Routledge, 2001.

Zurbrugg, Nicholas. *The Parameters of Postmodernism*. Carbondale, IL: Southern Illinois University Press, 1993.

Selected Journal Articles, etc.

Berressem, Hanjo. "Body-Wound-Writing." *American Studies* 43, no. 3 (January 1999): 393–411.

Bey, Marquis. "Cutting Up Words: Kathy Acker's Trans Locutions." *Transgender Studies Quarterly* 7, no. 3 (August 2020): 479–88.

Brimmers, Julian. "Kathy Acker's Library." *Paris Review* 225 (Summer 2018). Accessed January 14 2021. https://www.theparisreview.org/art-photography/7195/kathy-ackers-library-julian-brimmers.

Burke, Victoria. "Writing Violence: Kathy Acker and Tattoos." *Canadian Journal of Political and Social Theory* 13, nos. 1–2 (1989): 162–65.

Finch, Claire. "Kathy Acker's Dildos: Literary Prosthetics and Textual Unmaking." *Gender Forum* 74 (2019): 55–74.

Floyd, Kevin. "Deconstructing Masochism in Kathy Acker's *Blood and Guts in High School*." In *Critical Studies on the Feminist Subject*, edited by Gionana Covi, 57–77. Trento, Italy: Dipartimento di scienze filologiche e storiche, 1997.

Friedman, Ellen. "Now Eat Your Mind: An Introduction to the Works of Kathy Acker." *Review of Contemporary Fiction* 9, no. 3 (Fall 1989): 37–49.

Gabriel, Kay. "Nothing Until It Is Made Actual, or Acker versus Growing Up." *Transgender Studies Quarterly* 7, no. 3 (August 2020): 489–98.

Greaney, Patrick. "Insinuation: Détournement as Gendered Repetition." *South Atlantic Quarterly* 110 (1) (2011): 75–88.

Hauskneckt, Gina. "Self-Possession, Dolls, Beatlemania, Loss." In *The Girl: Constructions of the Girl in Contemporary Fiction by Women*, edited by Roth O. Saxton, 21–42. New York: St. Martin's Press, 1998.

House, Richard. "Informational Inheritance in Kathy Acker's *Empire of the Senseless.*" *Contemporary Literature* 46, no. 3 (2005): 450–82.

McBride, Jason. "The Last Days of Kathy Acker." *Hazlitt,* July 28, 2015.

Milks, Megan. "Janey and Genet in Tangier." In *Kathy Acker and Transnationalism,* edited by P. Mackay and K. Nichol, 91–114. Newcastle, UK: Cambridge Scholars Publishing, 2009.

Redding, Arthur F. "Bruises, Roses: Masochism and the Writing of Kathy Acker." *Contemporary Literature* 35, no. 2 (1994): 281–304.

Rickels, Lawrence. "Body Building." *Artforum International* 32, no. 6 (February 1994): 60–62.

Scholder, Amy. "Editor's Note." In *Essential Acker,* edited by Amy Scholder and Dennis Cooper, xi–xv. New York: Grove Press, 2002.

Sciolino, Martine. "Confessions of a Kleptoparasite" *Review of Contemporary Fiction* 9, no. 3 (Fall 1989): 63–67.

Sciolino, Martine. "Kathy Acker and the Postmodern Subject of Feminism." *College English* 52, no. 4 (April 1990): 437–45.

Sweet, Paige. "Where's the Booty?" *darkmatter,* December 10, 2009. Accessed August 3, 2020. http://www.darkmatter101.org/site/author/paige-s/.

Templeton, Ainslie. "Trans Smuggling in Genet's *Our Lady of the Flowers.*" *Tijdschrift voor Genderstudies* 20, no. 4 (2017): 399–414.

Trieu, K. K. "Building the Pirate Body." *Transgender Studies Quarterly* 7, no. 3 (August 2020): 499–507.

Vechinski, Matthew. "Kathy Acker as Conceptual Artist." *Style* 47, no. 4 (Winter 2013): 525–81.

Acker in Contexts. Selected Anthologies

Andrews, Bruce, and Charles Bernstein, eds. *The L=A=N=G=U=A=G=E Book.* Carbondale: Southern Illinois University Press, 1984.

Bellamy, Dodie, and Kevin Killian, eds. *Writers Who Love Too Much: New Narrative Writing 1977–1997.* New York: Nightboat, 2017.

Bergvall, Caroline, Laynie Browne, Teresa Carmody, and Vanessa Place, eds. *I'll Drown My Book: Conceptual Writing by Women.* Los Angeles: Le Figues, 2013.

Crawford, Ashley, and Ray Edgar, eds. *Transit Lounge.* Melbourne: Craftsman's House, 1997.

Dworkin, Craig, and Kenneth Goldsmith, eds. *Against Expression: An Anthology of Conceptual Writing.* Chicago: Northwestern University Press, 2011.

Ess, Barbara, and Glenn Branca, eds. *Just Another Asshole,* no. 6. New York: JAA Press, 1983.

Massumi, Brian, ed. *The Politics of Everyday Fear.* Minneapolis: University of Minnesota Press, 1993.

McCaffery, Larry, ed. *Storming the Reality Studio: A Casebook of Cyberpunk and Postmodern Science Fiction.* Durham, NC: Duke University Press, 1991.

McCaffery, Larry, ed. *Avant-Pop: Fiction for a Daydream Nation*. Kennebunk, ME: Black Ice Books, 1992.

Prince, Richard, ed. *Wild History*. New York: Tanum Books, 1985.

Robertson, Lisa, and Matthew Stadler, eds. *Revolution: A Reader*. Paris: Paraguay Press, 2012.

Rose, Joel, and Catherine Texier, eds. *Between C and D: An Anthology*. New York: Penguin, 1988.

Rosset, Barney, ed. *Evergreen Review Reader 1967–1973*. New York: Four Walls Eight Windows, 1999.

Scholder, Amy, and Ira Silverberg, eds. *High Risk: An Anthology of Forbidden Writings*. New York: Serpent's Tail, 1991.

Sussler, Betsy, ed. *BOMB: The Author Interviews*. New York: Soho House Press, 2014.

Vale, V., and Andrea Juno, eds. *Angry Women*. San Francisco, CA: Re/Search, 1993.

Wallis, Brian, ed. *Blasted Allegories: An Anthology of Writings by Contemporary Artists*. Cambridge, MA: MIT Press, 1989.

Index

abortion, 84, 85, 95

Acker, Kathy: as The Black Tarantula, 53–54, 162; death of, 7, 46–49; early life of, 33–34, 182n35; and language, 6; masculinity of, 20–21; and motorcycles, 18, 21, 26, 27, 30; as philosopher, 54; porn writings by, 10, 38; reach of work by, 170; remembrance of, 46; and sex toys, 23–24, 27, 35, 36–38. *See also individual works*

Acker-cities, 121

Acker-fiction, 159

Acker-field: agency in, 144; bodies/ gender in, 107–8, 109; as books that do, 156; cities in, 121; fame in, 129; incoherence in, 60; negative authority in, 56; nihilism in, 137; the penetrator in, 91; political complexity in, 139; psychogeography in, 122; the self in, 66; tactics of, 142. *See also* Acker-text; Acker-web

Acker-flow, 163

Acker-skin, 112

Acker-text: anticolonial revolutions in, 141; vs. bourgeois novel, 159; cities in, 120; eternal capitalism in, 130; family story in, 81; heterosexuality in, 99; labor in, 124; language in, 63, 74; love in, 112, 116; multiple genders in, 105; philosophical questions in, 56; pirate body in, 172; selving in, 55; as tactic, 130; as theory of self, 54; trans-ness in, 90, 155, 175; trans reading of, 171, 176;

and trans writing, 173. *See also* Acker-field; Acker-web

Acker/Wark relationship: clothing sharing in, 28, 35; email correspondence, 12–14, 16, 40, 41–42; fucking in, 8–9, 22–26, 27, 35–38

Acker-web: abortions in, 95; absent father in, 83; anarchy in, 148; and cishet fucking, 107; cities in, 120; death of gods in, 155; gender in, 173–74; genre/ gender spanning in, 163; girls in, 148; interiority/exteriority in, 62; limits of sexuality in, 90; and the marginalized, 170; the mother in, 84; philosophy of, 56; post-capitalism in, 133; rapists in, 96; revolutions in, 151; sex in, 126; sexual agency in, 97; whoring in, 145. *See also* Acker-field; Acker-text

Acker-work, 159

Adams, Douglas, 45

The Addiction (Ferrara), 40

After Kathy Acker (Acker), 22

agency, 144–48; and abortions, 95; of the girl, 149; of the penetrated, 97; of the trans body, 177

America Online, 13, 133

anal sex, 23–24, 27, 36, 93

anarchy, 123, 138, 148

anticolonial revolutions, 150, 151

Arachne, 53

art, 127, 128, 132, 134

artist, the, 126–27, 136, 145

art-work, 126–29; and capitalism, 132; détournement writing as, 160; and men, 145; S&M as, 101

assholes: in Acker/Wark relationship, 23–24, 36; roses as, 102, 104. *See also* cunts

Athena, 53, 54

author, the, 7, 55, 66, 138, 160

auto-plagiarism, 5

Badu, Erykah, 7

Bartlett, Neil, 44

Baudelaire, 6

beauty, 65, 85, 132

"being booked," 156–57

Bellamy, Dodie, 9, 28

Bey, Marquis, 173, 174

Blood and Guts in High School (Acker), 59, 68, 69, 70, 71, 72, 73, 89, 90, 91, 93, 99, 104, 114, 135, 136, 137, 143, 155, 157

bodies: alienation of, 143; and "being booked," 156–57; and body-work, 76; and class, 131; and commodification, 131, 135; concepts of, 19–21, 28; control and, 26; dysphoric, 172–73; and failure, 76–77; and holes, 154; and language, 174; and masturbation, 78; narrative inheritance of, 107; penetration of, 90, 95, 100, 104; poetics of, 111; and revolution, 155; and sexuality, 79, 91; and S&M, 101; and writing, 160

Bodies of Work (Acker), 54, 56, 57, 58, 59, 62, 66, 72, 73, 74, 76, 83, 84, 86, 87, 90, 101, 103, 105, 106, 108, 109, 112, 114, 117, 118, 120, 121, 123, 127, 128, 129, 132, 133, 140, 141, 143, 144, 148, 149, 151, 160, 161, 162, 163, 166, 167

bodybuilding, 75–76, 81, 119, 159

body-work, 75–77; and the dysphoric body, 173; and the hole, 156

Bohemia, 86, 173, 177

Bookforum, 14

boredom, 70–71; and dreams, 72; and fucking, 88; and null philosophy, 61

bosses, 102, 117–19

bottom, the, 29, 32, 36, 92

bottom theory, 48

Bound to Violence (Ouologuem), 150

boys, 55, 105, 109, 145–46

Brown, Pam, 11

capitalism, 130–33; and art, 128; and love, 113; and thanaticism, 137; and third philosophy, 60

cinema, 69

cis gaze, 171, 177

cis-lit, 171

citation, 7

cities, 119–23; and art, 127; colonial, 121; fame in, 129; and post-capitalism, 132, 133; and sailors, 148; and trans lit, 173

city-prison, 122

class, 81–82, 85, 121–22, 126–27, 131

cocks: in Acker/Wark relationship, 9, 24, 27, 35–36; and low philosophy, 55; as replacement for dicks, 104. *See also* dicks; dildos

collaborative writing, 162

coming: in Acker/Wark relationship, 9, 24, 38; and cunts, 103; as knowing, 79; of penetrator vs. penetrated, 91–92, 98, 154

commodification, 125–26, 128, 131–32, 134, 151

commodity form, 133, 144, 145, 161–62

communication, 156, 160–61

community, 125, 143–44

concepts: and the art world, 134; of the body, 20, 23–24, 105, 109; feelings as, 63; and fucking, 32, 36; of gender, 28, 93, 110; and the natural, 167; and post-capitalism, 135, 144; and selves, 58

control: and body-work, 76; and the bourgeois writer, 5; commodification as, 134; culture as means of, 142; and the father, 83; of nature, 166–67; and pain, 100; and the penetrator, 91; and S&M, 101, 152

copyright, 161

corporeal communism, 28

Crawford, Ashley, 7–8
Cross, Rosie, 13
culture, 142–44; and post-capitalism, 141; and third philosophy, 60
cunts: in Acker/Wark relationship, 9, 23, 24, 35, 38; assholes as, 104; and heterosexual relation, 104; and the penetrable body, 104; roses as, 102. *See also* assholes

death, 116–19; as bodily concept, 44; boredom as worse than, 70; commodification as, 151; of history, 138; and language, 76; of the mother, 84–85; obsession with, 143; as other side of sex, 89; and post-capitalism, 166; and revolution, 155; as world without love, 116
desire, 86–88; cities as made of, 122; extraction of surplus, 132; and fathers, 82–83; and memory, 64; for pain, 102
détournement, 160–63; in Huxtable's work, 177; in Ouologuem's work, 183n2
Dick, Leslie, 46
dicks: in Acker/Wark relationship, 9, 22–24, 36, 37, 38; denuded of aura, 104; as flesh vs. sign, 98; and the male body, 93, 95; and penetration, 154; refusal of, 153; sexual politics without, 152. *See also* cocks; dildos
difference, 83, 88, 91, 92
dildos: in Acker/Wark relationship, 23–25, 27, 35–36; and race, 36. *See also* cocks; dicks
Don Quixote (Acker), 57, 62, 63, 64, 67, 69, 70, 71, 73, 74, 79, 83, 85, 86, 88, 89, 91, 92, 95, 99, 100, 103, 106, 108, 109, 110, 112, 113, 114, 115, 116, 117, 123, 127, 128, 131, 134, 138, 143, 144, 148, 151, 152, 153, 154, 158, 164, 166
drag, 114, 120, 176
dreams, 71–72; Acker/Wark dreams, 3–4, 39, 42, 172; boredom as lack of, 70; and coming, 79; and the dead, 48; of death

of the mother, 85; and the imagination, 60; reading as similar to, 86
dysphoric body, the, 146, 172–73, 176–78

Ekwensi, Cyprian, 150
emotions, 63–64; and first philosophy, 60; and linear language, 72; and post-capitalism, 135; and solitude, 71
Empire of the Senseless (Acker), 54, 56, 57, 58, 61, 62, 64, 65, 68, 69, 70, 72, 74, 75, 78, 79, 81, 82, 83, 84, 87, 90, 94, 95, 98, 99, 100, 101, 103, 105, 109, 112, 115, 116, 117, 121, 123, 125, 126, 130, 133, 134, 136, 137, 138, 139, 140, 141, 142, 143, 144, 146, 147, 149, 151, 152, 165, 167, 168
engendering, 107–12
Ettler, Justine, 8
Euripides, 163
Eurydice in the Underworld (Acker), 56, 60, 63, 64, 70, 82, 83, 84, 86, 89, 94, 95, 96, 105, 108, 116, 146
exchange value, 132, 135
exteriority, 61–63; and nature, 166
eye, the, 69, 87, 154. *See also* I, the

fame-work, 129–30
family, the, 81, 85, 86, 121
fathers, 82–83; vs. boys, 20; and dreams, 72; and imagination, 73; as makers of death, 117; and power, 83; and theory, 6–7
female: bodies and penetration, 92, 93; bodies and sensation, 106; language, 59–60; nature as, 167; spiders, 53; workers, 126
femininity, 19, 107–8
feminism, 122–23, 156
femmunism, 150
fetishism, 127, 134, 142–43
fiction, 156–60
fifth gender, 109, 149
first philosophy: body vs. self in, 79; description of, 120, 178; tactics of, 142. *See also* second philosophy; third philosophy

Freilicher, Mel, 34
fucking: in Acker/Wark relationship, 8–9, 22–26, 27, 35–38; vs. being fucked, 22–23; and bodily concepts, 19–20; and closing vs. opening, 25; and fame, 130; as libidinal revolution, 152; and masculinity, 108; and power, 90; and sensation, 88; and sex-work, 126; and writing, 5

Gabriel, Kay, 176
gender: in Acker-field, 109–10; Acker's positions on, 95–96, 107, 108, 111; Acker's trans relation to, 170; in Acker-web, 107, 163; art-work shaped by, 127; and asymmetry, 31, 90, 104; as bodily concept, 19–20; and difference, 111–12; and dreams, 73; and the dysphoric body, 173; five concepts of, 110; fucking with, 5; and industrialization, 20–21; and love, 113, 115, 116; and memory, 65; and mother/father figures, 85; and myth of equality, 100; and nature, 167; penetration and theory of, 92; and pirates, 146–47; solutions to limitations of, 108–9; as technology, 21; as transitive, 29
genre, 5, 112, 132, 163
girl: "manning" as a, 39; Wark as Acker's, 25–26, 29, 35
girls, 148–50; in Acker-text, 105, 106; and the hole, 154; and penetrability, 104; and powerlessness/desirability, 124; and sex-work, 124
god: capitalism as, 130; death of in Acker-web, 146, 155; of history as dead, 156; the human as dead, 166; of language as dead, 67, 70, 75; love as dead, 115; and myth, 165
Greaney, Patrick, 6
Great Expectations (Acker), 33, 58, 59, 60, 62, 63, 64, 67, 71, 72, 84, 85, 87, 89, 90, 91, 92, 94, 95, 96, 97, 106, 109, 110, 112, 113, 114, 115, 125, 126, 127, 128, 130, 137, 145, 152, 155, 156

hand-jobbing, 77–78. *See also* masturbation

hand-writing, 79–80
Hannibal Lecter, My Father (Acker), 57, 59, 63, 64, 75, 77, 82, 87, 90, 92, 93, 94, 95, 101, 102, 108, 111, 113, 118, 122, 124, 125, 126, 132, 135, 137, 144, 145, 147, 154, 159, 165, 166, 168
Heaney, Emma, 171
Hemingway, Ernest, 170
Hepburn, Audrey, 31
heterosex, 91, 95, 96
heterosexual relation: and cunts, 104; and girls, 125; and penetration, 94; and possession, 110; S&M as philosophy of, 100; subject/object in, 96, 97
high theory: Plato as daddy of, 54; in post-capitalism, 138–39; thinking beyond, 57. *See also* low theory
history, 136–39; and Acker-field politics, 139; death of, 155, 156; and linear time, 66; and memory, 64
Hitchcock, Alfred, 17, 32
Hocquenghem, Guy, 36
holes, 153–56
human, the: Acker's lack of faith in, 71; as dead god, 166; gender beyond, 96, 107, 109, 110; and nature, 167; and sex, 89
Huxtable, Juliana, 169, 176–78

I, the, 69, 87, 107. *See also* eye, the
identity: as anti-revolutionary, 152–53; and culture, 143; end of as akin to death, 118–19; instability of, 66; panic about loss of, 157; refusal of, 147; writing against, 158
ideology, 25, 28, 32, 113
imagination, 73–75; and dreams, 72, 73; and masturbation, 79
I'm Very into You (Acker/Wark), 14–17
Indiana, Gary, 26
information, 135, 137, 141–42
inheritance, 81–82
In Memoriam to Identity (Acker), 55, 56, 57, 63, 70, 72, 73, 74, 75, 79, 81, 82, 87, 88, 89, 91, 96, 97, 99, 100, 102, 112, 114, 115, 118, 121, 123, 124, 125, 127, 132, 133, 137, 138,

139, 141, 143, 149, 151, 152, 153, 154, 155, 165, 167
internet, the, 133–34, 162

Kathy Acker Papers, 1, 54
Kaveney, Roz, 172
Kemp, Jonathan, 27
King, Nowl, 7
Kraus, Chris, 14, 22, 32

labor, 123–26
LambdaMOO, 13
language: absence of the girl in, 148–49; in Acker-fiction, 159; vs. acts, 39; and the body, 28, 174; and body-work, 75, 76; boredom and death of, 70; of death, 117; of dysphoric/ pirate body, 172; and fiction, 159–60; and flesh, 19; linear, 62–63, 68, 71–72, 74–75, 79, 108; and low theory, 55; and nature, 167, 168; as nothing special, 59, 61; as Oedipus's prison, 164; other ways of making, 68; as outside of nature, 168; and ownership, 160; play within gendered, 111; and poets, 6; and post-capitalism, 135; relation of to world, 67; trans relation to, 173; women's access to, 59–60; and writing, 58
language-work, 144
Lavery, Grace, 169, 175, 176
library, 85–86
Literal Madness (Acker), 51, 53, 56, 57, 58, 59, 62, 64, 66, 67, 68, 71, 72, 81, 82, 85, 87, 92, 93, 94, 98, 104, 105, 109, 115, 116, 121, 122, 124, 128, 129, 131, 132, 133, 135, 136, 138, 139, 140, 142, 145, 151, 152, 157, 158, 159, 160, 166, 167, 168
love, 112–16; and alternate forms of writing, 68; and commodification, 131; fathers and absence of, 83; lack of in cities, 122; materialism's negation of, 132; and mothers, 84; Oedipus's desire for, 164; as revolution, 152
low theory: after Acker, 178; of bodily spectrums, 92; description of, 54–55;

and the marginalized, 138–39; origins of Acker's, 126. *See also* high theory
Lucky Cheng's, 35
Lucretius, 47

Macquarie University, 12
"manning," 29, 37–39
Manzoni, Piero, 7
marginalized, the: agency of, 144; as cultural scapegoats, 142; and narrative, 68; philosophy for, 54; revolution of, 151; what writing can do for, 59
Marx, Karl, 21, 161
masculinity: in Acker-field, 107–8; Acker's, 20; Acker's desire/rejection/ fear of, 98; in Acker-text, 99; in Acker- web, 107; as bodily concept, 19; of city spaces, 120; dispensability of, 103; escaping, 7; and penetration, 29, 92, 93, 104; performance of in S&M, 100
masochism, 99–102; and death, 118; and the dysphoric body, 173; as rebellion, 152; and violence, 155
masochist, the, 102, 168
masturbation, 86, 173. *See also* hand-jobbing
materialism, 132, 139
McCarthy, Tom, 6
memory, 64–65; in Acker-web, 86; and emotions, 63–64; erasure of by desire, 87; as external to the body, 31; as genre of fiction, 44; and girls in Acker-text, 105; Oedipus as self trapped in, 164; personal vs. internet, 49; redundancy of, 42
men: Acker's feelings about, 93–94, 98; and art-work, 127; and dick as sign, 98; as gender in Acker-text, 105; as impossible desire, 94; language of, 59; and ownership, 160; as penetrator, 94; and rape, 97; and thanaticism, 137; violence of, 149
misandry, 93–96
modernist literature, 171
mothers, 84–85
motorcycles, 21, 96, 107, 149

Mucus in My Pineal Gland (Huxtable), 177
Murray, Charles Shaar, 42
Musée Mécanique, 30
Myles, Eileen, 11
My Life My Death by Pier Paolo Pasolini (Acker), 33
My Mother: Demonology (Acker), 23, 51, 55, 56, 57, 62, 63, 64, 65, 71, 72, 73, 74, 75, 77, 79, 81, 82, 83, 84, 85, 86, 87, 88, 89, 90, 92, 95, 97, 98, 100, 103, 104, 105, 107, 108, 111, 112, 113, 114, 115, 117, 118, 121, 122, 123, 125, 131, 134, 136, 138, 139, 140, 141, 142, 146, 147, 148, 150, 154, 155, 157, 159, 164, 167
myth, 163–65; of equality, 100; and gender, 109, 110; and masturbation, 79; tattooing as, 101–2

The Name of the Rose (Eco), 47
narrative, 67–70; and bodies, 75; and emotions, 63–64; fantasy as negation of, 72; and linear language, 66–67; and memory, 64
nature, 165–68
Needham, Joseph, 19
negative love, 115–16, 131
Nevada (Binnie), 174, 176
New York City, 121–22
"Notes in Writing" (Acker), 55
null philosophy, 60, 61

Oedipus, 164
oral sex: in Acker/Wark relationship, 9, 37, 55; and low theory, 55

pain, 64, 75–76, 100, 152
Peck, Gregory, 31
penetrated, the: and bodily limits, 100; the book as, 162; cities as, 123; and the dysphoric body, 173; as penetrator, 154; revolution of, 153; tattooing and power of, 102; and vulnerability, 96–97; wants of, 97
penetration, 90–93
penetration theory, 92, 93
penetrator, the: and failure, 96; and

power, 94; and rape, 97; as uninteresting, 91–92
Peters, Torrey, 174, 175, 176
philosophy, 54–55; of the emotions, 63; and naivete, 57; null, 60; without fathers, 55. *See also* high theory; low theory
Philosophy for Spiders (Wark), 171, 172
pirate, the, 104, 111, 146, 147, 172
Place, Vanessa, 7
Plato, 54, 163
The Poet and the Women (Aristophane), 163
poetry, 118, 127
poets, 6, 59, 73, 119
political economy, 135
politics, 139–41; and the city, 123; and masturbation, 78
porn, 10, 38, 177, 186n36
Portrait of an Eye (Acker), 55, 56, 57, 61, 62, 64, 65, 66, 69, 71, 77, 78, 79, 80, 82, 85, 88, 93, 94, 98, 103, 106, 108, 109, 110, 111, 114, 115, 120, 121, 122, 123, 124, 125, 126, 129, 130, 134, 145, 151, 152, 153, 165
post-capitalism, 21, 60, 133–36; artist vs. whore in, 145; and the city, 122, 123; and copyright, 161; and destruction of earth, 166; and exploitation, 143; forms of state in, 140–41; and the hole, 153; and imagination, 73–74; nihilism in response to, 137; revolutions against, 151; space of possibility in, 137, 140; and third philosophy, 73; and writing/reading relation, 162; writing under, 160–61
postcolonial literature, 150
power: and the city, 123; and control of nature, 167; death as weak point of, 119; vs. embrace of death, 119; and fathers, 83; and fucking, 90, 91; of girls, 149; masculine, 98; and media, 157–58; and the penetrator, 94; perception of girls by, 148; politics and refusal of, 140; tactics for confronting, 141
psychoanalysis, 117, 171
psychogeography, 18, 33, 120–21, 122

punk, 55, 57, 145–46
Pussy, King of the Pirates (Acker), ix, 8, 30, 62, 71, 72, 73, 74, 78, 79, 83, 86, 88, 89, 92, 104, 105, 106, 108, 111, 112, 121, 122, 144, 145, 146, 151, 152, 154, 158, 168

queer, 152–53, 171, 176

race, 36, 145–46, 177
radical feminism, 155
rape, 96–98
Redefining Realness (Mock), 176
revolution, 150–53; anticolonial, 141; vs. identity, 155
The River Ophelia (Ettler), 8
Rohy, Valerie, 170–71
Roman Holiday (Wyler), 31
Ronell, Avital, 22

sadism, 117, 152. *See also* S&M
sadist, the, 102, 152
sailor, 44, 147
Scholder, Amy, 10
Schulman, Sarah, 33
Schulz, Daniel, 45
Sciolino, Martine, 5
second philosophy: and cishet fucking, 107; and death, 116, 117, 119; description of, 120, 178; and desire, 87–88; and penetration, 93; and relation to others, 81; and S&M, 101–2. *See also* first philosophy; third philosophy
self, the: and boredom, 70; and death of the mother, 84–85; as derivative of events, 66; fiction of, 156; friendship and limits of, 115; and fucking, 88, 92; and language, 68; and love, 112, 114; and masturbation, 78; and penetration, 93; as product in sex-work, 125–26
selves: and the Acker-field, 60; and cities, 121; desire and inconsistency of, 87; and fucking, 88; and memory, 64; philosophies of, 60; relationship of writing to, 58–59; as residue of events, 63

selving, 55–57; and interiority/exteriority, 62; reading/writing relation as, 162
semiotics, 135
sensation, 60, 62–64, 77, 88
The Seven Sacraments of Nicholas Poussin (Bartlett), 42–44
sex, 88–90; in the Acker-web, 126; with cishet men, 99; and extortion of value, 132; and friendship, 114
sexuality: beyond categories, 112; beyond the human, 89; and the body, 79; in the bourgeois novel, 159; under capitalism, 131–32; and love, 115; mediation of in Acker-web, 86; new possibilities of, 111; as pain/ecstacy, 69; and pirates, 146–47; and sailors, 148; as site of confusion, 10; as transformative, 89; women's, 106
sex-work, 123–26; vs. art-work, 129; and capitalism, 132; and fame-work, 129–30; and politics, 139; and trans lit, 173. *See also* whoring
sex-workers, 125, 145. *See also* whore
Shaviro, Steven, 48, 186n37
signified, the, 135, 136, 142
signifier, the, 135, 136, 142–43
S&M, 9, 37–38, 100–103. *See also* sadism
solitude, 71; vs. being with an-other, 114; and masturbation, 77; and third philosophy, 70
sophia, 53, 54, 55, 59
spiders, 53–54; kleptoparasite, 5; and masturbation, 78
Streeter, Alex, 39
Stupart, Linda, 48
Suthon, Hayne, 35

tactics, 142, 143, 157, 158, 167
tattooing, 101–2
thanaticism, 137
third philosophy: and Bohemia, 86; description of, 120, 178; and post-capitalism, 73; and the social field, 73; and solitude, 70; tactics of, 142. *See also* first philosophy; second philosophy
Tillman, Lynne, 19

time, 65–67; dreams as escape from, 72; and exchange value, 131; fiction of, 156; and history, 138; and masturbation, 78; and sex, 89

topping, 22, 29, 32, 48

Trans | Acker symposium, 169, 170, 171, 172

trans body, the, 104, 178

trans lit, 170, 173, 174, 176

trans-ness: of Acker's writings, 171, 174; in the Acker-text, 90, 175; and coming, 79; of some Ackers, 109

trans women, 155, 174–75

Trieu, Kato, 30, 169–70, 171, 172

21C, 7–8

use value, 132, 135

Velasco, David, 14

Vertigo (Hitchcock), 17

Viegener, Matias, 7, 9, 16, 23, 28, 46–47, 169

violence, 114, 120, 140–41, 155

Wark/Acker relationship. *See* Acker/ Wark relationship

weaving, 53, 54, 55

Wendling, Amy, 21

whore, 146, 161. *See also* sex-workers

whore pride, 145

whoring, 145

Why Are We So Blest? (Armah), 150

women, 103–7; in Acker-text, 105; lacking language, 59–60; sexuality of, 106; writing of, 159

wonder, 57–58; and desire, 87; and the dysphoric body, 172; and structure/ content play, 162

writing, 58–60; in the Acker-fiction, 158, 159; alternate forms of, 68; as art-work, 161; and body-work, 75–76, 77; bourgeois, 5, 6; and commodity form, 161–62; and desire, 87; as détournement, 160; double nature of, 67; and fucking, 5; and gender norms, 171; in/ against revolutions, 150–51; and masturbation, 25, 78; materiality of, 125; in networked era, 12; as non-penetrative, 106; and sailors, 148; and sensation, 64–65; and sex-work, 126; vs. tattooing, 101–2; and time, 66; trans, 172–75; and transition, 111–12

Zambreno, Kate, 38